The History of
REED
TRANSPORT

First published in 2009 by Roundoak Publishing,
The Old Dairy, Perry Farm, East Nynehead,
Wellington, Somerset, TA21 0DA. United Kingdom

Tel. +44 (0)1823 461997
email: info@nynehead-books.co.uk
www.nynehead-books.co.uk

Origination: Roundoak Associates
Printed by Amadeus Press
Cleckheaton, West Yorkshire
ISBN 978 1 871565 51 5

This page: Arthur Bryant and his Foden FG6/24 S20
eight wheel rigid, no.52 - 108 BKP, by the Export Shed
at Aylesford's East Mill alongside the River Medway.
Arthur transferred to Reed Transport when the BRS
Larkfield Depot was acquired in 1955.

Front cover: Maudslay badged Mammoth Major
MkIII no.47 - LUV 240 was captured on film by
Arthur Ingram in January 1951 in Fountayne Road,
Tottenham with a four-high load of reels for John
Dickenson's who were located in Broad Lane,
Tottenham off which Fountayne Road ran.
It is wearing the original early 1950s livery and
would have been in the Perkins & Glover fleet as an
Albert E Reed subsidiary at the time.
Harry Stratford was its regular driver.

The History of
REED
TRANSPORT

including

Perkins & Glover,
T.R.T.S. and
Cropper & Colthrop

John Marsh

Roundoak Publishing

Contents

Acknowledgements

When I set out to write this History, one of my objectives was to identify as many vehicles as possible that the Company and it's predecessors operated. As a consequence within the Appendices are details of some 1400 vehicles.

Much information was available from Company archives but there were periods in time for which records no longer existed. In fact, some of the early records merely listed a registration number, nothing more. I am therefore indebted to the many organisations who hold transport related archives and I commend the use of these facilities to any transport enthusiast or historian. Long may those records be preserved and available for all to use. Those organisations I am particularly indebted to are:

Cambridge County Council, County Record Office, Huntingdon

Centre for Kentish Studies, Kent County Council.

Cheshire County Council, Record Office Chester - keeper of Foden archives

Essex Record Office of Essex County Council Heritage Services.

The Kithead Trust.

Motoring Archive Research Service, Beaulieu for the interpretation of Ford chassis numbers.

Register of ERF Vehicles Society - REVS.

West Yorkshire Archive Service.

I would also like to record my thanks to London Borough of Southwark Local Studies Library for access to their records which helped me piece together the Perkins & Glover history.

Now to those past employees of the Company who have contributed stories, photographs, hard copy and generally trawled through their memories for information.

First and foremost, I must mention Stuart Wise, Thatcham Archivist Extraordinaire, who has contributed virtually all of the history relating to that Depot, either from his own records or by contact with former Thatcham employees. Furthermore, his vast collection of photographs has formed a major part of the pictorial presentation within this History. My sincere thanks, Stuart.

My sincere thanks are also directed to my former boss for over thirty years, Ron Adkins. Ron was able to elaborate on and add to that most important period of the Company's History, the Perkins & Glover years, from his own experiences. He filled in the many gaps which I was left with after the first draft and then read the final draft cover to cover to ensure no glaring errors had been made.

Graham Day, Fleet Engineer to Reed Transport and SCA Transport since 1986, provided much of the engineering related contribution for Chapter Seven together with access to the 'Black Book' - details of all vehicles purchased since 1974. Also his responses to the endless letters and e-mails between us as I pieced together the vehicle details in the Appendices. Finally for his perusal of the Appendices, amending where errors were found and generally ensuring that no 'howlers' had crept in. Many thanks for your patience and help, Graham.

Grateful thanks are due to my old 'Northern' colleague, Chris Halliwell, for assisting me with that area's pieces of the jigsaw including many archives and photographs which he, like myself, had saved over the years which otherwise would have been destroyed.

Other contributors must be mentioned, hoping that no one has been missed out:

Peter Allen, Ron Cooper, Jack Howlett, Ron Mulford, Digby Staples, Derek Appleby, Colin Dumelow, Alan Jones, Ed Murray, Jim Sullivan, George Blackman, Stan Ellison, Rita Lewis, Jimmy Myler, Len Valsler, Sid Brenton, Tony Gliddon, Basil Lucking, Pat Oswald, Sid Vaughan, Ted Brooker, Elizabeth Glover, Les Marsh, Keith Parks, Sid Whittaker, Charlie Brooks, Michael Glover, John Mollett, Bill Parr, Steve Wimbush, Dave Buxey, John Grierson, Terry Martin, Gordon Pease, Ken Wratten, Harry Chittenden, Mike Houle, Ron Moore, George Smith, Mick Cook, Philip Howe, Dennis Morgan, Steve Smith.

The loan by Donald Charlesworth of the two volumes 'Albert E. Reed and the Creation of a Paper Business 1860 - 1960' and 'Reed International Developments in a Company History 1960 - 1974' by Philip Sykes proved invaluable particularly in checking dates and the order of key events.

John Sanderson, Foden Historian from Sandbach, helped to identify model codes and provided many interesting Foden photographs. My grateful thanks, John.

Thanks on the photographic front also go out to Adrian Cypher, Peter Davies, Arthur Ingram, the late Roger Kenney, Malcolm Mortimer, Phil Moth, and ATPH.

Finally, to my dear wife, Megan, a real transport wife who put up with endless evenings of me tapping at my PC and the countless meetings and telephone calls with former colleagues as the History built up, my warmest thanks for your patience.

John Marsh
Boughton Monchelsea, Kent

Preface & Introduction

I began my employment with Reed Transport in April 1956 as a Trainee Traffic Clerk at Aylesford and had the privilege of experiencing first hand the development of the Company from it's early days. Apart from an absence of two years between 1960 and 1962 for National Service and a gap of 21 months at the end of the Seventies, I was a part of the Company's culture and ethos, and well into the ownership change to SCA Transport from 1991.

Reed Transport was a great Company to work for and so inevitably the researching and writing of this History was to become a labour of love, not only for my own satisfaction but for the benefit of, and on behalf of those thousands of people who at one time or another worked for it. It has put me in touch with many ex employees - my former colleagues, many of whom have been long retired. What has surprised me is the extent to which so many of them still held clear memories of vehicles or events or operations dating back thirty, forty or more years. In every instance, it was obvious that all still held great affection and respect for the Company.

The layout I finally settled upon was to break the History down roughly into decades, interspersed with chapters covering specific subjects, engineering for instance, or operational events which I considered worthy of special record. I have also described how things were done, for example vehicle programming and the allocation of cost and income. There are occasions when I have had to backtrack or repeat some item of detail where it is relevant to more than one part. I hope this is not too irritating to the reader.

Inevitably there are inaccuracies, hopefully very few, but when one relies upon memory only, some poetic licence may have crept in. The main point is that the spirit of the story has been maintained. I have tried to tell it as it really was, warts and all. I sincerely hope that the readers enjoy the story, be they former employees, transport historians, diesel in the blood transport people, enthusiasts or just plain Joe Public.

Finally, a memory from myself to set the scene. As a rather naive 16 years old trainee, I was told by one of my respected colleagues to go down to the Yard and tell a particular driver (in fact Alan Stephens) to tranship a load. I recall that it was a Friday afternoon and I guess Alan was hoping for a prompt finish. I expected that I would be greeted with some hostility. I guess that Alan realised that I had been set up but after a somewhat chilly response, went off to tranship without further ado. I was relieved to say the least but it was part of the learning curve for all new entrants into the transport industry and an experience overall which I would not have missed for the world.

Any person standing on Gorse Hill by the side of the A20 at West Kingsdown in Kent on a weekday afternoon in the mid Fifties could not fail to notice and be impressed by those Maudslay and Foden eight wheelers laden with reels of newsprint from Aylesford Paper Mills, destined for delivery to the London press rooms the next morning, as they powered up over the North Downs. Those magnificent vehicles resplendent in mid green livery with gold lettering were returning to their London Depot squeezed under and between railway arches in Southwark, just down from Blackfriars Bridge. The convoy would also have comprised various fixed artics and one or two Maudslay or Austin four wheelers.

The scene is much changed today. The M20 Motorway has reduced the A20 at West Kingsdown to relative quiet except on Brands Hatch racing circuit days and no longer are the national dailies printed in Fleet Street and the Southwark area printing houses. No longer is there a need for a staging post in central London, also carrying a reserve stock of reels in case of emergency. Deliveries are made direct into the large printers in south and east London using automated discharge system curtainside trailers. Sheets and ropes have long been an encumbrance of the past. One aspect of the operation has not changed though - the expectancy of the customer towards the haulier to be able to deliver a first class service with meticulously timed deliveries and damage free product.

This is the story of one of those hauliers, primarily serving the paper and packaging industries, from it's creation in 1954 to it's finale, in name, in 1991 - Reed Transport Limited. A legend in it's own right, this book also traces the Company's roots in south London and Berkshire between the Wars, through the implications of 1947 Nationalisation and 1954 Denationalisation, it's steady development in the 1960s and 1970s followed by a period of uncertainty in the 1980s and into the 1990s. With the story comes many hitherto unpublished photographs of vehicles, people and events, which became the cement between the building blocks of what was a unique haulage company in so many ways. Enjoy the story.

Chapter One

The Perkins & Glover Years

If one studies an A to Z London Street Atlas for Great Suffolk Street, off Southwark Street which is the link on the south side of the River Thames between Blackfriars Road and Southwark Bridge Road, a triangulation of railway lines will be found. One runs south to north into Blackfriars Station, another runs east to west from London Bridge to Waterloo East Station, whilst a third curves up to Blackfriars from London Bridge. Beneath the arches thus created within the triangle, a thriving independent haulage company operated.

The name of the Company was Perkins & Glover Limited and it was founded on 7th July 1930. A copy of the Certificate of Incorporation no 249321 is at Appendix 1. The entrance to the Depot and the address of the Company was 38 Great Suffolk Street, London SE1. A copy of a large scale Ordnance Survey map published in 1951 is featured below and covers that part of North Southwark which includes the triangulation of railway lines and no 38.

To the rear of the Depot was an office which opened out into Gambia Street, built in about 1951 or 1952. The property was owned by the Railway Executive to whom a rent was paid. A ledger entry reveals the October 1954 rent for Great Suffolk Street was £42.10s.0d and that for Gambia Street £4.5s.0d, a total of £46.15s.0d.

The General Election of July 1945 resulted in a landslide for the Labour Party. Within their manifesto was the intention to nationalise railways and long distance transport. The due Parliamentary processes dragged through 1946 culminating in Royal Assent in August 1947. The Transport Act 1947 was then on the Statute Book.

Albert E. Reed, the Aylesford, Kent based paper manufacturer was the principal customer of Perkins &

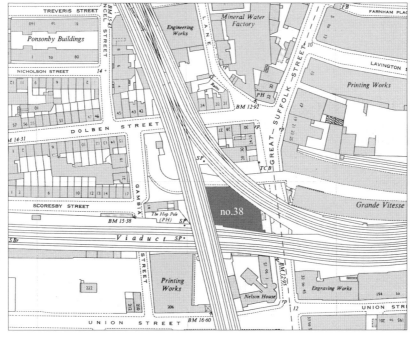

Glover. The threat imposed by nationalisation became a threat in the mind of Reed to the continuity of the all important level of service and in 1947 Perkins & Glover became a wholly owned subsidiary of Albert E. Reed, surrendering it's A Licence and becoming a C Licensee. Quoting from Philip Sykes' 'Albert E. Reed and the creation of a paper business 1860 - 1960', "At this point the Reed group consolidated its position with two small but important acquisitions. .... (The other deal) involved the acquisition of Perkins & Glover whose transport business was engaged primarily in carrying the company's paper. The price paid was £50,000, payable as to £30,000 immediately and the remainder over ten years. It continued under it's current management".

The other acquisition referred to was the paper agents Friedman & Wescott and were both made following the announcement of a consolidated trading profit of £580,000 in the year to 31st March 1947 for Albert E. Reed and the subsequent dividend payable.

Philip Sykes was Deputy Chairman of Reed Paper Group from 1963 and a Deputy Chairman of Reed International from 1970 and was the author of two volumes covering the history of Reed from 1860 to 1974.

The Company continued in the Perkins & Glover name until 14th October 1954 when changed to Reed Transport Limited. A copy of the Change of Name Certificate is featured at Appendix 2. Following that date, a small fleet of 'Reed' vehicles based at the Mills at Aylesford known as the Local Fleet combined with the P&G fleet to create the embryo Reed Transport fleet. The initial fleet comprised 47 vehicles based in London and 11 vehicles at Aylesford plus the Local Fleet. Also included within the new Company was a fleet of 150 cars managed at Aylesford on behalf of the parent company. Appendix 3 lists all known vehicles operated between 1945 and 1956 whilst Appendix 4 covers the Aylesford Local Fleet between 1954 and 1956.

To illustrate the importance of the Albert E. Reed Aylesford Paper Mills business to Perkins & Glover, a study has been made of a ledger covering the years 1945 to 1949, particularly the revenue figures or in the ledger terms 'cartages'. The cartages recorded for the above period are as follows:

Year	Total	Aylesford Paper Mills	% of Total
1945	£29,071. 4s.11d.	£23,873. 2s. 2d.	82%
1946	£35,762.12s.10d.	£30,803. 5s. 2d.	86%
1947	£43,033. 9s. 2d.	£33,546. 5s.11d	78%
1948	£57,853. 0s. 7d.	£49,796.15s. 7d.	86%

(to March 1949)

When referring to the customer base for 1947 below, those with an eagle eye will spot a discrepancy of about £686, this sum probably lost in the opening and closing balances.

Net profits for the same period recorded in the ledger are as follows:

1945	£1625.2s.2d	=	5.6% return on revenue
1946	£3116.7s.7d	=	8.7% return on revenue
1947	£3972.7s.9d	=	9.2% return on revenue
1948	£4556.11s.5d	=	7.9% return on revenue

Summary of Cartages 1947

Customer	£	s	d
Albert E. Reed, Aylesford Paper Mills	33546	5	11
Southern Paper Stock	3199	5	6
W. Soanes	1848	13	9
Albert E. Reed, Tovil & Bridge Mills	1675	8	1
Hugh Stevenson & Sons	1219	12	7
Samuel Jones & Co	668	8	10
Lloyds Shipping Gazette	340	19	8
South London Press	192	15	10
Hackney Gazette	167	5	1
J. Hill	131	6	7
United Wire Works	112	0	0
George Newnes	86	2	2
Daily Mirror	85	9	10
Surrey Advertiser	72	3	1
Winner Publishing Co	37	18	10
St Pancras Chronicle	27	15	9
Oury Miller	26	1	3
Albert E. Reed, London Paper Mills	11	18	8
Henry Ling	11	8	1
Sundry cartages	248	4	11
	£43719	4	5

Most, if not all, of these customers were paper related businesses. Southern Paper Stock was a Reed subsidiary sourcing wastepaper and based at Tovil, Maidstone. The remaining companies were printers, publishers, paper merchants or suppliers to the papermaking industry such as United Wire Works who supplied machine wires.

Origins of Perkins & Glover

So what were the origins of Perkins & Glover Limited? At the Local Studies Library of the London Borough of Southwark, in Borough High Street, a search was made through the Post Office London Street Directories - Kelly's. The lineage of P&G has been traced back to 1858 when George Perkins had a corn dealer's business at 20 Gravel Lane, Southwark. More about Gravel Lane later.

The 1857 Directory lists 20 Gravel Lane as occupied by Charles Potter, a corn chandler. Moving forward to 1870, the occupier is listed as George William Perkins. Was this the same Mr Perkins or a son perhaps? Also in 1870, the same George William Perkins occupied nearby 136 Union Street. The year earlier, 1869, listed 136 Union Street as occupied by Mrs Martha Purser. By 1873, George William had moved to 54 Gravel Lane but still had the premises in Union Street, still trading as a corn dealer.

In 1881, 136 Union Street was occupied by James Loughlin, a coal dealer, whilst another change was imminent. Next door, 56 Gravel Lane was occupied by Kingston & Son, listed as railway agents. A year earlier, 56 was the address of John King, a confectioner. 1882 saw diversification. 54 continued to be listed as George William Perkins, corn dealer, but 56 showed George Perkins & Co as railway agents, clearly the takeover of the Kingston & Son business. The next year, 1893, it appears that the corn dealer business had been abandoned as the Directory shows 54 and 56 occupied by George Perkins & Co., railway agents.

The demise of George William saw Mrs Mary Ann Perkins & Son listed in 1896 as railway agents and in 1897, Perkins & Son, railway agents. Such was the listing until 1906. The year 1907 saw the first move in name to the transport business notwithstanding the associated role of railway agents. Perkins & Co were listed as carmen, continued to 1919.

The following year, 1920, saw the first mention of the Glover name with two entries against 54 - Perkins & Co., carmen and Sidney John Glover, carman. A dictionary definition of carman is 'one who drives a cart', reflecting the Company's early reliance on four hooved power. In 1928, the Directory changed, listing Perkins & Co and Sidney John Glover as 'motor haulage contractors'. The 1931 Directory showed Perkins & Glover Ltd - motor haulage contractors - for the first time as well as Sydney

John Glover - motor haulage contractor.

But this was to be more than just a business relationship. Sidney John had married Nellie Perkins, presumably the daughter of George and Mary Ann. Ledger entries suggest that Sidney and Nell were active in the Company up to July 1948. Certainly Nell Glover was a force to be reckoned with in the Company in the immediate post War years. Her word was law. She had a dog called Chuckles who inevitably became the object of a scam. Often, a driver would be detailed to take Chuckles for a walk. Occasionally Chuckles would go 'missing' and a reward would be posted. Miraculously the dog would be 'found' and the reward duly claimed. An unofficial rota appears to have been operated to decide whose turn it was to lose Chuckles!

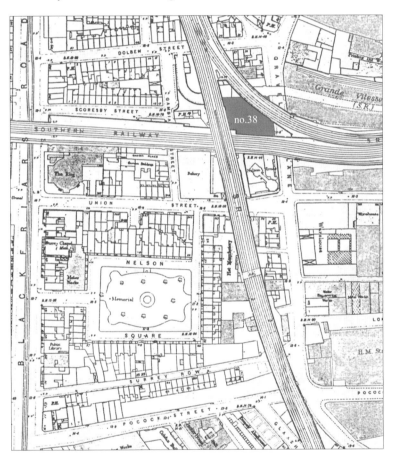

During the War, Nell and Sidney lived on the top floor of the Strand Palace Hotel, from where they ran the business, shuttling to and from Great Suffolk Street amidst the bomb damage.

Nell was a beautiful singer and pianist and counted amongst her friends Nellie Melba and Ivor Novello. Sidney was a great sportsman and was active in high diving, motor racing, especially at Brooklands, golf and bowls. He was also a Margate Bowls Champion.

Nell and Sidney's son, Alan Curtis, was born in January 1914 at 54 Gravel Lane and in 1932 went to Peterhouse College, Cambridge. Alan studied Law, a profession which he intended to pursue rather than join the family business. He did however join the Company briefly before the War. During the War he served as a tank commander in North Africa, was captured in the desert and was a prisoner of war in Italy and Germany until his return in 1945. He was mentioned in despatches. Reference is made of Alan in a ledger from January 1945 presumably about the time he rejoined the Company. He became General Manager, a position which he held after the Reed purchase and the change of name to Reed Transport in 1954. Thereafter, Alan continued as

Managing Director until his retirement in early 1969. He died in 1984. His father, Sidney, died aged 77 in February 1961.

And what about 54 Gravel Lane? The London County Council abolished the name of Gravel Lane by a Date of Order of 7th July 1939 to take effect as from 1st January 1940, becoming an extension of Great Suffolk Street. For 54 read 38. Presumably a house originally stood on the site. Previously, Great Suffolk Street ended, northwards, at the junction with Wellington Street, now called Pocock Street and Gravel Lane extended up to and across Southwark Street into what is now Sumner Street. Today, Great Suffolk Street extends from Borough High Street across South-wark Bridge Road and Union Street up to Southwark Street. Thus Perkins & Glover and predecessors had been based 'under the arches' since 1873.

A copy of an Ordnance Survey map is featured left this revealing Gravel Lane extending north from Great Suffolk Street. It also shows the tram lines as well as railway lines.

There is also another Southwark address which needs to be brought into the story - this being Bullstairs Wharf, a warehouse on the River Thames. There is no listing of Bullstairs Wharf in 'London Wharves and Docks' published by Temple Press in association with 'Commercial Motor' in it's second edition form in 1954. Neither can it be found in the latest A to Z, but it formed a key part in the Perkins & Glover, later Reed Transport operation. However, reference to the London County Council 'Names of Streets and Places in London' for 1929 and 1955, lists Bull stairs, Bull alley, Upper Ground Street, Southwark. A close study of the A to Z just west of Blackfriars Bridge will reveal an entry for Bull All. (Alley). For those familiar with London will recognise the site between the Bridge and the Oxo Tower. A copy of an early Ordnance Survey map indicating Bull Stairs Wharf is featured overleaf.

It is not known when P&G first occupied Bull Stairs

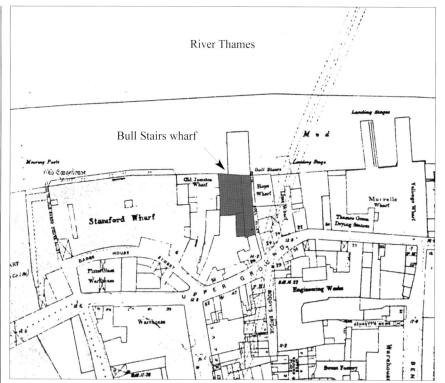

River Thames

Bull Stairs wharf

Wharf but it was in full use during the 1950s for the warehousing of smaller consignments - paper in reams for example - and also the parking of trailers as the articulated fleet increased, together with some vehicles. There is no ledger record of rental payments for the premises.

Another Southwark landmark played an important part in the Perkins & Co and P&G business - Bricklayers' Arms Goods Station. Originally built in 1844, 'The Brick' was finally closed in June 1981. Back in 1921, Bricklayers' Arms handled 800,000 tons of traffic, employed 1000 people to handle the freight plus a further 300 who acted as clerks, etc. A sentence in Malcolm Tucker's 'Bricklayers' Arms Station' published in 1989 reads 'Some manufactured products travelled inwards, such as building materials, paper from the mills of North Kent for London's packaging and printing industries ...' Aylesford Paper Mills shipped paper by the South Eastern Railway to Bricklayers' Arms which the Company then distributed throughout London, before and after the War.

As well as the Glover family, in the early post-war years the staff included Ted Holwill and 'Val' Valentine on the administration side whilst Frank Brown was the Supervisor looking after the day to day operations in the Depot including the vehicle programming and warehousing. Fred Parton looked after the maintenance and repairs of the fleet. In February 1949, Ron Adkins joined the Company fresh from two years National Service with the RAF. Ron, who had been based in Berlin and subsequently Wahn near Bonn, had

found his interest in transport matters as a consequence of the challenges presented by the Berlin Airlift working with the distribution of food and other supplies flown into that city. After some initial training from Frank Brown, he took over the fleet programming.

Prior to the building of the office opening into Gambia Street the Company was run from small offices just inside the depot on the left. The left and centre railway arches to the rear were used for the warehousing of reels, the right hand arch providing access to the new office. The repair bay was to the right hand side, again under an arch. A study of the Ordnance Survey map of 1951 on page seven can visualise the layout as described.

It is not known when P&G last relied upon horse drawn transport but two stories have been recalled by Ron Adkins from long serving drivers who worked with the horses. When Ron asked Tom Killick how he liked his new vehicle, Tom replied that "it was not a patch on Babs and Beattie", his beloved horses. David Diss recalled how they struggled with the horses to cross Blackfriars Bridge en route to Fleet Street in icy conditions. The Bridge in those days was paved in wooden blocks which became very slippery. Their solution was always to follow the tram lines because the tram drivers always carried a small sack of sand which more often than not was used to release cart and lorry wheels from the tracks.

Little is known about early motor vehicles other than those listed in Appendix 3. Michael Glover, the son of Alan, recalls that the fleet included some steam wagons "definitely not Sentinels, probably Fodens". Harry Chittenden (of whom more later) recalls possibly two Diamond T four-wheel rigids in the fleet around 1938/1939. They were of normal control layout with prominent chrome radiator grilles "very modern for their time". Harry also recalls one or two Foden six-wheel rigids at that time.

The P&G livery was brown with white lettering but as the Company moved towards the change of name to Reed Transport, so the livery changed to the familiar 'Reed' green with gold lettering, described in greater detail in Chapter Twenty. The post War vehicle supplier was Maskells of Brixton, Bill Maskell being a great friend of Alan Glover. The relationship was so close that annually a joint Sports Day including a cricket match was held at Warlingham, Surrey by the two companies. Maskells continued to supply many vehicles to Reed Transport well into the 1960s.

The implications of Nationalisation excepted, so what was so special about P&G which caused one of the UK's fast developing manufacturing companies to buy it? It was all about those three key factors - service, reliability and commitment. Virtually every newsprint customer demanded a timed delivery. 8.00am meant 8.00am and an 8.15am or 8.30am arrival was not good enough. Streets were narrow and even in the Forties there was congestion and parking difficulties particularly in London. There were street markets to beat, tight entrances and primitive unloading facilities. There was War damage and reconstruction to be avoided. A second to none level of service and reliability was paramount. Certainly P&G's commitment to Albert E. Reed was never in doubt with an average of 83% of it's business from Aylesford Paper Mills alone. Added to the above factors was the close proximity of Great Suffolk Street to Fleet Street, and P&G becoming a wholly owned subsidiary of Reed became a reality.

Thus we have a small family owned business with a turnover of £43,000 in 1947 which was to expand and develop over the next 44 years into a nationwide operator of high standing and repute within the haulage industry and reaching a turnover in 1991 of £13.2 million. The Perkins & Glover name survived for seven of those years until the name change to Reed Transport. Throughout the

44 years, it was those three vital factors which were to be the parameters by which the Company was to be judged by the parent Company and by which it was able to survive the pressures of 'big group' ownership. It was never to become a financial burden, always achieving an acceptable profit and return on capital despite all the traumas and setbacks on the way. The route through those 44 years begins at the next Chapter.

Left: A group of former P&G, later RT London Depot drivers. Pictured left to right are: Frank Brown - Depot Supervisor, Fred Humphreys, Dan Jenkins, Bill Humphreys (brother of Fred) and Tom Killick on the occasion in 1962 of the five collectively achieving 200 years of service.

Below: This photograph was probably taken during the Lord Mayor's Procession of November 1926. Perkins & Co. were entrusted with the carrying of this De Havilland DH 50J hauled by Fordson XU 9930. The aircraft had been used on return survey flights to Capetown and Melbourne made for Imperial Airways being flown by Alan Cobham. The flight to Capetown began on 16th November 1925 when he took off from De Havilland's factory at Stag Lane, Edgware Middlesex, arriving in Capetown on 17th February 1926. He landed back in London on 13th March. Then on 30th June 1926 Cobham took off from Rochester to survey a route to Australia, landing in Melbourne on 15th August. The return flight was made between 29th August and 4th October, in time to appear in the procession the following month. Alan Cobham's achievements were recognised by a knighthood conferred by His Majesty King George V.

Chapter Two

Return to 'Hire and Reward'

Having abandoned A Licences and the ability for 'hire and reward' operations in 1947, the Company then took a dramatic u-turn in 1955, with history repeating itself but in reverse. The Conservative Party returned to power in October 1951 committed to denationalisation and consequently The Transport Act 1953 was given Royal Assent in November 1953. Although it was intended for BRS to continue but on a greatly reduced scale, a Road Haulage Disposal Board was established to dispose of a large number of depots and vehicles in units by tender.

One depot scheduled for disposal was BRS Larkfield, one mile away from Reed Transport's Aylesford base and a prime supplier of vehicles to the Aylesford Mills and factories. Prior to nationalisation, Thomas Tilling, the London based bus and goods vehicle operator, owned the Larkfield Depot. On nationalisation, Tilling became a 'lead company' and Larkfield Depot became part of 2A Mid Kent Group within South Eastern District, later during reorganisation becoming 61F Mid Kent (Maidstone) Group.

The Tender Document for the disposal of Unit 66/6554, as it was designated, listed 39 vehicles of which four were described as additional vehicles. There were also 10 trailers, one being listed as additional. One trailer was a drawbar whilst two others were 'fixed' to AEC tractors. A further one not identified would also have been 'fixed' but to a Vulcan tractor, later to be converted to full automatic coupling. See Appendix 5 notes.

In 1955, Reed Transport successfully tendered for this unit and so returned to being a 'hire and reward' operator with a Special A Licence. Thirty-nine vehicles had been acquired and transferred down the road to Aylesford. The Company had gone the full circle.

Drivers and Staff who transferred to Reed Transport with the acquisition of BRS Larkfield Depot in 1955 (as remembered)

Drivers

Jack Ackrill	Jack 'Ginger' Lawrence
Albert Basden	George Lewis
Johnny Basden	Charlie Luck
Fred Broderick	George Maile
Arthur Bryant	George Martin
Tommy Cresser	Charlie Mitchell
'Titch' Crittenden	Bert Norley
'Pop' Driver	Percy Ottaway
Eric Edmonds	Charlie Patston
Bill Featherstone	Arthur Plummer
Charlie Hawkins	Johnny Reader
Bill Hepper	Ken Sackett
Johnny Jell	Alan Stephens
George Jones	Joe Westaway
Stan Kelk	Len Woods
Tommy Knight	

Staff

Jim Atkinson	Wally Wraight
Frank Davis	Elsie (later married
Joe Smith	Fred Broderick)

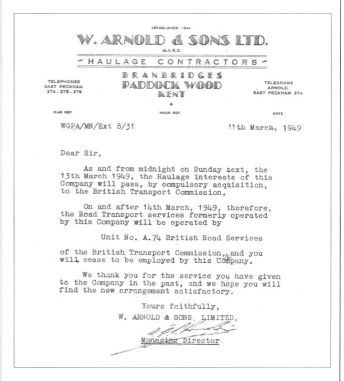

Above: George Martin was a driver with Mid Kent haulier W. Arnold & Sons Ltd. Above is a letter dated 11th March 1949 advising George that, as from 14th March, the road transport services would be by Unit A74 British Road Services as part of nationalisation. This must have been one of thousands of similar letters sent to transport employees about that time. George later joined Reed Transport when the BRS Larkfield Depot was acquired. His regular ex BRS vehicle was Atkinson six-wheeler 215 - HKK 445, followed by replacement Foden eight-wheeler - YKP 105, this also carrying fleet number 215. For many years later George was a permanent night trunk driver on the Aylesford to Wigan service.

Left: These two AEC Mammoth Major MkIIs had a chequered life. New in March 1939 to Greenwoods of Ramsey, they were transferred then or at a later date to subsidiary Medway Transport of Rainham. They are shown as requisitioned into the British Ministry of War Transport. Note the camouflaged shed, the MoWT drivers' uniforms and white edging to the wings. Released back to Medway, on nationalisation they became a part of BRS Mid Kent Group based at Larkfield. BEW 486 as 61F259 and BEW 535 as 61F260. When Reed acquired BRS Larkfield as Unit 66/6554 in 1955 they became Reed Transport's nos. 217 and 218. By the time BEW 486 arrived at RT, it had gained a more streamlined cab with an unusual three-piece windscreen. Regular drivers were Jack 'Ginger' Lawrence and 'Pop' Driver.

Below: The actual ledger entry detailing the purchase of the 39 vehicles, licences and ancillary effects of BRS Larkfield Depot.

It is not known whether all 39 vehicles saw operational service from day one. They were allocated fleet numbers 201 to 239 and are confidently listed at Appendix 5. The land on the A20 in Larkfield was subsequently sold, initially becoming a car dealership and is now occupied by a Filling Station and B&Q store. An entry in a ledger suggests a purchase price of £63,500 for the ex BRS vehicles. The ledger itself makes for interesting reading:

June 13, 1955.

Motor vehicles ex BRS	£63,500
Licences ('A' Fleet)	£1721.11s.3d.
Plant	£8
Furniture & equipment	£142
Petrol & oil ('A' Fleet)	£286.1s.
(charged sic) to	
A.E. Reed & Co Ltd (loan a/c)	£65,000
A.E. Reed & Co Ltd (Kingsway)	£651.15s.5d.
BRS Maidstone Depot	£5.16s.10d.

Being purchase considerations for 'A' Licence Fleet purchased from the British Transport Commission together with agreed take over values of fuel, licenses, etc.

The next ledger entry follows:

June 13th 1955:
Depreciation of Fixed Assets (M/Vs) £29,500
(charged sic) to
Depreciation on Motor Vehicles £29,500
(ex BRS)

Amount required to reduce 'A' Licence Vehicles to present commercial value.

It appears that £29,500 in value was written off from day one. Was this the value of goodwill? There is no entry related to the value of the BRS Depot land. Perhaps this was taken into parent company Albert E Reed as an asset valued at £651.15s.5d, then to be resold?

By the end of the financial year 31st March 1958, only 10 of the original acquired vehicles remained in the fleet. The replacements were 10 Foden eight-wheel rigids of which four were 'secondhand' transfers from the Perkins & Glover London fleet, two Foden six-wheel 'Chinese Six' twin steer rigids, six Austin / Scammell tractors and eight Austin four-wheel rigids. Apart from the four transfers, the 21 others were all new purchases. Details of these replacement vehicles are at Appendix 6.

So the Company now had C Licences for Aylesford and London in the name of A.E. Reed & Co Ltd and a Special A Licence in the name of Reed Transport Ltd. But it was that combination which was to find the

Above: Arthur Ingram was there in London's Archway Road in July 1957 with his camera when Reed's AEC Matador 3472 no.235 - LKT 752 with its fixed Dyson single-axle trailer passed by hauling this well sheeted load. The AEC was one of those acquired in 1955 by Reed when the vehicles and assets of BRS Larkfield were purchased. The AEC first went on the road in September 1949 being owned by H.J.Manwaring, 'The Nortons', Maidstone Road, Collier Street, Marden.

Company before the Transport Tribunal before long. In December 1955, an Application was made to the South Eastern Licensing Authority for an A Licence to carry 'General goods - primarily paper and paper products such as finished paper including newsprint, corrugated boxes, paper sacks, towels, tubes and the like paper products for Albert E. Reed & Co Ltd., and it's subsidiaries, and return loads of general goods being machinery, raw materials and other goods for Albert E. Reed & Co Ltd., and it's subsidiaries, <u>and general goods for independent concerns'</u>.

It was this last phrase, underlined, which was to create controversy over the coming months. Out of the 18 vehicles that were the subject of the Application, the Company intended that six would replace some of the 39 vehicles which by now were held on the Special A Licence whilst the remaining 12 were to be additional vehicles. A new newsprint machine, no 13, was being built at Aylesford to come into production in 1957 with an annual capacity in excess of 80,000 tons and that was going to need extra vehicles. The Application was refused by the LA, even the substitution was refused for the six vehicles. There followed a Public Inquiry in early

1956 when the decision was upheld.

Under the Road and Rail Traffic Act 1933, the Appeal Tribunal had argued that whilst Section 12 of the Act allowed for a Company and it's subsidiaries to be regarded as one for the purpose of B and C Licences, companies could not hold an A Licence allowing them to carry their own goods as well as those of other companies. An earlier case in 1947 had seen the Appeal Tribunal uphold a refusal to grant an A Licence to W.H.S Transport Ltd, a subsidiary of W.H. Smith & Son Ltd

The decision included the statement "It is not appropriate or desirable that the company operating the transport should carry goods for hire or reward for the parent company, and also for other persons under an A Licence." Accepting the principles of the W.H.S.

decision, the LA held that, because all the companies in the group were members of a 'family', an A Licence should not be granted and that the work should be done under C licence. There was a suggestion that Reed Transport had gained the Special A Licence through an oversight by Parliament and that the vehicles should be operated on a C Licence.

The Company appealed against the refusal to the Transport Tribunal which now, since 1951, included the old Appeal Tribunal. The Tribunal sat for three days in January 1957 to consider the case. The respondent was the British Transport Commission. Mr Gerald Thesiger QC representing the Company submitted that Parliament intended that BRS vehicles should be operated under Special A Licences when disposed of and that the holders were in no worse position than those of ordinary A Licences when seeking replacement or additional vehicles and the fact that Reed Transport was a subsidiary made no difference.

Mr Beddington for the BTC said that the Commission had not objected to the replacement vehicles but opposed the grant of further A Licence vehicles. The Reed Group held C Licences and would be able to afford to charge lower rates for return loads than ordinary hauliers. He did not agree with the LA's view that it had been an oversight by Parliament by which the Special A Licence had been obtained. Special A Licences were perhaps a bait to attract customers to help in the disposal of the BRS undertaking. Reed Transport had paid for the Special A Licence and were entitled to it's privileges. It was clear that Reed wanted A Licences for additional work because

the work could not be undertaken economically with C Licence vehicles. While it was perfectly legitimate for Reed to ask for this licence, it was against the public interest that it should be granted.

The Tribunal announced at the end of the Hearing that the appeal would be successful in so far as the six replacement vehicles were concerned. The matter of the additional vehicles was to be referred back to the LA so that both parties could produce additional evidence. No record of the next stage of this case exists in the archives but it must be assumed that a successful outcome was achieved by the Company from the LA.

There was a backlash from within the transport press. 'Motor Transport' for 15th March 1957 carried a headline "Domination and dictation by big business." The column 'Signpost' commented in a lengthy article "Where does this decision lead? Every C licensee, large and small, can now do what Reed Transport has done." In 'Commercial Motor' for 29th March, Political Commentary by Janus under the heading "Letter and Spirit" carried a whole page on the Tribunal decision. The final paragraph started "The damage that the new decision may cause to the haulier is obvious, although the extent of the damage remains to be seen."

Certainly, the general haulage industry saw Reed Transport and it's A Licence as a threat and probably all without exception were critical of the Transport Tribunal's decision. Drivers fed back comments from on the road about 'Greedy Reed' but the Company weathered the sour grapes and was to prosper up to and beyond the introduction of Operators Licences.

Right above: No.26 - JXL 199 was one of six Maudslay Maharanee tractors with single axle fixed trailers in the fleet with a 12 ton payload. It is pictured refuelling at the North Site Depot in Aylesford.

Left: A very smart Maudslay Mogul no.27 - JXP 549 passing Blackfriars Tube Station on it's way back empty to London Depot over Blackfriars Bridge in the early 1950s.
Photo: A Hustwitt (c) NA3T

Reed Transport was a general road haulier. Thus, between October 1954 and June 1955, the P&G London and Aylesford based fleets, the Aylesford Paper Mills Local Fleet and the acquired fleet of BRS Larkfield were brought together under the General Management of Alan Glover.

A.J.(Bert) Bryant was Commercial Manager London and W.C.(Bill) Dale, who had joined the Company in 1955, was Commercial Transport Manager Aylesford. Fred Dowlman relinquished his responsibility for the Local Fleet to concentrate on the management of the Mills' Yard Department, responsible for raw materials. Eric Atkins was Maintenance Superintendent and Eric Clegg the Accountant. Another Director for a short period was Fred Lewis who joined from Aylesford Paper Mills where he had particular responsibilities for the car fleet. He retired in 1959.

The fleet by mid 1956 comprised 124 vehicles and 52 semi-trailers. 'Commercial Motor' for 16th and 23rd November 1956 carried a feature article on Reed Transport titled "Transportivity in Top Gear" - the Company was on it's way.

Right: Alan Glover, Managing Director Reed Transport Ltd.

Above: Maudslay badged Mammoth Major MkIII no.47 - LUV 240 is pictured awaiting unloading in Fountayne Road, Tottenham with a four-high load of reels for John Dickensons, sheets neatly rolled up on top. John Dickenson's address was Broad Lane, Tottenham off which Fountayne Road ran. It is wearing the original early 1950s livery and would have been in the Perkins & Glover fleet as an Albert E Reed subsidiary at the time. Harry Stratford was its regular driver. This Arthur Ingram view dates from January 1951.

Left: Seen later in its career, this 1954 Bedford S-Type no.63 had been relegated to local work and is seen here at the Quarry, Tovil Mills being loaded with towelling probably comprising six small deckel (width) reels wrapped as a single roll ready for delivery to Kimberly Clark at Larkfield. Note the long forks on the forktruck. This would have been after the acquisition of the Tovil & Bridge fleet and operations in 1959 described in chapter four.

Left: Photographed when new and before receiving it's plate this Austin 7K/FED3 four wheel rigid was one of a batch bought in the summer of 1956. No.14 is believed to have received the registration number XKO 267.

Below: UKE 515 was one of four Austin Loadstar six tonners and was used on the many small newsprint deliveries to London or down to the West Country and Cornwall. This late example of the type was bought in December 1954.

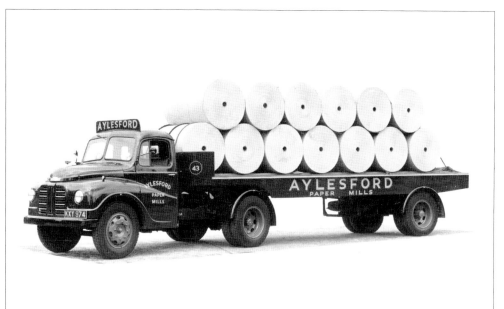

Left: P&G for several years favoured Austin tractors with fixed semi trailers with a 9-ton payload. No. 43 and it's sister no.44 were the last into the fleet as full articulation then took over as vital to provide the flexibility needed with pre loading of trailers in the Mills.

Below: No.69 - UKP 155 was one of seven Foden FG6/12 six wheel rigids purchased in 1955 for the C Licence fleet at Aylesford. It is here depicted in No.9 Reelstock Shed at Aylesford Paper Mills, West Mill being loaded by overhead crane with wrapped reels of newsprint. No.9 machine was one of the newsprint machines at Aylesford. The hessian sacks against the wall would have held wooden reel centre bungs.

Above: No.60 - NGN 52 was one of two Fodens exhibited at the 1952 Motor Show. Its companion was no.61 - NGO 52, a tractor with single-axle fixed trailer. Both had cream steering wheels, just discernible in no.60, for the occasion. It looks as if the load - being sheeted up by driver Chris Mallett - comprises 20 reels of newsprint loaded three tiers high, possibly for delivery to the Daily Mirror at Back Lane, EC4.

Left: No.17 became the first of four Foden FE6/15s which were transferred into the A Licence fleet, renumbered 220. It replaced the ex BRS AEC Mammoth Major of the same number which was stolen in 1955. Seen here being tidily loaded with newsprint - eight reels on the floor, seven as the second tier and then six reels on top - it was itself replaced by an FG6/24 in 1956.

Above: What it is all about, or was - Fleet Street. A busy post-war scene looking towards Ludgate Circus with St Paul's Cathedral in the distance. At the extreme left are the distinctive offices of the Daily Express, now known as River Court, whilst further down are the offices of the Irish Independent and the Methodist Recorder, also now long gone as is the building they occupy.

Left: Another view of No.60 - NGN 52, probably taken around the same period as the picture taken in Aylesford sheeting and roping up. The vehicle's location is approximately the same as that depicted in the Fleet Street picture above. Undoubtedly the load's sheeting has been removed for dramatic effect in this publicity image that appeared in the Reed Paper Group's 50th Anniversary brochure published in 1953.

Chapter Three

Progress During the Early Years

During the five years 1955 to 1959, the operational activities were rationalised. For a while, the three fleets referred to within the Company as the A Licence Fleet, the C Licence Fleet and the Local Fleet continued to operate independently, but from the same Traffic Office. Many of the vehicles acquired from BRS were, to say the least, somewhat decrepit and a replacement programme had been undertaken. Many ex BRS vehicles were disposed of still in red livery with Reed fleet numbers only added in white in a white circle.

Typically, an A Licence vehicle would leave Aylesford on a Sunday for a north west destination, backloading and back empty by Wednesday afternoon. A short Midlands run was then programmed for Thursday and Friday - remember these were 20 mph days! A vehicle leaving on Monday for the North, back on Thursday, needed a 'local' for Friday or else was backloaded for tipping out on the following Monday.

For those drivers heading for the north west on the A5, the 'Jubilee' at Brownhills was the usual stopover whilst the 'Goats Head' at Towcester was another favourite. When ex BRS Larkfield driver Albert Basden - 'Yahyah' to his colleagues - died, he left instructions for his ashes to be scattered along the A5 at the top of Tramways Hill north of Towcester. Albert's vehicle from BRS was AEC Matador four-wheeler no 212 with the Carrimore drawbar trailer in tow. Later he took over the AEC Mammoth Major MkIII eight-wheeler no 221.

The fleet movements were planned on a blackboard and there was constant speculation amongst the more cynical traffic staff that if someone swept against the board and inadvertently wiped off the detail, the fleet would be 'lost' for a week. Vehicle programming was soon to become more sophisticated.

Leading sources of backloads included Williams Bros of Queensferry, N. Wales (now part of TDG), Trowbridge of Sheffield, Starr Roadways of Bilston, the Clearing House, Berkeley & Long of Bordesley Green, Birmingham and the inevitable brickfields of East Anglia. Bagged fertilizer was collected from Billingham for delivery to various farms in Kent on behalf of several agricultural merchants. Contact continued with many BRS depots still left in business. In many cases, drivers were left to find their own return loads, their knowledge all part of the skill. On occasions, vehicles were 'lost' until the driver phoned into the Traffic Office when empty for new instructions.

The largely London based C Licence fleet operated on generally a local basis, delivering in London or the Home Counties in the morning, running to Aylesford for reloading, to return to Great Suffolk Street in the afternoon with the next day's delivery. Back loading was minimal, often returns of reel centres to the Mill for reuse being the norm.

The four-wheel rigids were regularly used on six-ton newsprint deliveries into Cornwall - Launceston and Liskeard for example. They were backloaded with bagged china clay from St. Austell for Aylesford Paper Mills. Other 'in house' return loads would be machinery, particularly machine rolls, and spare parts from Walmsleys in Bury and other paper machinery suppliers, machine clothing i.e. drying felts again mainly from Lancashire, and bagged alum from Avonmouth, all back to Aylesford Paper Mills. This traffic was the priority for the

Left: No.202 - XKR 107, an Austin 7K/FED3 four-wheel rigid which first went on the road in July 1956 is pictured later in that year being washed down in the original Aylesford Depot by Sid Brown.

The eight wheel rigid still had a major role to play in the Reed Transport fleet when this picture was taken by the River Medway in 1958. No.52 - 108 BKP, a Foden FG6/24 S20 is seen posed at Aylesford's East Mill by the Export Shed with driver Arthur Bryant at the wheel.

Right: No.19 - YKN 419, Austin 5K/FED3 was new in 1957. This photograph was used by Carrimore Six Wheelers Limited for publicity purposes.

Right below: Reed was a large user of Austin based four wheel rigids. This example was a one off with an attractive fibreglass cab and wrap round windscreen. An MKC/FED3 model and registered 109 CKR it was allocated to the Aylesford A Licence fleet in 1958 given no.231.

C Licence fleet with any excess mopped up by the A Licence vehicles.

A further source of backloads was Reed's factory at Feniscowles near Blackburn, Sun Paper Mill. W.H. Bowker was the local haulier looking after Sun's deliveries. However, with the growing Reed Transport fleet increasingly running to the North West, inroads into this Reed Company's traffic flows was inevitable. This Mill produced paper for the Corrugated Cases factories, including Brentford (soon to be closed and relocated to Thatcham), Aylesford and Histon near Cambridge.

Until 1956 the C Licence fleet continued to be programmed from London Depot. Each day a traffic clerk based in Aylesford Depot would meet with Aylesford Paper Mills, agree the next day's traffic requirements and then transmit the information by telex to London Depot. This role was initially filled by Fred Riley, followed by 'Val' Valentine from London Depot from early 1956. Fred transferred to London Depot.

The teleprinter was affectionately called the 'Wurlitzer'. Later in the day a return telex message would confirm the traffic allocation by fleet number for both the London and Aylesford based C Licence fleet. This information was then

passed back to the Paper Mill. Surplus traffic, mainly the longer distance, was identified as available for RTC.

Confused? In this context, the 'C' did not mean C Licence but Country. The so designated 'Reed Transport Country' fleet was of course the A Licence fleet! Added to that surplus traffic was some traffic from Medway Paper Sacks, predominantly middle and long distance work, and any other traffic from site factories. More about MPS later. Once that fleet was fully programmed the surplus was then subcontracted by the Aylesford Depot Traffic Office. The term 'programmed' was always used rather than 'planned'. From late 1955, Ron Adkins began spending more time at Aylesford,

commuting from North London when necessary. From June 1956, Ron was based at Aylesford Depot and thereafter the fleet programming was undertaken at Aylesford.

With rigid vehicles predominating the fleet, the Mill loading facilities were underutilised in the mornings whilst the mass influx of London based rigids arriving at the loading bays from mid-day created a pressure which could not be sustained. In 1952, a start was made to ease the problem. Two Aylesford based shunters were employed, Ted Brooker from the Local Fleet (of whom more later) and Bill Burridge. One or two 'spare' vehicles were in the system at Aylesford which were then

Left: Aylesford depot S20 cabbed FG6/15, no.215 - YKP 105, replaced a 1945 Atkinson six wheeler of the same number - that vehicle being an ex BRS Larkfield acquisition. George Martin continued as its driver.

Left below: A technically interesting rear view of S20 cab Foden no.52 - 108 BKP which particularly demonstrates the method of securing the overropes to the tie bars on the rear of the body.

On bad days, one or two vehicles never made it back to SE1, this resulting in 'dodgy' nights out for the drivers between Swanley and south London and the shortening of available hours for the next day. A review of the optimum size of fleet which could be sustained by a base in London resulted in the transfer to Aylesford in late 1956/early 1957 of a significant number of the vehicles, the actual number unknown.

A few London drivers did relocate, the names of six can be recalled - Bob Axford, Fred Bissett, Len Jones, Fred Pooke, Bill Stewart and Harry Stratford. Others took redundancy. It was becoming clear also that the introduction of more articulated vehicles with spare trailers to allow off peak morning loading at Aylesford was essential. That said, there were already several Bedford S tractors in the fleet with single-axle Scammell type trailers, later to be replaced by Austin 5K tractors. 10 tons was the limiting carrying capacity.

preloaded for changeovers later in the day as the London drivers arrived, followed by more night changeovers again from London.

Ted, later in 1952, became the first Aylesford based P&G driver 'on the road'. Using no 58 - MXL 740, a new Bedford S/Scammell artic, Ted's first job was to report one Monday morning to Frank Brown at Great Suffolk Street with a load of newsprint for Daily Mirror at Stamford Street, just around the corner. He was progressively followed by many other Aylesford based drivers, a total of 11 vehicles as mentioned earlier by the formation of RT in late 1954. No 58 was later to be stolen from Aylesford.

One regular, almost daily, operation involved three Aylesford based tractors each delivering three loads of sackkraft reels to APCM at Northfleet - 90 tons in total, trailers being preloaded. The regular drivers were Arthur Fenwick, Albert Malyan and Bill 'Mac' McKenzie. Today, if such traffic flow existed, four heavies would comfortably clear the same tonnage. But it was vital to start replacing the traditional 15 ton eight wheeler with full articulation. Seven Foden S20 tractors with 14 Eagle tandem-axle 27ft air suspension trailers entered service in late 1958 and January 1959, nos 91 to 97, which made a significant start towards solving this problem.

Reed Transport became one of the first operators to try

Left: Parked on the forecourt of RT's Head Office is no.91, the first of seven Foden FGTU6/20 tractors introduced in 1958 with 14 Eagle tandem axle air suspension trailers as the first stage of reducing the reliance on eight wheel rigids for heavier loads. The ability to preload trailers eased the peaking of loading at Aylesford Paper Mills caused by a predominance of rigids and 'fixed' artics.

Left below: Rear view of one of 14 Eagle air suspension trailers bought in 1958/59 for working with its fleet of Foden FGTU6/20 S20 tractors. The beginning of the end for the eight wheeler fleet.

Ron Adkins introduced a practice of loading an extra reel in the back dock which was then offloaded in London Depot before the vehicle then proceeded to Holborn. Not only was maximum loadability again achieved (and income) but at least once a week a full load of 20 reels was delivered direct to Holborn from London Depot, saving the collection from Aylesford. Such deliveries could be fitted in to suit the vehicle programme depending on whether the fleet was fully occupied or short of work on a particular day or dependant on the customer's time delivery needs.

After the 24ft bodied rigids, tractors with 27ft trailers were used. It was not uncommon on a quiet day to move a full load of Daily Mirror reels into London Depot for temporary storage. It also allowed the customer to call off extra loads at a moment's notice to meet, say, the extra demand due to the breaking of a major story.

It was not until 1969 that longer vehicles were accommodated at Holborn. A trial one day involved two ERF 30 tons gvw units with 33ft trailers which were successfully manoeuvred into the unloading bays at Holborn, each with 22 reels on board. The drivers Johnny Bull and John Grierson with nos 153 & 155 were the heroes of the day and within a week the Daily Mirror started ordering specific timed deliveries for the longer and heavier vehicles. In due course, Holborn closed and the printing of the Daily Mirror for the south was moved to Watford.

out air suspensions with the Eagles. When Bill Dale asked Ron Adkins for his view on how many artics the Company should buy, Ron's response was "as many as the Company could afford". The future of the eight-wheel rigid at Aylesford was doomed and the last entered service in 1960, about which more in Chapter Twenty.

The storage facility within London Depot enabled maximum loadability to be achieved on some vehicles which otherwise would have been light loaded. For example, one major newsprint customer was the Daily Mirror at Back Hill, London EC1. Reels could only be delivered two tiers high, eight on the floor of an eight wheeler, seven on the second tier, which weighed about 10½ tons. To achieve maximum payload, a further six reels were loaded at the Mill as the third tier which brought the payload up to an acceptable 15 tons. This tier was then offloaded into the store before the vehicle proceeded across Blackfriars Bridge to Back Hill. Then, the Daily Mirror opened a new printing house at nearby Holborn, closing Back Hill. This allowed three high loads to be delivered but the back dock on the top tier was to be left empty in accordance with Daily Mirror instructions.

Left: An aerial view of the complex that was Aylesford taken sometime before 1953. To the left the River Medway and to its right East Mill sandwiched between the river and the Medway Valley railway line. To the right of the railway is the much larger West Mill, unrestricted in its expansion.

known as East Mill and West Mill. That physical separation of the Mills in itself created a need for round the clock internal transport operations. Paper was made from a multitude of grades of woodpulp, much of which arrived by barge up the River Medway from the ports of Rochester and Chatham. East Mill was built on the west bank of the Medway and was therefore, literally, sandwiched between the River and the railway line. Pulp needed at West Mill was moved from East Mill pulp yard or direct from the barges by the Local Fleet, initially using Bedford/Scammell tractors and trailers. The same fleet moved finished product from the machines to the stockrooms. This was a 24 hour operation. The total site occupied 450 acres.

The so called Local Fleet based at Aylesford merits special attention as it played a vital role in providing service support to the various factories on the Aylesford site. At the height of it's activities, Reed had thirteen paper machines at Aylesford, producing a variety of product from newsprint and softback book paper to various grades of packaging, paper bag and envelope papers, tissue paper and sackkraft paper for the cement factories' own cement bag production.

The Mills occupied both sides of the Medway Valley railway line between Maidstone and Strood and were

In addition to the Paper Mills, Reed owned several smaller companies on the site. These included Brookgate Industries (later to become Aylesford Conversion Section) which produced high quality coated paper and also a fibre product used by printers and Brookgate Industries Towelling Division manufacturing absorbent paper for industrial towels, later to become a part of Kimberly Clark of Kleenex fame when Reed took a one third interest in this American owned company's new factory on the Aylesford site in the mid fifties. This move in itself produced an opportunity for Reed Transport by supplying four pantechnicon sized vans in full Kimberly Clark livery on C Contract Licences. Details of these vehicles are included at the beginning of Appendix 17. Other Reed Companies included Medway Paper Sacks (later to become Reed Medway Sacks) and Medway Corrugated Paper Company which became part of Reed Corrugated Cases.

Left: YKJ 725, an Austin 5K/FED3 boxvan with a 1,650 cu.ft capacity. One of four vans - three rigids and an artic / pantechnicon trailer - that entered the Reed Transport fleet in 1956/57 on C Contract Licences for Kimberly Clark. It was known as KC1.

Far left: A 1950 Austin Loadstar K4WA four-wheel pantechnicon of the Medway Corrugated Paper Company Ltd. It probably transferred to Reed Corrugated Cases in 1953 but by 1958 when the RCC fleet became the responsibility of Reed Transport it had been disposed off.

Above top: This early Austin 5K/FED3 tractor and flat trailer was allocated no.6 in the Reed Corrugated Cases Aylesford factory's own fleet. Registration number unknown, it certainly transferred into the RT fleet in 1958 along with possibly two other tractors and several pantechnicons.

Above: This Commer D91A four wheel van joined the Reed Corrugated Cases fleet in November 1956. The vehicle, along with two similar examples, transferred to Reed Transport in 1958.

Left top: YKO 348 Austin 5K/FED3 tractor with a pantechnicon trailer - it was new in 1957 along with three rigid pantechnicons. On C hire to Kimberly Clark it was known as KC3; Johnny Francis was it's driver.

Left centre: YKO 348 and its van trailer in what is believed an earlier Kimberley Clark product livery, Delsey Toilet Tissue. Note the wheel spats, typical of 'modern' styling of the mid 1950s as is the livery and product illustration.

Left: This cheerful grouping of Reed Corrugated Cases drivers in front of three pantechnicons dates from after Reed Transport acquired the RCC fleet in 1958. The vehicles behind the grouping are YKT 944 and YKT 481, Austin 4K/FED3s and 118 DKO, an Austin DER/15.

It was in March 1956 that Reed Corrugated Cases had been formed to take over all the Company's corrugated cases activities which also included National Corrugated Paper Company and Thompson & Norris. The factory at Aylesford operated it's own small fleet which during 1958 was to be merged into Reed Transport. In the 'Commercial Motor' feature of 16th November 1956, this fleet is described as comprising "32 vehicles .... 27 of which are in the 2 - 7 ton class" Appendix 10 attempts to identify this fleet but falls short of many vehicles.

Brookgate Industries was the source of one particularly unusual operation. Every few days a 24ft trailer was requested to load 500 bundles of ticket coils, weight about nine tons. The trailer was then shunted up to Bullstairs Wharf, often at night via London Depot. The load was then broken down and the ticket coils delivered to London Underground stations - and there were a lot of them. This was invariably carried out at weekends, with rigids and sack barrows.

The Local Fleet comprised a variety of vehicles in addition to the articulated fleet mentioned above, including tippers to clear boiler house flue dust, a gully emptier, various vehicles moving raw materials, stock and machinery on site, a 'town van' collecting parts from Maidstone factors and the surrounding area for the factories and a small Karrier with crew cab for use by the Building Department, such was the specialised nature of this fleet. Some vehicles were fitted with two-way radios, a feature to become standard for the 1990s but RT had them in the 1950s.

When Reed Transport was formed, both the Perkins & Glover and the Local Fleets were numbered in the series 1 upwards. As a consequence, the Local Fleet had '100' added to their numbers. Appendix 4 attempts to identify this varied fleet. Included are three Dennis rigids of prewar vintage and one Austin. Basil Lucking, who joined A.E. Reed in 1947 as a fitter, ex REME, recalls that there were four Dennises, generally by then used on internal Mill movements and presumably prior to the advent of the Bedford/Scammells. The listed three were identified in the LTO archives.

No further information has come to light regarding the Austin. However, one driver who does recall the four Dennises is Ted Brooker who joined in 1950. Three were used on 24 hour shifts within the Mill, were petrol engined and started on a handle - no self starting.

Basil recalls that three of the regular Dennis drivers were Cecil Dean, Bob Allingham and Bob Freeman, the latter two certainly continuing with RT from 1954. Ted has added to the list of drivers a further five - Jim Goodger, Albert Malyan, George Mannering, Aubrey Mills and 'Speedy' Tolhurst, excluding himself from 1950. The three middle named also joined RT. Ted believes that the three Dennis rigids were numbered 7,8 and 9. The fourth, number unknown, was driven by Cecil Dean and was nicknamed 'The Pig', being of normal control. It was used primarily to deliver reel centres within the Mill, a task later taken over by Commer 14A no.10, later no.110. See also Appendix 4.

This pre Reed Transport Local Fleet was managed by Fred Lewis with Moss Craddock as the Foreman. The early maintenance facility is described later, in Chapter Seven.

Right above: No.131 - 566 BKJ was an Austin 7K/FEDS and the last tipper to be provided for Aylesford Paper Mills for use in clearing boiler house flue dust. Given her role in life it was certain that she would never again be quite as pristine as she is in this picture taken in September 1957 just before entering service.

Right: This delightful crew-cabbed Karrier Bantam of 1954 vintage - a non Reed Transport vehicle - was used on site maintenance work by Aylesford Paper Mills Building Department. It would have been RT's responsibility for maintenance and repairs along with vehicles of many other Group companies.

An interesting innovation occurred in 1957. The Nation was involved in the Suez Crisis. Fuel rationing was imminent. The Carrimore drawbar trailer stood idle in the Depot. The former BRS AEC Mammoth Major no 226 was modified for drawbar trailer operation and so, it could be argued, Reed Transport had it's first 20 tonner. This honour would at a later time be attributed to an ERF LV cab 64CU tractor, fleet no 15, in 1965. 226's regular driver, Bert Norley, together with 'Titch' Crittenden, another driver set sail. 'Titch' was not enjoying the best of health at the time so probably welcomed the chance to go as mate. Regular runs were to Castleton near Sheffield and Padeswood near Mold with 20 ton loads of sackkraft paper for the cement factories. Special A Licence rules, based on unladen weight, were satisfied by a Vulcan seven-tonner being taken off the road in exchange for the drawbar trailer. Bert was later appointed Night Foreman in Aylesford Depot.

A major step was taken in 1957 when a new two storey Head Office and Vehicle Workshops was built in New Hythe Lane at a cost of £125,000. The then Minister for Transport and Civil Aviation, the Rt. Hon. Harold Watkinson performed the official opening ceremony of the building on Friday 15th November 1957. The importance, skills and versatility of the Workshops is covered in Chapter Seven. The Traffic Office was downstairs, the clerks seated around a purpose built console, looking out onto New Hythe Lane. The disadvantage at the time was that the fleet remained at East Mill, a half mile away and under the supervision of a Foreman. There was no face to face contact with drivers.

This was to be short lived for, in 1959, a new Aylesford Depot was created on waste ground 300 yards away from the Head Office. A new building with Manager's Office, Traffic, Subcontracting and Administration Offices together with a Driver's

Messroom were downstairs and toilets, showers and locker room upstairs. Alongside this building was an open fronted but covered structure with about five bays where unsheeted vehicles could be parked and with a bank to one side where transhipping could take place. A secure Equipment Store was incorporated to one side of the structure. The whole parking area was tarmaced and lined out. This became an excellent new home for Aylesford Depot, bringing staff and drivers back together and allowing the traffic staff to 'see' what vehicles were entering and leaving the Depot. Ron Adkins had been appointed Depot Manager.

During the early days of the Company, some of the Aylesford based Reed Companies, particularly Medway Paper Sacks, continued to subcontract traffic themselves which was not covered by Reed Transport's own vehicles. In 1958, the Company assumed responsibility for all traffic emanating from the Aylesford Companies.

One early problem was that the yard was prone to flooding which caused unrest at the time with drivers literally paddling in water whilst roping up and coupling and uncoupling trailers. This was resolved by laying new drainage which caused much disruption at the time but was worth it in the end. The continual lowering of trailers and increased vehicle weights resulted in the landing legs and, in the case of auto coupling trailers, the bogie wheels making deep indentations into the tarmac, especially in warm weather. Initially steel plates were laid down to take the weights but the eventual solution was to incorporate concrete strips into the surface. At a later date a purpose built two-bay vehicle wash was added to the Depot facilities.

The year 1958 was to include a further landmark in the Company's history. Apart from traffic flows within the south east, the most significant flow was to the north west. Profitable backloading was the key to a viable operation to that area and the move to establish the first base outside of the south east was taken, with the opening of an office in Kingsway, Manchester. Jim Atkinson, who had joined the Company with the BRS Larkfield fleet, was appointed Manager.

Left: The traffic office at Aylesford located on the ground floor of the new head offices opened in 1957. Those featured are: a very young John Marsh (Trainee Traffic Clerk), Ken Fuller (Traffic Clerk C Licence Fleet), Bert Stickens - at rear - (Depot Foreman), W.C.(Bill) Dale (Commercial Transport Manager later to become Managing Director) and Jim Atkinson (Traffic Clerk A Licence Fleet) later to become Depot Manager at Wigan. Jim was ex Greenwoods / Medway Transport and BRS Larkfield.

'Big Jim' or Claude as he was known as, was to become a legend within the subsequent north west developments, more a little later. One of Jim's early priorities was to take responsibility for the total transport needs of Sun Paper Mill at Blackburn. Then, in April 1959, Reed Corrugated Cases opened a factory in Warrington Road, Goose Green, Wigan in premises previously occupied by British Celanese. This followed the closure of the former National Corrugated Paper Co factory in Old Trafford, Manchester, which Reed had purchased in September 1944.

Initially, all deliveries were handled by a small 'own' fleet augmented by independent hauliers, one of which, Eric Rosborough, was to continue to work as a subcontractor throughout Reed Transport's time at Wigan and into the SCA Transport years. Subsequently, Reed Transport was invited to take over the responsibility for the factory's delivery needs. The Manchester Office was closed and a fully fledged Depot was opened on the factory site at Wigan in February 1960.

At the time of takeover, the Factory's 'own' fleet comprised two Commer TS3 tractors, an Austin four-wheel rigid flat, a Bedford four-wheel pantechnicon, a small van for delivering samples and an Albion four-wheel rigid with Dyson drawbar trailer. Seven drivers and one fitter were employed by RCC and the fleet was controlled by Despatch Foreman George Trail. One of the drivers, Bill Parr, recalls that the Albion was fitted with a massive radiator and had been originally built for operating in the heat of Africa on the groundnut scheme.

This vehicle with trailer was transferred to the RCC Factory at Histon in the April. During February 1960, a further four Commer TS3 tractors were purchased. The Commers operated with Hands 27ft fifth-wheel trailers, unusual as all other trailers were 24ft or less. An attempt to identify this fleet is detailed at Appendix 11.

According to Bill Parr, the six Commers carried the fleet numbers 964 to 969. Bill drove no 968 and well remembers two characteristics of the TS3.

"If the tickover was regulated too slow and you were starting off in 1st gear, at times when you revved up the engine with it being a two stroke, it would spin in the reverse direction. Thus 1st gear and all the other forward gears became reverse ones. The same applied if you were in reverse gear which would become a forward gear. You had to stop the engine immediately and start up again.

The TS3 ran on a special oil, Shell Rotela, which aided the decarbonisation of the engine. The deposits built up in the silencer which unusually ran across the front under the bumper. When the engine was working hard and the silencer got very hot, it used to decarbonise and on a dark night you would see a stream of red hot sparks of carbon being sprayed out, quite a sight."

Reed Transport's early contribution were two 'secondhand' Austin 5K/FED3 tractors and trailers with Scammell couplings transferred from the South. These were followed by a further number possibly up to a total of eight. The exact number and the identification of these vehicles is not known. They remained in green livery. The early mixing of 5th wheel and auto couplings must have created some inflexibility at times. Some of the Austins developed chassis cracking in front of the rear spring hangers, perhaps as a result of their being hard worked on paper deliveries from Sun Paper Mill as well as the corrugated cases operation. The chassis had to be plated to overcome the cracking, a problem related by Les Marsh who was Wigan Depot's first Engineer.

Les joined RT from St Helens Corporation in 1960, leaving in April 1963 to join the Ministry. The Commers, in blue livery, were merged into the fleet for programming purposes but for a period continued to be owned by RCC. Eventually through persuasion they were transferred to RT but this protective approach to the ownership of commercial vehicles by Group Companies was to feature throughout Reed Transport's history and even into the SCA ownership of the 1990s.

At the start there was no workshop facility at Goose Green, the Commer TS3s being maintained by the local dealership. However, a building adjacent to the entrance of the site previously used for the recharging of the factory electric trucks was taken over and developed into a workshops for the growing fleet. During the early years, the Manager's Office and Traffic Office were within this building. Later the operation was rehoused into a portable building including a drivers' messroom which allowed more space for the workshops. The Company had staked it's claim in the north west!

Sadly, on 1st December 1967, Jim Atkinson passed away. He had just given a driver a rollicking for not applying the handbrake on a parked trailer, returned to his office, sat down at his desk, collapsed and died. His successor was B.J 'Tommy' Atkins who had been one of the first two drivers recruited when the Depot opened, later promoted to Depot Foreman and had previously worked for BRS Manchester.

Until inroads were made in the early 1960s into the packaging part of the Reed business - Aylesford, Thatcham and Wigan - P&G / RT would have been described as specialising in paper haulage. In particular, it was the newsprint business with all it's idiosyncracies on which the Company built it's early reputation.

In 1960, the 'perfect' newsprint load would have been 15 reels of 36 inch diameter, loaded two tiers high, eight on the floor and seven on the second tier, on a 24ft platform. The payload would be in the region of 11 tons, depending on the deckel (width) of the reels. However, there were very few 'perfect' loads, and special loading requirements were commonplace and furthermore all

demanded timed deliveries. Some examples were:
Two high, back dock empty, i.e. eight reels on the floor with six on the second tier.
- this requirement allowed for the bottom rear reel to be comfortably removed leaving platform space for the rear first top tier reel to be 'broken down' or eased down gently as the next bottom reel was removed rearwards.
Two high on boards.
- this allowed slings to be passed under and round the bottom reels after the top tier reels, slung when loaded, had been removed by overhead crane.
Skids required.
- like brewery deliveries, there were the occasional deliveries where reels were lowered onto the road/pavement or down into a cellar.

Many deliveries were to small London and provincial newspapers each with their own press rooms. In London for example, in addition to the large national dailies and evening papers, there were many small newspapers - Hackney Gazette, Hampstead & Highgate Express, Ilford Pictorial, Ilford Recorder, Islington Gazette, St Pancras Chronicle, Stratford Express and Tottenham Herald. Perhaps one delivery per week was sufficient. Then there was Lloyds List printed in narrow Leadenhall Street, EC3 in the heart of the City, definitely a small lorry job.

Then there were the Home Counties deliveries. For Surrey, there were Surrey Advertiser and Surrey Times, both at Guildford and Surrey Comet at Kingston. For Surrey Comet, P&Gs last fixed artic, Foden no 61 - NGO 52 - had it's single-axle trailer built with an unusual bow front to allow for an extra two reels, one on the floor, one on the second tier, to be carried. It's regular London based driver was Johnny Anderson Junior. Father Johnny Senior was also a P&G driver. Then there was Middlesex Chronicle at Hounslow, Herts Advertiser at St Albans and Herts Express at Hitchin. Moving further clockwise, in Essex was Essex Weekly News at Chelmsford whilst in

Kent, Kentish Gazette at Canterbury and Kent & Sussex Courier at Tunbridge Wells brought the circle of regular newsprint deliveries around. There were many others in London and the Home Counties and a great many into the Provinces.

It is appropriate at this stage to mention briefly the origins of the parent Company. Albert Edwin Reed was born in 1846 in Cullompton. His first job at the age of 14 was as a clerk at Lower Wookey Mill which produced newsprint from straw and wastepaper. Several moves later, within the West Country and in between at a Mill near Edinburgh where he stayed for only three months, Albert with two others purchased Ely Paper Company at Cardiff in 1877. He managed the Mill for 12 years before parting from the other owners.

Ely had become the UK's largest producer of newsprint with 130 - 150 tons per week output. His move to Kent came in 1889 when he became Manager of a new Mill at Northfleet owned by Ekman Pulp & Paper Co. Also in 1889 he bought the assets of a bankrupt company which included Riverside Mill at Dartford. That Company was incorporated in 1890 as the London Paper Mills Company.

By 1894, Albert had still not realised his ambition - to wholly own a mill or company. However, in that year and following a fire in 1893, Tovil Paper Company's Mill on the south west side of urban Maidstone, was offered for sale by auction. Albert's brother, Ernest, put in a successful offer on behalf of Albert. Albert at the same time was negotiating to buy Glory Mill at Wooburn in Buckinghamshire for £13,000 but preferring the Tovil option, promptly sold Glory Mill (the next day?) to Wiggins Teape for £13500! Tovil Mill was re-equipped and on his 50th birthday in January 1896 the third machine started up. In 1897, Albert severed his connection with the Northfleet Mill.

By 1903 Albert had bought a former oil seed crushing mill known as Bridge Mill, about 500 metres from Tovil Mill and on the bank of the River Medway. The incorporation of Albert E.Reed & Co Ltd took place on 28th May 1903. As soon as Bridge Mill had been established in 1904 with one machine, Tovil & Bridge Mills became one operating unit. Albert retained his shareholding of London Paper Mills until 1909 when total control was achieved. More about this Mill later. It was in 1917 that he turned his sights to Aylesford with the purchase of land. Building commenced in 1920 and production started in 1922 with two machines.

Albert Reed died on 21st February 1920. His sons, Ralph and Percy, took over as joint managing directors.

Left: Earlier times at Aylesford Paper Mills' East mill. A pair of Southern Roadways' Scammell artics leaving well laden. The Mill was free to use any haulier for it's deliveries in the early days. Perkins & Glover became another haulier in due course.

Chapter Four

Albert's Other Transport Fleet

At the end of Chapter Three, the origins of the parent Company have been described with the emphasis on Tovil & Bridge Mills being the first wholly owned Mill of Albert Edwin Reed. We have reached 1960 with the story but it is now necessary to backtrack to around 1947 to bring in a most interesting part of Reed Transport's history which involves Tovil & Bridge Mills' own transport operation.

Les Dougal, who had first joined the Research Department at Aylesford Paper Mills in 1933, returned from his wartime service as a Major in the 6th Armoured Division to become Mill Manager of Tovil & Bridge, a position he held until 1955 when he was appointed Director of Operations for a Company in New Zealand in which Reed had an investment.

Mr Dougal and the local management were extremely proud and protective of it's transport independence. Remember that Perkins & Glover had been saved from nationalisation in 1947 by Reed as the main haulier for nearby Aylesford Paper Mills but not Tovil & Bridge. Alan Glover had his eye on the T&B business - and it's fleet. Mr Dougal's response to the courting was that if P&G and from 1954, Reed Transport, wanted the fleet, then they had to take over total responsibility for cranes, fork trucks, shovels and all other moving equipment throughout the Mills. But Alan was not interested in the ancillary plant.

In early 1951, Alan was seeking capital from the Main Board to fund new vehicles. Mr Dougal, also present at

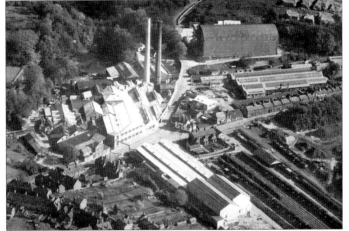

The Tovil and Bridge Mills of Albert E. Reed & Company Ltd at Tovil, Maidstone in the early 1950s.

the meeting, took the stance that if P&G had funding for new vehicles, then T&B should also be granted funds as it also had an old fleet. Appendix 3 shows new Foden S18 eight-wheelers coming into the fleet from June 1951, whilst Appendix 9 confirms one new Albion HD57 six-wheeler entering service for T&B in December of that year. The independence of Tovil & Bridge Mills had been preserved.

Typically, the T&B fleet was old. Prewar vehicles included a Tilling Stevens petrol electric and three Dennis 4-cylinder petrol engined four-wheelers. The Tilling Stevens was used to move pulp from the Bridge Mill wharf well into the post-war period. The Albion tradition began after the War when four six-wheel rigids entered the fleet, two having been transferred from Aylesford Paper Mills presumably surplus to requirements as P&G were by then Reed owned and serving that Mill. All were ex War Department, with diesel engines and four-speed gearboxes with boosters, promising a top speed of around 28mph. They had single rear wheels with balloon tyres and carried 21ft flat platform bodies.

When the body of one was stripped back by Archie Mungeam and Ken Parks in the T&B Garage, presumably prior to repainting, a 9mm shell hole was found together with camouflage. They were nicknamed 'Bull Elephants'. There was evidence of machine gun mountings on the cab roofs - the gunners' or observation hatches had been blanked off. Charlie Brooks and Ken Wratten recall the canvas seats

Left: The Tovil & Bridge love affair with Albions began soon after the War with four ex WD six wheel rigids. Here we see JXB 120 being roped up by Charlie Brooks whilst it's driver Sid Geering strides out to assist.

Below: SKM 412, one of the six Albion HD57 six wheel rigids prior to acquisition from Tovil & Bridge Mills in 1959. It was later to become fleet no.4 and is pictured minus a cab logo.

the bottom and progressing almost military style. With an array of ancillary equipment attached to any Mill, a new driver at T&B started on the dumper clearing boilerhouse ash and other bi-products from the paper machines. He would then graduate via the various cranes, the Ferguson tractor with scoop, the Austin tipper, the 'flivver' - a Ford one tonner FVU 319, hence the name, used as the local runabout, finally becoming relief driver for the 'road' fleet. When a

and that the roofs dripped rain in wet weather. They did not have front brakes either. A photograph of JXB 120 has been provided by Charlie and is featured on this page. Details of these and other early T&B vehicles have been included in Appendix 9.

Mr Dougal's successor was W.F.(Fred) Amies for two years when, in 1957, Dan Marsden became Mill Manager. Mr Marsden, perhaps needing to concentrate on Mill matters and with less sentimentality towards his transport fleet, had a change of heart, so in 1959, it was agreed that Reed Transport took over the T&B fleet and it's operations.

The T&B fleet had been engaged in four distinct activities, deliveries of reels to customers throughout the UK primarily with it's six Albion six-wheel rigids, deliveries to the various Aylesford factories, returning with waste paper, using the Albion and Bedford/Scammell tractors on a round the clock shuttle, internal movements of raw materials and stock between the Tovil and Bridge Mills and fourthly, the collection of wastepaper in the area using four-wheel rigids and one artic. Thus, on 28th September 1959, the six Albion HD57s transferred to Aylesford Depot to be followed soon after by two rigids and some of the Albion and Bedford tractors.

Before moving on to the post 28th September period, the culture within the T&B Transport Department and many of it's operational activities are most worthy of recording. Anyone wishing to join T&B as a driver was to expect a rigorous 'apprenticeship', literally starting at

vacancy occurred, if he was lucky he was given the choice of a 'journey' or a 'local' fleet vehicle. A typical Saturday morning saw all the drivers working on basic maintenance, a washdown and polish, then lined up for Monday morning.

Perhaps influenced by Mr Dougal's military background together with the return to civilian life of many seeking driving jobs after demob, the T&B transport operation was run with military precision. The Transport Supervisor was George Ransome, an ex REME Sergeant. The Foreman was Bill Lomas, an ex infantryman. The fleet of HD57s had grown to six by 1954, it's driver allocation makes interesting reading :

OKM 35
 Norman Edwards Ex Royal Army Service Corps
PKM 726
 Ernie (Chum) Stannett Ex Ministry of War Transport
SKE 411
 Bonnie Francis Ex RSM, Royal Military Police
SKM 412
 Ken Wratten Ex RAF
SKR 71
 Sid Geering Ex Royal Artillery
TKJ 157
 Laurence (Charlie) Weeks Ex Seaforth Highlanders

Such was the allocation on 28th September 1959 on transfer to RT. Within the total driving strength of the Mill, Ken Wratten recalls that perhaps only three were from a non military background. Other drivers who transferred in October were Doug Arnold, Charlie Brooks, Frank Brown, Harry Chittenden, Gordon Cooper, Robert (Paddy) Fitzsimmonds, David Hughes, Charlie King, Ron Packham and Derek Smith. Three fitters also transferred - Dougie Gilkes, Archie Mungeam and Fred (Dick) Whittington. So RT inherited and benefited from a team of well trained and highly experienced drivers and fitters.

The Albion HD57s were certainly the pride of the fleet. At one Saturday lineup, George Ransome became convinced that SKE 411 was finished in a slightly lighter shade of green and demanded that Bonnie Francis presented the vehicle to Mr Dougal at 9.00am on Monday morning for inspection. The lads meanwhile gave SKE a thorough polish. Mr Dougal emerged from his Office at 9.00am, straightened his tie, approved of what he saw and with his words 'Off you go, Francis', Bonnie left for his delivery leaving George rather embarrassed.

Right: This Bedford S type / Scammell artic - JJG 112 entered service with Tovil & Bridge in October 1954. Acquired in 1959, it appears in its Reed days to be carrying the fleet no.6 but this was issued to Albion HD57 - TKJ 157. It would appear that the sunlight was playing tricks when the photo was taken.

Although a C Licence fleet, the 'journey' fleet was worked rather like general haulage vehicles. Regular runs would be to Bristol with bagged alum back from Avonmouth for the Mills including Aylesford; to Reed owned National Packaging at Manchester, later to be closed when the Wigan factory opened, returning with machinery and machine felts, and occasional deliveries to Scotland. Mr Dougal saw his drivers and fleet very much as ambassadors and an occasional run back empty from Scotland was acceptable as the Tovil & Bridge Mills name was clearly shown on the vehicles. There was one occasion when Mr Dougal's father saw an Albion passing through Glasgow and rang his son to congratulate him.

The HD57s were fitted with 58 gallon tanks, unheard of locally in those days. To be appreciated by any Albion enthusiast reading this story, when asked why by the drivers, the Albion representative said that being built in Glasgow, they had to carry sufficient fuel to reach Aberdeen and back as filling stations were few and far between. Although originally delivered on Firestone tyres, replacements were early Michelin Xs. Often, drivers were flagged down and told that the tyres were down. A spare was always carried and drivers were responsible for tyre changes.

George Ransome was committed to running an efficient operation using every trick available but ensuring absolute legality. For example, a delivery to Bristol and a backload from Avonmouth in the 1950s was not quite achievable in two days. By arrangement with P&G, the driver of the day would reach Great Suffolk Street by 5.45pm on day two. The relief driver would travel up by train from Maidstone and return vehicle and driver to Tovil. Ken Wratten recalls that, as the relief driver, he was given 4/6 for his train fare and 2/- for the tram and a snack!

One interesting innovation prior to takeover took place in 1958 or 1959 when, for two weeks, there was a night operation to the north west. George was desperate to prove that a night operation could be sustained. The then relief driver, Harry Chittenden, travelled up to Stafford on Sunday to stay over. Bonnie Francis and Ken Wratten trunked with their HD57s alternate nights from Maidstone to Stafford and Harry delivered to Manchester reloading with machinery, machine felts and chemicals for the Mills. Each did three round trips each week for two weeks but the operation was ceased. It had resulted in other vehicles in the fleet standing idle through lack of work. Prior to the transfer, T&Bs Transport Department produced for RT a weekly schedule of the expected movements of the HD57s for the following week. Where there were days without work or there was a backload opportunity, then RT would give priority over subcontractors to utilise this extra capacity.

So, with Reed Transport taking over T&Bs operations about 12 vehicles with 16 drivers

and three fitters transferred in late 1959, some vehicles being allocated fleet numbers from 1 upwards. In Appendix 9, an attempt has been made to identify as many vehicles as possible, both pre transfer, those involved in the transfer and subsequent vehicles. Tovil & Bridge Mills had retained the internal Mills operation with some vehicles. The Mills to Aylesford shuttle proved impractical to manage from Aylesford and after a short period, embarrassingly, it was agreed that the Mills' management would take that operation back 'in house'. None of the drivers returned to T&B.

For years after the fleet takeover and with the responsibility for non Aylesford deliveries now with RT, the Foreman, Bill Lomas, would always announce himself as 'Main Mill here' when contacting the Aylesford Traffic Office, such was the rivalry with the Aylesford Mills, but also the pride of working at those Mills where Reed began.

It was to be sixteen years later that a sub depot to Aylesford was established at Bridge Mill to manage the total T&B operation.

As a footnote, when Ken Wratten after transfer to RT was asked by Aylesford's Len Woods (of whom more later) how he was finding life at Aylesford, he replied that it was like comparing the Grenadier Guards (i.e. Tovil) with the Pioneer Corps!

Top: This Albion Claymore of Southern Paper Stock, Tovil near Maidstone, was most probably WKL 614 new in December 1955. It became no.29 when, along with part of the Tovil & Bridge Mills fleet, it transferred into Reed Transport in 1959. It was regularly seen in the Maidstone area collecting wastepaper which became very much the basic raw material for the two Mills at Tovil. Southern Paper Stock was a small waste paper subsidiary of Albert E. Reed and is listed in Chapter One - Summary of Cartages as a customer of Perkins & Glover 1947.

Right: 660 YKL was one of several LAD cabbed Albion Chieftains operated by Tovil & Bridge Mills between 1959 and 1976.

Chapter Five

The Thatcham Connection

IT was inevitable that much of the Company's development would be directly related to the expansion programme of the parent Company, which was continually undergoing change, with many acquisitions as well as a few disposals. It's name changed many times, reflecting the nature of it's business. Albert E. Reed became Reed Paper Group, Reed Group, Reed International and, finally, the manufacturing part became Reedpack, following a management buyout in 1988.

A major acquisition by Reed in September 1956 was to have a significant effect on Reed Transport by 1960. Carton manufacturers, Cropper and Co Ltd and their associated companies Colthrop Board & Paper Mills Ltd and Containers Ltd occupied an industrial site at Thatcham, Berks. There were remarkable similarities with the Aylesford site - the River Kennet on the south side, a mainline railway line to Paddington through the middle and the A4 trunk road (before the advent of the M4) on the north side. A transport company was owned - Cropper & Colthrop Transport - which, similar to Reed Transport, had a history stretching back to 1921.

Nationalisation in 1947 and denationalisation in 1954 played a key part in the story. It was very much a case of history repeating itself. The story behind this company must be included as it formed another important root from which Reed Transport was to develop.

Sidney Ashman and Wilfred Street formed a company in June 1921 called The Thatcham Road Transport Station, a somewhat strange name, to become known throughout the transport industry as TRTS. The factories in Colthrop Lane, Thatcham were it's principal customers. Mr Ashman had previously started to work

Top: 'Super' Sentinel six-wheel artic with a carrying capacity of 10 tons, delivered new in August 1923.

Above: One of twenty-six Sentinel steam waggons to have worked in the TRTS fleet in the 1920s / early 1930s.

for Colthrop Board Mill in 1919 with a petrol engined Saurer lorry but because the rate was too low, he turned to general haulage, meeting Mr Street in 1920.

The first premises were an office and garage in Thatcham Broadway. New and larger premises were finally completed by 1934 facing the A4 Bath Road on the Reading side of Thatcham. The entrance was around the corner in Colthrop Lane. The new premises were next door to the main customers' factories. In September 1936, a private limited company was founded to take over the business called Thatcham Road Transport Service Ltd. At least the capitals remained the same.

No records have been traced regarding the first vehicle, or vehicles, which Mr Ashman and Mr Street had in their possession on the formation of the Company in 1921. TRTS historian and retired Thatcham staff member Stuart Wise suggests that it was one Sentinel which the founders took turns to drive. When Stuart met Mr Street in 1977, he told him that TRTS acquired a fleet of 27 steam wagons before moving on to purchase internal combustion engined vehicles. It is believed that 26 were Sentinels and one was a Foden. Twenty-seven was probably the maximum number of steam wagons operated at the peak of the steam haulage era rather than the total the company ever actually owned.

It is possible that others were operated in service for a short period or purchased for cannibalisation for spares to keep the others running. There is also the suggestion that registration plates were transferred if licences were still current. People who Stuart has spoken with have suggested that there was more than one Foden but there is no proof to verify. One thing for sure is that Mr Street spoke categorically to Stuart about the one Foden.

Left: This Standard Sentinel was the victim of an accident at Colnbrook, Slough whilst en route to London in July 1929.

Below left: Albion JB 4006 loaded with timber, it's driver George McBain is on the left with his mate Len Walker on the right.

Below: JB 9928 was one of sixteen Albion 7½ tonners introduced into the TRTS fleet in 1936, all registered consecutively commencing with JB 9924. Its radiator is well muffled for winter work in this post-war view.

Bottom: A splendid line-up of six of the seventeen Albion six-wheel rigids introduced into the TRTS fleet in 1934/35. JB 4006 is nearest the camera beyond which is JB 4005 and JB 4003.

Right: JB 4006 again, fully loaded being sheeted up by its crew in this pre-nationalisation scene.

Right: New arrival AJB 707, an Albion four-wheel flat at Thatcham Carnival in 1937 with the float of the Thatcham Silver Band.

Below: JB 5242 is pictured here at Colthrop's premises a year after purchase bedecked in bunting and Thatcham made products ready to parade throught the town on the occasion of the Silver Jubilee celebrations of King George V in 1935.

Right: The Thatcham premises just before the Second World War. The impressive newly-built garaging featuring T.R.T.S. lettering on its facade. Loaded four and six-wheel Albions are parked in the yard.

Below: ERF ballast tractor CRX 674 when new, prior to painting. It would live on at Thatcham into the Sixties under another guise.

Below right: ERF breakdown tractor CRX 675 was new in 1946 and fitted with an AEC 7.7 litre engine. Note the incorrect registration and Ministry of War Transport detailing carried at the time.

Left: ERX 249, an Albion CX7 eight-wheel rigid that entered service with TRTS in November 1948. Rated for a 15-ton payload it survived into 1960 being part of the Cropper & Colthrop fleet acquired by Reed Transport. Note the sturdy headboard in this bodybuilder's view.

Right: ERX 249 in the process of being sheeted up having just loaded with reels from Colthrop Board Mill. It is pictured outside the bottom garage at Thatcham along with this group of TRTS drivers.

Above: This Philip Hine picture dates from October 1947 and this TRTS Albion four-wheel rigid appears to have seen a lot of use in the years since 1936, the first year of its registration. There is plenty of tread on the tyres of JB 9930 though and its load of large and sturdy packing cases carry the - now rare - stencil of 'Made in England'.

Right: EJB 470, a Bedford OSB four-wheel tipper, seen being loaded here by a Ruston-Bucyrus, also lasted through into 1960 and Reed Transport acquisition.

The Sentinels were acquired secondhand with the possible exception of one purchased new. Unfortunately, very little detail is known of the model types or their previous owners. The early acquisitions were Model A six-tonners of post First World War design, but mostly still on solid tyres. Certainly all had been disposed of by 1936. Some photographs have been included from Stuart's collection. One of the early TRTS employees, George 'Darkie' Amphlett lodged in a company owned cottage next to the Depot until the early 1970s. His job was to start at 4.00am each day to fire up the boilers of the steamers ready for the drivers starting at 6.00am.

During the War, the company was given the responsibility for operating and maintaining a fleet of 62 Bedford QLs based at local army depots for the Ministry of War Transport. This included the supply of drivers.

Above: Some of the TRTS drivers and mechanics who operated and maintained a fleet of 62 Bedford QLs based at local army depots for the Ministry of War Transport. They are pictured here with U.S. Army personnel in front of a line-up of Bedford OWLs.

Above: CRX 675, the ERF recovery tractor in its BRS days in Gatliff Road, London SW1 in June 1950 having just winched the Aveling roller onto a drop-frame trailer. Why it was engaged in such a procedure so far from its Berkshire base remains a mystery as does the fact that it retains its TRTS markings. Whatever, it is fortunate that Arthur Ingram was there to record the occasion.

Left top and left: EJB 470 again photographed in the two later liveries it carried during its lifespan in the Thatcham area.

Left below: It is believed that this picture was taken at the time of the purchase by Cropper & Co. of BRS Thatcham depot and its assets in 1954, the previous owner's markings having been painted over. The vehicle closest to the camera could well be EJB 637, a Foden DG with a tag axle to increase the payload to 11 tons. It lived on into the 1960s under the ownership of a showman.

Right: BRS Thatcham staff at their Christmas party held in Thatcham Drill Hall, probably 1952.

In 1949 TRTS was nationalised as a 'lead company' within Reading District as part of 40F Reading Group with it's Thatcham Depot. It's dark blue livery was changed to BRS red but in October 1954 the then fleet of 89 vehicles and premises were acquired for approximately £225,000 from the British Transport Commission by Cropper & Co to become Cropper & Colthrop Transport Company Limited. The fleet was quickly painted back to dark blue. Of course, the fleet all had Special A Licences.

Sidney Ashman continued to work in the Thatcham Depot during BRS ownership whilst his partner, Wilfred Street, became Reading District Manager but based in the Thatcham Depot. On the purchase of the BRS Unit by Cropper, Sidney Ashman was appointed Managing Director of the new company, Cropper & Colthrop Transport, a position he held until his retirement on 31st March 1960.

After the Reed purchase in 1956 Cropper & Colthrop had continued to operate independently. There was no immediate merger into Reed Transport although there was progressive interworking and co-operation between the two companies. Finally, on 1st April 1960, Cropper &

Left: Three of Cropper & Colthrop Albions with drivers and mechanics at Thatcham. MMO 209 and LRX 402 were Albion Chieftain tractors purchased in the mid 1950s and fitted with Scammell coupling gear - they were to later to receive Reed fleet nos 780 and 773. GBL 573, an Albion Chieftain four-wheel rigid was new in 1950. The seven ton payload flat would in Reed days be allocated fleet no.755.

Below: FBL 48, a Foden FG6/15 S18 eight wheel rigid rated for a 15-ton payload started its working life with TRTS in 1949. It is pictured with its load of packing cases and 'I' beams well secured alongside no.770 one of the ex BRS 'Nellies', a Guy Otter Perkins P6 four wheel rigid, one of sixteen similar examples in the C&C fleet.

Colthrop Transport ceased to exist and the fleet and premises became Reed Transport's Thatcham Depot with Tom Cantwell as Depot Manager. On that date, the fleet totalled 88 vehicles plus a recovery tractor and mobile crane. Progress in repainting from dark blue to green had already started prior to the change and many vehicles already were operated in green livery with Cropper & Colthrop on the headboards but the Reed Paper Group logo on the cab doors.

It is apparent that Reed Transport had influence long before 1st April 1960, particularly with regard to vehicle specification. For example, in late 1958 seven Foden S20 tractors nos 91 to 97 were purchased for Aylesford Depot, see Appendix 17. At the same time, Cropper & Colthrop placed in service two similar tractors which became nos 798 and 799. They were Berkshire, not Kent, registered. See Appendix 7. For the Aylesford tractors, 14 Eagle tandem-axle trailers were purchased, nos 351 to 364. For the C&C tractors, four similar trailers were purchased, numbered 43 to 46 prior to 1st April 1960.

Above: A family group at Thatcham in Cropper & Colthrop livery. Austin BMC tractors, Albion Chieftain tractors, ERF no.718 - CRX 674, the AEC 7.7 engined C15 ballast unit now configured as an artic tractor and, to the right, the two Foden FGTU6/20 tractors No's 798 and 799.

Left: Reed Cartons (formerly Croppers) manufactured cardboard cartons on the Thatcham site as part of the Reed Paper Group. This Austin LD van, registered in 1957 as OBL 186 was used to deliver samples and small orders. It was sold out of service to Reed Transport driver Sam Scutter who converted it into a caravanette. He later sold it to a garage at Beech Hill, and it was then purchased by a gentleman who required a vehicle that he could drive as far as practical to Australia, just how far he got in the van we will probably never find out.

Left below: An impressive line-up from an earlier era. Drivers and their Fodens in Cropper & Colthrop Ltd's days prior to Reed's acquisition of the company. The vehicle nearest the camera is FJB 952, a Foden FG6/15 S18 eight-wheel rigid capable of a 15 ton payload new to TRTS in 1949. Further down the line-up are four of the early post-war Foden DGs operated by the company.

'Motor Transport' for 1st September 1961 published an article in the series "Improving the Breed" which featured several innovations introduced by Reed Transport. One paragraph began "Reed Transport was one of the first operators to try out air suspension and 18 tandem-axle lightweight Eagle semi-trailers with Andre twin-pillow air suspension are in service". There is another clue. C&C was already a committed Foden user for heavies. For the middleweight range, and some rigids, Albion Chieftain was favoured, but in 1957/1958

Left: One of only two Commer TS3 rigids acquired from Cropper & Colthrop Transport was No.714 - SMO 640. It is depicted here loaded with baled rags, a raw material for the old Colthrop Paper Mill (not Board Mill) at Thatcham.

Below: MMO 296 was converted in 1963 to a sludge tanker for use around Colthrop Mill. It retained its Reed Transport livery (and fleet number) despite being owned by Colthrop Board & Paper Mill. The picture was taken in 1967.

there was a switch to Austin tractors with one rigid, in line with Reed Transport policy at that time. Or was this mere coincidence?

Apart from a BMC boxvan, no.720, purchased one month after the merger and registered in Hampshire, the first new vehicles for Thatcham were Commers - two rigids and three tractors - in July 1960 and were Kent registered. To finally close this debate, there exists one more clue. Like Reed Transport, Cropper & Colthrop Transport enjoyed the benefit of an article in 'Commercial Motor'. The article in the 23rd October 1959 issue was titled "Personal Service for Paper Trade" and subtitled "A 40-year old Haulage Business, Recovered Intact from B.R.S., Becomes the Transport Organization of a Big Thatcham Paper Group". The article confirms the acquisition of the Group by Albert E. Reed on 1st September 1956. It continues "There is now close co-operation between Reed Transport Limited and Cropper & Colthrop Transport, particularly on traffic movements and the Reed maintenance system has been introduced at Thatcham".

Mention needs to be made of

three small local non Group customers which C&C had. First was Florco based next door to Colthrop Board Mills. Originally known as British Floorcloth, it's name was changed to Florco during the Fifties. There were two related engineering companies, Plenty, based in Newbury and Pulsometer Pumps in Reading, both manufacturing pumps and valves, particularly for the oil and gas

Reed TRANSPORT

Left: Thatcham garage. Evident in this post 1960 view are the fixing positions of the T.R.T.S. lettering and that the roof had been raised.

Below: Tired looking Albion Chieftain LRX 402 nearing the end of her time in the Thatcham fleet.

industries. All three customers generated small consignments which were integrated within the Group distribution. All continued well into Reed Transport days.

Cropper & Colthrop had an office in London. It was in the premises of Mounts Wharf, off Fulham Palace Road. Significant volumes of traffic took the Thatcham fleet into the London area and there was a need for a reporting base for drivers for backloading. For instance, the Mills at Thatcham used wastepaper as a raw material so wastepaper merchants rang the Fulham office with their daily needs. Drivers particularly liked to be at Mounts Wharf on boat race day as it was a good viewing point. Jack Dracey was C&C's man in Fulham and eventually moved into Reed Transport's Depot in Southwark after the takeover, a logical move.

Appendix 7 identifies those Cropper & Colthrop vehicles merged into the fleet in 1960. They were numbered into the 700 series. Appendix 8 lists vehicles operated by TRTS and C&C between 1934 and 1959, which were not acquired by Reed Transport, these being included for the sake of interest. Of the 58 vehicles listed, 57 were Albions. Referring to Appendices 7 and 8 together, a close study of the last two numbers of each registration number shows how TRTS was able to identify vehicles without fleet numbers, i.e. 01, 02 etc. Superstition reigned as there was no number ending in 13.

By the end of 1960, with the Thatcham vehicles now added, Reed Transport's fleet had grown to a total of 223 vehicles.

Right above: The original TRTS Colthrop Depot is seen here in this view looking north from Colthrop Lane in February 1975.

Right: Colthrop Board Mills was a major customer of Reed Transport, this February 1975 view shows the engineer's stores and workshops of the North Mill. Photographer Stuart Wise's Ford Capri is parked at the left.

49

Left: This picture dates back to the days of Cropper & Colthrop and their Coles crane equipped Thornycroft Amazon. Dating from 1942 the Ex RAF unit (right) is being assisted with another of its kind unloading this girdered assembly from a BRS owned trailer. The Cropper vehicle which was first registered in 1948 appears to have been 'customised' in the course of its civilan life having received modifications to its bonnet and fitted with a non-standard radiator of apparently French origins. It also has storage capability on the cab's roof.

Below: EMO 683 the Thornycroft Amazon, minus its Coles crane which has been transferred to a Foden chassis, picured parked up awaiting disposal in September 1966.

Above: In 1964 the ageing ERF C15 tractor unit CRX 674 was taken to Aylesford and rebuilt as a site shunt unit. A second-hand Atkinson cab and ERF badging (!) were fitted as part of the rebuild. Its original AEC 7.7 litre unit was replaced with a Gardner engine at this time. The ERF started its revenue earning life as a ballast tractor with TRTS in 1945 and is seen in June 1969 during a break from site shunting duties at Colthrop Mills.

Right: Whilst the Ex RAF Thornycroft Amazon was seen as being time expired, its Coles crane was still regarded as an asset. It is pictured fitted to a cut-down OBL 502 Foden KG6/24 S20 which began life as an eight-wheel rigid flat in the Cropper & Colthrop fleet dating from October 1957. Now numbered 701, as an eightwheeler it carried no.785.

Chapter Six

The Sixties and Further Expansion

Reed Transport entered the Sixties with four Depots under it's belt - Aylesford, London, Thatcham and Wigan. Mention has already been made in Chapter Three of Albert E. Reed's paper mill at Dartford, London Paper Mills. But there was a second one in north Kent - Empire Paper Mills on the bank of the River Thames at Greenhithe which had come into Reed ownership on 1st August 1952. Both had local hauliers serving their needs and London Paper Mills also had it's own small fleet.

One regular haulier serving Empire was Cope's Express. Reed Transport had started to make inroads into their business as just another haulier. This situation, where Group Companies remained free to play the haulage market, frequently caused Reed Transport's traffic staff a level of irritation especially when there were vehicles looking for work. Undoubtedly, the same feelings were held by it's senior management. It was a situation which was hard to accept and understand. It was not only the two Mills in North Kent to which this applied; the same situation existed elsewhere and was to repeat itself time and time again and even into the late Nineties. It was all part of Reed Transport's growing pains.

Following the parent Company's trail of acquisitions, another opportunity presented itself in 1960. Amalgamated Press owned Imperial Paper Mills, another Thamesside mill, at Gravesend. In 1959, Amalgamated Press was purchased by Daily Mirror, changing it's name to Fleetway Publications. In 1960, agreement was reached whereby the Mill passed into Reed ownership. Subsequently, Imperial's fleet of vehicles passed to Reed Transport together with a small workshops and became it's Gravesend Depot, Depot no 5.

Ted Holwill was appointed Depot Manager as from 2nd October 1961, moving down from London Depot. Traffic staff transferred from within RT were Frank Pearce from Aylesford and Fred Riley also from London who, in turn, was replaced by Ken Fuller who had transferred from Aylesford earlier, from 31st July. The

The Empire Paper Mills at Greenhithe on the River Thames

Imperial Foreman, George Blackman, continued in that position. George had previously spent 25 years with bus company Maidstone & District as an engineer before moving to Imperial when the fleet comprised only six vehicles. Local haulier A & H Hardy of Northfleet was Imperial's local haulier.

Internal letters suggest that the Imperial fleet comprised 20 vehicles at the time of acquisition. Twenty vehicles registered between 1952 and 1957 have been identified and are listed at Appendix 12. Nineteen AEC rigids from three original batches were involved in the transfer of which 16 were six-wheelers, three were eight-wheelers. Two, RKR 915 and RKR 917, were originally built as six-wheelers but had later been returned to AEC by Imperial for conversion to eight-wheelers. The LTO archives confirm that the third one, VKP 925, was originally built

Imperial Paper Mills Drivers at the time of Takeover in 1961

NKL 1	Bert Jarvis	RKR 913	Bill Coggar
NKL 2	Bill Lingham	RKR 914	Bert Bradshaw
NKL 3	Maurice Sayer	RKR 915	Basil Reader
NKL 4	George Ralph	RKR 916	Alf Spratling
NKL 5	Roger Turner	RKR 917	Len Valsler Snr.
NKL 6	Bill Hart	RKR 918	Doug Christie
PKM 7	Vic Donovan	VKP 919	Charlie Fewtrell
PKM 8	Ginger Maddon	VKP 920	Vic Albone
PKM 9	Bill Spunner	VKP 921	Jack Saunders
PKM 10	Harry West	VKP 922	Ray Colenutt
PKM 11	Barry Hunt	VKP 923	Jim Coggar
PKM 12	Percy Bance	VKP 924	Ted Adams
		VKP 925	Bill Greaves
Foreman		Fitter	
George Blackman		Ralph Dawson	

- Compiled from information supplied by Len Valsler -

Full details of the original fleet are at Appendix 12.

Above: This line-up features old Imperial Paper Mills drivers at their sports club. Len Valsler's Dad is pictured fourth from the right.

Left above: Imperial Paper Mills AEC Mammoth Major 3671 - no.21 - VKP 921 is parked close to Harry's Café in Liverpool Road, Holloway awaiting the return of it's driver. Harry's was a favourite of the Imperial, Reed and Hardy drivers before it closed. No.21 carries a fly sheeted load of reels for one of the Watford printers - Odhams Press or Sun Printers. It became Reed Transport Gravesend Depot's no.195 on acquisition in 1961.

Left: RKR 914, pictured here as number 188 was one of nineteen AEC Mammoth Majors acquired from Imperial Paper Mills in 1961. This being one of sixteen six wheelers acquired, the other three vehicles being eight wheelers.

as an eight-wheeler. It is believed that the 20th vehicle was the Dodge tipper, OKR 692 used by the Mill Yard Department.

Also included in the Appendix are details of an earlier batch of six AECs from 1951 believed to have been disposed of very soon after the acquisition. Photographic evidence suggests that they were replaced by at least two Fodens and two of the former Tovil & Bridge Mills Albion HD57s transferred from Aylesford.

During the late Forties and well into the Fifties, it was the practice for paper mills' fleets in Kent to have side and rear body panelling on it's flat platform vehicles, as shown in many of the photographs. This at least allowed for the mill name to be emblazoned on the sides. Imperial joined Reed and Bowater with this fashion. The Imperial livery was a mid to dark blue with gold leaf lettering. George Blackman recalls that body and paintwork was generally sent out to a local Northfleet Company - Barney, Sands & Hartridge.

It was not long before this new Depot took over total responsibility for the tonnages from the other two North Kent Mills and so, at last, justice was done! The small London Paper Mills fleet, believed to have originally comprised 11 vehicles, was also merged into the Gravesend based fleet. Information about this fleet is lacking but what detail has been unearthed is included at Appendix 13. For a short while, perhaps three or four weeks, Ted Holwill moved up to London Paper Mills but then returned to Gravesend. An ex London Depot driver, Bill Wetten, was based at LPM as traffic clerk.

Above: The London Paper Mills at Dartford which specialised in the manufacture of white papers. Known as the Riverside Mills, Albert E Reed & Company Ltd acquired more than 50% of the share capital in 1909, a controlling interest which ultimately became 100%. It was not until 1961 that it's own small vehicle fleet was merged into the Gravesend fleet of Reed Transport. The London Paper Mills was to close in 1968.

Below: London Paper Mills' Austin K/FED3 four wheel rigid was one of four similar examples of which one was definitely taken into the RT fleet in 1961. RYO 578 carries LPM's no.6.

Far left: Gravesend in 1961. AEC Mammoth Major 3671 six wheel rigid No.198 - VKP 924 which entered the Imperial fleet in January 1957 but now featuring Reed Green livery and signage instead of Imperial's blue is pictured at the extreme left alongside other examples of the then Reed fleet including two more AECs, an Austin four wheel rigid and two Albion HD57s - originally acquired from Tovil & Bridge Mills in 1959 - soon after the takeover of Imperial. Note the old West Street railway line.

Left: Another picture dating from 1961 kindly provided by Len Valsler features this line up of four ex Imperial Paper Mills AEC Mammoth Major 3671 rigids and a solitary Foden at New Mill. The AECs include no's 197, 192, 188 purchased in the early to mid 1950s whilst the Foden, no.16 - 76 BKR, a FG6/24 S20 eight wheel rigid was purchased new by Reed in January 1958.

This History will show that Reed Transport was ever the innovator and in 1961 an unusual and, literally, small fleet was provided for Kimberly Clark. Seven Morris 5cwt vans towing Reed Transport built steel framed two-wheeled trailers entered service in the customer's Hi-Dri livery. A photograph has been included. Hardly the general haulage vehicle, the idea was that these vans would be used by salesmen with the option to leave the trailer at, say, an exhibition where a bulk order needed to be left whilst the van would be used for multi drop small quantity sales. These vehicles have been included at Appendix 17. This innovative fleet was featured in an article in 'Motor Transport' of 1st September 1961. Also included is a photograph of an Austin mini van from 1960, in a Kimberly Clark Hi-Dri livery. A number of Austin A35 vans and Morris 1000 Travellers were registered as goods vehicles in the name of Reed Transport in 1959 and 1960. In the absence of information regarding their useage, they have been omitted from the Appendices.

Above: This Morris J Type van was photographed by Roger Kenney in Rochdale. It began its life in June 1952 with a company called Hygiene Products (Great Britain) Limited. Later in life it entered the Reed fleet and was believed to be allocated to Thatcham sometime after 1961/62 although no one can actually remember it - another suggestion being that it actually was based in the London depot. The same fleet number - 820 - was previously allocated to a Bedford shunt unit acquired from Reed Corrugated Cases at Brentford.

Top: Not what might be called a general haulage vehicle, nevertheless this Morris van with trailer - 273 NKT, was one of seven such outfits built for and contracted to Kimberly Clark in 1961.

Above: Another vehicle hired to Kimberly Clark was this Austin Mini van 562 MKJ which dates from 1960. An early example of the type, the Mini van remained in production until 1982.

At Thatcham, the Corrugated Cases factory, Containers Ltd, became a part of Reed Corrugated Cases. That Company already had a factory at Brentford which had been one of five previously acquired from Thompson & Norris in 1954. The decision was taken to close Brentford and transfer production to Thatcham. The move was spread, it is believed, over the period between November 1961 and August 1962. Included in the closure and transfer were 23 vehicles, all of which were transferred to Reed Transport. Details of this fleet are at Appendix 14. The operational implications of this development were both significant and interesting and have therefore been included separately as Chapter Eight.

Bert Bryant was appointed Fleet Engineer on 25th March 1963, relocating to Aylesford. On 1st April 1963, Bill Dale was appointed Assistant General Manager.

On 1st August 1963, Albert E. Reed & Co Ltd became Reed Paper Group Ltd.

The significant moves towards full articulation in the early Sixties put a strain on the space available within London Depot. No longer was it a rigids orientated depot. Gravesend Depot was rapidly receiving tractors and trailers as replacements for the inherited ex Imperial rigid fleet. Aylesford Depot's fleet was also changing with it's six and eight wheel rigids being replaced by tractors and trailers.

Left: AEC Mammoth Major MkV no.225 - 417 KKT, new in June 1960 to Aylesford, at an unidentified corrugated cases factory. The main sheet is being prepared for pulling off; the flysheet lies neatly rolled by the rear wheels. Sister Mammoth Major, no.227 joined the Aylesford fleet a couple of weeks after no.225.

Left below: Commer 512 VKK was one of a batch of six of the type delivered new to Thatcham Depot at the end of 1962.

Below: No. 748 - 619 SKM was one of 11 Foden S21 cabbed tractors based at Thatcham. This example being new in January 1962. The trailer is sporting a new 16oz TCS black mainsheet with yellow flysheet for this photo.

Great Suffolk Street. A hut was provided for the supervisor appointed who was Percy Grant, the driver from Foden six-wheeler no 57.

Percy was a highly respected employee now responsible for security, assistance with parking and exchange of trailers, the handling of the delivery notes and general communication to and from the drivers. A telephone was installed together with the statutory kettle and teapot. At night time, delivery notes were posted through a letterbox flap. This arrangement at Vauxhall lasted until 1976 or 1977 and eventually, as the London based fleet reduced, the site was vacated and a smaller area rented at Potters Fields off Tooley Street, between London Bridge and Tower Bridge. The new Greater London Assembly building, City Hall, has now been built on the site. Percy Grant went on to become a chauffeur at Reed International's Headquarters at Reed House in Piccadilly.

There was a large volume of traffic from both depots for customers within a few miles radius of Great Suffolk Street, both national as well as local London newspapers, magazine printers and the many paper bag manufacturers. The possibility for night shuttles from both depots up to London which articulation now provided was a superb opportunity for maximum utilisation. The downside was the large number of extra trailers needed at both ends and the space to accommodate them in London. A large area was rented from National Car Parks by Vauxhall Bridge on the south side. This was primarily used by Aylesford Depot whilst Gravesend Depot fed into

Above: The unmistakable frontage of The Carlton dance hall in Rochdale's Great George Street acts as a backdrop to this Roger Kenney picture of no.123 - 244 NKL, a Commer HDY/Scammell artic parked having almost certainly just undertaken a delivery of newsprint to the premises of the Rochdale Observer. Dating from February 1961 it was one of a number of vehicles transferred north to Wigan. The Carlton, later to become a bingo hall, finally closed its doors in September 1999 reopening two months later as Liquid Rock.

Left: Atkinson 'Silver Knight' no.60 - 612 KKT was new in 1963 and is seen coupled to a fifth wheel 'four in line' trailer at Aylesford.

Above: Saturday afternoon in the mid Sixties at Thatcham, tractors - mainly Atkinsons - parked up outside the traffic office as captured through the gates by a young Stuart Wise.

Right above: A quartet of Thatcham's Atkinson FC 5LW/Scammell tractors. All bar no.762 - 626 VKN, pictured second left and the oldest vehicle dating from December 1962, were later converted to fifth wheel coupling. They were underpowered and not regarded with affection by those who had to drive them.

Right: The time is up for no.799 - RJB 329, a Foden FGTU6/20 S20 tractor new to Thatcham Depot in 1958, pictured loaded for transport to Aylesford and disposal in 1968.

Below: Both these units entered the Reed Aylesford fleet in 1961. No.44 - 619 PKL, an Atkinson FC 5LW tractor with Scammell couplings and no.223 - 256 SKE, a Foden FGTU6/24 6LX S21 tractor receive their drivers' attention at Aylesford before departure with their loads.

In 1965, legislation was changed to vehicle gross weights and dimensions which was to allow 30 tons gross vehicle weights on five axles and therefore articulated vehicles of 20 tons carrying capacity. Reed Transport's 'first' 20 tonner was fleet no.15 - EKK 482C, an ERF LV cab 64CU tractor, this was to be followed by many others. Les Crick was it's driver. See Appendix 17 for the details.

The next significant development was to come also in 1965. Reed had again been on the acquisition trail when, in that year, Wallpaper Manufacturers was purchased. WPM as it was known owned three paper mills, wallpaper factories and a paint factory, centred in the Lancashire town of Darwen. The paper mills were Darwen Paper Mill, Lower Darwen Paper Mill and Hollins Paper Mill. The wallpaper manufacturing was centred both within Darwen

Top: Nos 707 and 708, two of the newly arrived ERF LV cabbed 64CU NHE180 units. These 1966 arrivals are pictured along with Foden S21 and Atkinson tractors in the lorry park at Thatcham.

Left above: Part of a crowded Aylesford Depot in the mid 1960s showing a wide range of it's Atkinson, Austin, ERF and Foden fleet.

Left: Thatcham's first 20-tonner was this 'A' series LV cabbed ERF which was allocated to Bob Fidler in 1967. No.154 - FKE 607D had been first allocated to Aylesford in January 1966 when new. This oversized load was destined for the USA via Southampton Docks. GKO 239D, another Thatcham ERF 'A' Series, follows behind with another part of the consignment.

and beyond, whilst the paint factory was next door to Hollins, also in Darwen. WPM had well-known brand names in those days such as Walpamur and Duradio paints, these were promoted under the Crown name. Arthur Sanderson fabrics and wallpaper were mostly marketed under the Crown and Sanderson names.

A 12 page handwritten report exists in the archives almost certainly written by Jim Atkinson. Unfortunately it is undated but it would have been prepared in 1966 or 1967. It identifies the three Paper Mills and follows: "which all operate their transport independ-

ently and without any reference to each other's requirements, there is therefore the situation that one Mill will hire a contractor to go to Manchester whilst the other is hiring to bring pulp from Manchester. There is an extremely strong case for central control of transport within the organisation but, in my opinion, an even stronger one for a transport control in the North Western Area to co-ordinate and operate all Group needs, particularly medium distances, one instance is Hollins Mill delivered 535 tons to Oldham during April, whilst Maybanks, Oldham deliver 500/600 tons wastepaper

from Oldham to Sun Paper Mills, Feniscowles monthly."

The Report goes on to describe the three Mills' individual transport operations in detail. A 50% share in wastepaper merchant J&J.Maybank Ltd had been purchased by Reed in 1965 and is described in greater detail later, in Chapter Thirteen.

In April 1969, Len Woods was appointed Northern Area Manager "responsible for Reed Transport activities in Darwen and Blackburn".

Len Woods had been a driver with BRS Larkfield, joining RT in 1955. After becoming involved with a lengthy works study project following the raising of the speed limit from 20 to 30 mph, he had succeeded Ted Holwill as Gravesend

Above: Taken outside of Aylesford Depot is this publicity photograph of Atkinson FC 5LW tractor of 1962, no.102 - 140 TKE with a typical load of 15 reels of newsprint for major customer Express & Star at Wolverhampton.

Left: one of the twelve Seddon 13:four tractors purchased in 1966. No.26 - HKE 923D was in the Aylesford fleet, initially in RCC livery - dark blue cab and light blue wheels.

Left: No.719 - GKO 238D an ERF LV 64CU NHE180 tractor with a tandem axle trailer was new into service when Stuart Wise took the opportunity of photographing the unit at Thatcham in May 1966.

Transport continued as a prime haulier to Crown even through the periods of changes of ownership - Williams Holdings and later Akzo Nobel - it wasn't until 1998 that the Company as SCA Transport finally acquired the trunking fleet of five 38 tonners.

Depot number six was now established. Thus the Company's presence in the north west was greatly strengthened by this move which also enabled the transport needs of nearby Sun Paper Mill to be adequately covered in total. Later, in June 1969, a portable building was purchased for the Traffic Office. Then, in 1972, the operation was moved into a lovely old and typical Lancashire stone two storey building known as Hollins Cottage, affectionately called the Farmhouse. Other moves followed as the prior needs of Hollins Mill had to be honoured. The Old Laboratory was the next Office in 1978 followed by a move in 1988 into the former Sports Pavilion.

During 1968 or 1969, Reed Paper Group's name was changed to Reed Group, reflecting the diversity away from paper. The old Mill at Dartford, London Paper Mills, was closed by April 1968 with a loss of 350 tons per week.

In 1968, the Company severed it's connections with

Depot Manager. In October 1967 he was appointed Manager responsible for Personnel, Training and Safety. One anecdote attributable to Len concerned his command of the English language. His daily obsession was to search for spelling and grammatical errors in the Daily Telegraph.

At the same time Ron Adkins took over responsibility for both Gravesend and Aylesford Depots with Ken Lewis and John Marsh appointed as Deputy Depot Managers to those depots respectively. Ken transferred from London, although was originally from Aylesford.

Following several meetings with the Darwen Mills' Management, it was agreed that Reed Transport would take over the three operations as from 28th July 1969. Included in the transfer were 23 drivers (on eight different rates of pay), three fitters and an apprentice.

Twenty-one assorted vehicles and a total of 48 auto and 5th wheel trailers were acquired, full details at Appendix 15. Darwen Paper Mill retained one tractor and three trailers for internal mill movements; Hollins one tractor and six trailers for the same need. Ken Sackett, a Traffic Clerk in Aylesford Depot and also formerly a BRS Larkfield driver colleague to Len Woods, moved to Darwen as Traffic Manager. Included in the transfer was the continued use of the garage at Hollins Mill for an annual rent of £750. Within the garage was an office which became the Darwen Traffic Office.

The fleet of trunking and small deliveries vehicles operated by the paint factory was retained by the factory, a situation which prevailed throughout that Company's Reed ownership. No amount of persuasion could change the minds of the Management. Ironically, although Reed

the sourcing and administration of the Group's company car fleet as a move was made towards leasing. At the same time all new commercial vehicle purchases were to be funded by leasing contracts. RT embarked upon a massive replacement programme to the value of £330,000 completed by March 1969 to be followed in 1969/1970 by a further investment of £200,000. A feature on RT in the in-house paper 'Reed News' of April 1969 headed "Geared to meet the transport challenge of the '70s" and subtitled "Five year replacement programme will increase productivity", the new Company policy was described thus:

"In choosing the new fleet, the management team was also influenced by the recent Ministry of Transport legislation requiring all vehicles and trailers to be tested annually. As a result, they have decided to discontinue buying expensive custom-built general purpose vehicles intended, with intensive servicing, to operate for 10 years." It followed on "Instead they are leasing mass-produced vehicles with a life of seven years in the heavy range and five in the lighter. But the new trailers should last ten years".

Thus Atkinson, ERF and Foden were out of favour. Appendix 17 shows the influx of 28 AEC Mercury and Mandator tractors together with Bedford and Ford lightweight tractors for the corrugated cases operations and also rigids - at least 78 in total. As Chapter Twenty later confirms, the AEC Mandators did not stand the pace so by 1970/1971, Scanias were being introduced and Fodens were back in favour. The Bedfords and Fords did, however, prove satisfactory for five years relative to the payloads and trailer lengths at that time.

Alan Glover retired in 1969 and was succeeded by Bill Dale as Managing Director. Ron Adkins had been appointed General Manager in August or September 1968. At the

same time, Ken Lewis and John Marsh took over as Depot Managers at Gravesend and Aylesford.

The next part of the History begins in Canada. In July 1963, Reed entered into a joint venture with Canadian Forest Products to build a pulp and paper mill in British Columbia. The mill was completed by July 1966. By 1967 it was producing sackkraft for Reed Medway Sacks and, as a consequence, No 6 Machine at Aylesford which was producing sackkraft was closed. After modification and twenty weeks later, No 6 Machine was producing test linerboard for Reed Corrugated Cases as a part substitute for more costly imported kraft linerboard.

The route from British Columbia to the UK involved a voyage of over 9000 miles via Panama. Canadian Forest Products shipped pulp and lumber via Seaboard Shipping, the largest charterer of dry cargo vessels in the world. A contract with Star Bulk was entered into from January 1969 for six years, shipping from Vancouver to the UK and Germany. The German terminal was at Brake on the River Weser but a new terminal was required in the UK. By now, the PLA was moving away from the London Docks to Tilbury. Reed took the initiative in setting up a jointly owned company, Seaboard Pioneer Terminal. The 'Pioneer' part of the name was derived from Reed's small in-house freight forwarding company, Pioneer Shipping & Forwarding Company Limited. Pioneer was to become a Division of Reed Transport in 1970, more later.

SPT took a 25 years lease from the PLA from February 1969. The PLA undertook to construct 46 Berth

Left: This RCC liveried Bedford TK, no.784 - PKO 793G was one of 20 units that arrived in 1968/69. It is pictured at Thatcham coupled to one of the 'pallet carriers'.

Right: No.49 - KKN 269E an AEC TGM4B Mercury tractor being unsheeted at Thatcham. It entered Reed service in June 1967. Note the use of overropes over the top front reel.

to SPT's requirements. Unfortunately, during the whole of 1969, the use of 46 Berth was frustrated by the actions of the unofficial union body known as the No 1 Dock's Group at Tilbury over container operation. This was all about the non acceptance of productivity agreements proposed by Devlin Stage II. SPT, not having a demand for continuous labour, had employed a stevedoring company, Scrutton Maltby, who had successfully negotiated a productivity agreement with the Unions and therefore suffered the actions through no fault of it's own. As a consequence, SPT had to wait for the dispute to end and 46 Berth came into operation in April 1970.

In preparation for the start of the operation and to cope with this new business, during 1969 George Blackman transferred from Gravesend to Tilbury as Supervisor. He was succeeded as Foreman at Gravesend by George Ralph. During the early Tilbury days, an office was shared with Samuel Williams, the haulier responsible for the Seaboard timber deliveries. Ironically, there were occasions before the dispute was settled when SCA's Terminal next door, 44 Berth, was used at weekends to handle Reed products. It was to be over 20 years later that SCA was to become so significant to RT's history.

In due course, the operation was moved into a converted secondhand exhibition trailer (a semi-trailer) surplus to requirements from a Group Company. One side, capable of being opened and lowered to form a demonstration platform, was sealed, the whole structure repainted green and fitted with a traffic desk and seating area, forming a very comfortable and practical office. By now, George had two drivers with shunt units and

trailers. At a later date, the trailer was replaced by a Portakabin.

Initially, the operation relied upon the backloading of it's own fleet from various depots supported by subcontractors. For example, Aylesford Depot was provided with three new Scania LBS110 tri-axle tractors with 38ft 6in flat platform tandem axle trailers to operate a three loads each per day shuttle from Tilbury of sackkraft to Reed Medway Sacks at Aylesford. Although operating at 32 tons gross, it was widely anticipated at the time by MD, Bill Dale, that gross weights would be increased, hence the specification of the Scanias. Unfortunately, these tractors were never able to operate to their full potential - 38 tonnes gross not coming until 1983. Their unladen weight gave them a payload of only 19 tons. Nevertheless, these vehicles were impressive for their day and many more Scanias were to follow into the fleet although only 4x2s. Depots gained greatly from the ability to backload from Tilbury, usually straight back to their 'home' sites.

In 1970 or 1971 the first delivery vehicle was based at Tilbury, maintenance facilities being provided from Gravesend Depot with the help of a mobile workshops.

Above: The exhibition trailer that provided the offices at Tilbury when purchased new by the Reed Paper Group for Reed Corrugated Cases..

Left: Two of the three Scania LBS110 tri-axle tractors purchased to operate with 38ft 6in flat platform tandem-axle trailers to operate on the shuttle hauling sackcraft between Tilbury to Reed Medway Sacks at Aylesford. Legislation of the day denied them operating at their designed capacity.

Chapter Seven

Engineering

The centre of engineering activities for the Company was at Aylesford. The original maintenance facilities on the formation of the Company were primitive and totally inadequate to meet the needs of a growing fleet. The maintenance bays were at the end of an open fronted structure next to the original Head Office of the Company, known as North Site, and alongside the River Medway at East Mill. A vehicle park and fuelling facility were adjacent and the total depot was within chainlink fencing.

As mentioned earlier, a new purpose built Head Office and adjoining Workshops was built in New Hythe Lane and formally opened on 15th November 1957 by the Rt. Hon. Harold Watkinson. The Workshops had been in use from around May of that year. The facilities provided were more than just for routine maintenance and repairs. There was a fully equipped diesel shop where pumps and injectors were maintained as well as an electrical shop which overhauled starters, dynamos, magnetos and other sundry pieces of ancillary gear.

The Workshops in particular were the subject of much Industry Press coverage. 'Commercial Motor' of 22nd November 1957 headed an article "Novel Pit Design in Fleet Workshops." 'Motor Transport' for 22nd November began "Minister opens Reed Transport depot" followed by "Maintenance Facilities For Over 400 Vehicles." What seemed a contradiction came with 'Modern Transport' of 23rd November with "Maintenance of 200 Vehicle Paper Fleet. Functional Depot Layout and Equipment." Both were correct. 'Motor Transport' included 100 cars, 80 trailers and 50 pieces of plant in it's calculation; 'Modern Transport' did not. It was the five bay service dock with tiled inspection pit which attracted most attention.

A ground floor plan of the Workshops is shown above. The 'L' shaped office area carried a second floor

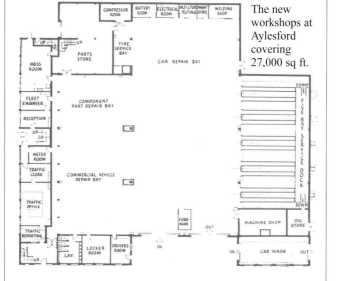

The new workshops at Aylesford covering 27,000 sq ft.

above. There was also a second floor area above the Parts Store for spares, particularly heavy items, access by a hoist above the entrance.

There was already a second maintenance facility on the Aylesford site, which supported the original small but growing Mill Local Fleet together with the fleet operated by the corrugated cases factory, Medway Corrugated Paper Company. In fact, it was always known as the MCPC Garage, even after the factory's name was changed to Reed Corrugated Cases in 1956. Fred Church was responsible for this facility with Basil Lucking as his number two. Others included Ray Keeley and Don Steel who both departed for National Service, returning to serve Reed Transport for many years, Ray into SCA ownership. Tom Flight and Charlie Bignell were two other names recalled.

In addition to the commercial vehicles, a fleet of cars from Rolls Royce down, site agricultural tractors and plant, together with an elderly Dennis fire engine were all maintained within this garage.

A photograph of the Dennis fire engine has been included, believed to have dated back to 1921 or 1922. The solid tyres were later replaced by pneumatics. Basil Lucking recalls the four-cylinder engine and magneto and the absence of

Aylesford's original Dennis fire engine and crew when on solid tyres.

front brakes. Two large squats or wedges were carried to add extra assistance to the handbrake and rear brakes. It's registration number is not totally clear but certainly began MF 68xx, possibly 6806 or 6896. This fire engine survived into the post-war years to be replaced by a 'modern' Dennis, mentioned later.

As soon as the new Workshops were fully operational, the corrugated cases fleet became a part of it's responsibility transferring to RT anyway in 1958. The MCPC Garage was thereafter used for the factory fork trucks maintenance. But back to the new workshops and it's role in the growth of Reed Transport. Maintenance Superintendent Eric Atkins left the Company and was replaced by Ken Smalley as Fleet Engineer followed by John Whittaker and then by Bert Bryant in March 1963 as mentioned in Chapter Six. Support to the Fleet Engineer was provided by Ron Cooper although Ron spent three intervening years at Thatcham, as mentioned later.

The first Garage Foreman was Scotsman Tom Mackie. At a later date this was to become a 6.00am to 2.00pm / 2.00pm to 10.00pm shift position with Don Baker and Tim Cooper as Supervisors. Much later, year unknown, the Garage ceased to be a cost centre and became a profit centre. A Garage Manager was appointed, Vic Chambers firstly and when he left, John Smith took over and remained in post into SCA days.

It needs to be recorded that Aylesford Garage dealt with the repairs and maintenance needs of several Group Companies' commercial vehicles and fleet cars as well as several non Group commercials and many privately owned cars. It was an MoT Test Station for private cars. Preferential labour rates were applied to all Group vehicles, higher rates for private transactions. It was practice to charge the appropriate depots and their vehicle groups for all work carried out. The vehicle costing procedures are described in greater detail in Chapter Eleven. Thus a monthly Financial Statement was produced for Aylesford Garage.

Left and above:
Night and day views outside the new Aylesford workshops. Two of the then current fleet of Fodens have been used by the photographer to dramatic effect along with one of the company cars, an Austin A55. The Foden in the night view - S18 no.214 - WKN 311, new in January 1956 was a replacement for one of the ex BRS vehicles. The other Foden, S18 six-wheel rigid no.72 - VKE 741, dates from May 1955.
Note inside the well-lit workshops can be seen the rear of the Aylesford site's ambulance.

Left and below: Inside the new workshops. Along the rear wall in front of the rooms that include the battery store, electrical shop, welding shop and compressor rooms are the servicing bays for the company cars whilst to the left are heavylift gantries of the component part repair bay for removal of engines, transmissions and similar mechanicals. The five-bay service dock (below), where no.214 is one of the five vehicles positioned, is located to the front and right of YKT 481, an Austin 4K/FED3 four wheel pantechnicon of Reed Corrugated Cases. Ray Keeley is the young technician in the foreground.

Back to the practicalities. Engines, predominantly five and six-pot Gardner LWs and later the 150LXs with Foden two strokes added, were regularly overhauled on the shop floor. Gearboxes, drive axles, steering boxes and all manner of chassis components were fully overhauled. These were the days before off-the-shelf service exchange parts. A comprehensive spares facility was included within the Workshops. Extensive vehicle modifications were carried out. For example, some 'oil braked' Atkinson tractors were converted to air over hydraulic systems to improve performance, nicknamed 'boilerhouse brakes' after reference to Westinghouse!

As will be seen from the ground floor plan, initial access to the Workshops was through either one of two front entrances. The sunken bays were at right angles to the entrances which meant a skillful manoeuvre within the shop floor area. One fitter achieved notoriety when an eight-wheeler was reversed across the pits instead of along one of them which left the drive axle dangling in the gap. It made for quite a recovery job.

The Workshops was not only involved with the Company's own 'straight forward' fleet. It was also responsible for special vehicles and equipment owned by the parent company and it's many subsidiaries. These included a Dennis fire engine with Rolls Royce B80 straight eight engine and a Dennis trailer fire pump with a four-litre side valve petrol engine. The Aylesford site, not only was dissected by a mainline railway, it had it's own railway network either side, moving raw materials on rail wagons and loading some despatches by rail. The Ruston-Hornsby diesel shunt engine was maintained by Reed Transport's mobile workshops Bedford no.127. Even the emergency diesel pump for the Mill sprinkler system came within the orbit of it's responsibility.

YKT 173

Left: Foden no.240 - YKT 173, a Foden FG6/15, had a flat fronted fibreglass cab, builder unknown. It is pictured here in the commercial vehicle repair bay in the new workshops at Aylesford. It's regular driver was Bill Featherstone.

Opposite page: Just some of the tasks undertaken by the mechanics and workshop staff in the Aylesford workshops plus a well stocked store room with an ample supply of leaf springs. Staff identified: top left - Trevor Johnson with an AEC AV505 engine; top right - B R Perrins of Rootes of Maidstone; middle left - Tom Flight, he was never without his cap; middle right - Basil Cleggett; bottom left - Cyril Bovis; bottom right - G H Lavender.

Right and right above: Foden eight wheeler no.15 - LYP 177, a 1951 acquisition, wearing another RT built cab, clearly a publicity picture, this shot was used by The British Steel Frame Co. Ltd of Cambridge Heath Road, London E2 to advertise their curved windscreens.

Chapter Five refered to a 'Motor Transport' article published on 1st September 1961 in the series "Improving the Breed" and a further innovation. To quote: "Reed is a bodybuilder of no mean prowess. The Company was one of the first operators to have cabs with wrap-round windscreens, building its own on Foden and AEC eight wheelers. These cabs have aluminium panels on ash frame". Four vehicles thus rebuilt have been identified - AEC Mammoth Majors no 47 - LUV 240 and no 49 - LYF 575 together with Fodens no 15 - LYP 177 and no 55 - MXD 544. There may have been others. Photographs of nos 49 and 15 are included. It is not know whether these

rebuilds were following serious accident damage or due to wear and tear. A photograph of no.15 was used by The British Steel Frame Co Ltd of London E.2 to promote it's curved windscreens. A close study of the photographs of nos 49 (see page 68) and 15 - AEC and Foden - show the close similarity of design.

Another product of the Workshops at this time was a recovery vehicle completed by early 1960. The Reed in-house magazine, 'Papyrus', featured this vehicle in an article published in the Spring 1960 edition. It was based on an ex WD AEC Matador chassis, as can be seen from the accompanying photograph on page 68. Again, a close

Above: Re-cabbed no.49 - LYF 575 AEC Mammoth Major MkIII dating from 1951 featuring a Reed Transport built cab of aluminium panels on an ash frame.

Left: The newly completed Aylesford AEC Matador recovery unit in 1960 outside the company's offices.

Below: A later no.15 being manoeuvred by the Matador recovery at Aylesford Garage with John Sullivan supervising. The Foden S21, 629 SKN, was not a write-off but was rebuilt by Aylesford Garage. It was renumbered 747 and transferred to Thatcham.

comparison with the photos of nos 15 and 49 clearly shows the similarity of the 'family' cab design.

The Matador ran on large 'track grip' tyres which were said to be so far out of balance that a speedo was not needed! At 29 mph all was fine but at 30 mph the steering gained a mind of it's own, the cab shook and the driver knew that he was speeding. Woe betide any driver who needed to select low box when on the move. He would

Right: More than a decade later a replacement for the now aged - and slow - AEC Matador was needed. Aylesford workshops used the cab, gearbox and cab of ERF no.155, mated it all to a bought-in tipper chassis, fitted their own bodywork and equipped it with a Harvey Frost crane. It is pictured here when newly outshopped. Standing in front are (left to right), John Smith, Garage Manager; John Cooper - later to become Thatcham Depot Engineer and Don Baker, Shift Supervisor.

Right below: Another example of the in-house capabilities at Reed Transport was the building of a considerable number of 'pallet carriers', these being fitted with Scammell auto couplings. A newly built example is featured here.

never get it out without stopping and taking a hammer to it. Such was the reputation of no. 500 (later 105).

Still on the subject of recovery vehicles, sometime in the Seventies a replacement was needed. A secondhand six-wheel tipper chassis was acquired, found by Vehicle Inspector Jim Sullivan. By now, the 1966 ERF no 155 - FKP 220D had been taken off the road. It's Cummins engine, gearbox and cab were fitted to the chassis and a recovery body with crane was built by the Workshops. The number 155 was retained but it operated on trade plates.

At around 1960, pit doors were added to the side of the building so vehicles could enter from outside directly on to the pits thereby eliminating the need for 90 degree manoeuvring within the building, a major advantage. At the same time, an extension was built incorporating a Body Workshops capable of undertaking the most complex rebuilding, for example cab replacement after a major accident. Hand painting to a very high standard together with copal fixed transfers was undertaken and a skilled signwriter was a part of the garage staff.

Anxious to portray itself as a responsible operator, the Workshops were made available to the Kent Police Training School who would attend on a quarterly or so basis bringing groups of Officers for familiarisation training before becoming fully fledged Road Traffic Officers. In advance of annual testing for HGVs in 1968, the Company helped to train the testers for Gillingham HGV Test Station.

Reed Transport became a trailer manufacturer in 1966 which continued until 1969. Trailers built ranged from 25ft single axle flats with Scammell auto couplings using Mereworth pre-pressed frame members to heavies, brought about by the Transport Act of 1968 which permitted 32 tons, which were 33ft 6in tandem-axle flats with 5th wheel couplings and full air brakes. The Company also designed and built what were called 'pallet carriers' for own use as well as for those Corrugated Cases factories that ran their own fleets. Based on 25ft and 27ft 6in single-axle chassis, a superstructure was built with front and rear bulkheads and a roof. To the cantrails were hung reinforced vinyl sheets (curtains in today's language) in tracks which merely kept the weather out. The bottom edge was secured using rubber bungees to rope hooks whilst the pallets were fixed using conventional roping methods.

Trailer manufacture ceased in 1969 due to relatively

high production costs, both labour and materials, at a time when the trailer industry was rapidly developing. At least one local Kent haulier, Mumfords of Marden, purchased Reed Transport built trailers. The total number of trailers built could not been determined. Five ex employees were asked for their views on numbers but the final tally has not been discovered. Records no longer exist. Digby Staples, one of the Bodyshop staff, was actively involved in the build programme and at it's height remembers completing the flooring of flat platform trailers at a rate of two each week. It is safe to assume that at least 300 trailers were built over the four years but it could have been as many as 400. In addition, Thatcham Garage was to build about 12 trailers including two 'pallet carriers' from kits sent down from Aylesford, whilst a further two were built at Wigan Garage. More about those two garages later.

Designs were subsequently transferred to the embryonic Fromant Trailer Company with whom a long and close relationship was maintained until it's eventual demise. It was in 1969 that Fleet Engineer Bert Bryant left to join Fromant and they were to become the main supplier of trailers, certainly for 100% of the heavies.

mechanical and electrical repairs and maintenance could be carried out. Indeed, in the later Fifties, Cropper & Colthrop Transport held a Foden franchise. As far as can be ascertained, it was for a 24 hour Recovery and Repair Service only, covering an area from Kidlington to the North to Winchester in the South and from Marlborough in the West to Maidenhead in the East. Sales Service was not included. It is not known when this franchise ceased.

Major bodybuilding and repainting was carried out at Thatcham. Not to be outshadowed by Aylesford's building of a versatile recovery vehicle, Thatcham Workshops in 1962 built it's equivalent, also onto an AEC Matador chassis previously owned by bus company West Yorkshire Road Car. The principal contributors to this vehicle were carpenter Louis 'Lew' Lilywhite and fitter Gordon Bowden. Reed

Another innovation by the Workshops is worthy of mention at this point. The progressive switch in the 1960s from Scammell auto couplings to 5th wheels created a nightmare for site shunting with the two types of trailer. To overcome this one or more Atkinson auto coupling tractors were modified with 'flip over' 5th wheel couplings so becoming dual purpose shunters.

The Company had Workshops at other Depots - Darwen, Gravesend, Thatcham and Wigan. London Depot retained a capability for running repairs as the fleet diminished in size. After Aylesford, Thatcham had the broadest range of facilities, albeit until 1984 in an old building. Nevertheless, practically any

Transport inherited an ERF based four wheel recovery vehicle no 719 - CRX 675 from Cropper & Colthrop in

Above: CRX 675 after a sale to a Colnbrook garage. It still retained its Reed Transport green when photographed in 1969.

1960. The winch and Harvey Frost crane were transferred to the Matador. Later, when the Matador was replaced by a Foden S21 cab six wheeler, again built by the Workshops, this time onto a former concrete mixer chassis, the crane was again transferred for continued use. The former ERF no.719 - CRX 675 at the time of writing this book is in preservation restored in T.R.T.S. livery.

The Depot Engineer at the time of the 1960 acquisition was Max Langden, succeeded by Ron Cooper from Aylesford in 1961. After three years, Ron returned to Aylesford, eventually to become Company buyer. Ken Pearce also from Aylesford replaced Ron, followed later by Peter Ashby. Peter was replaced by John Cooper in August 1980. John had started as an apprentice at Aylesford in 1957 and continued at Thatcham with SCA Transport as it's Depot Engineer until retirement in 2003 - 46 years service, marvellous.

Above: The replacement for Thatcham's Matador no.700 was this Foden S21 originally built in 1963 as an eight-wheeled mixer. It is pictured in the wash at Thatcham in the 1970s and carried trade plates 372 MO.

Left: In 1957 it was necessary to find a rugged replacement for the elderly Bedford O and S type tractors used on internal operations within the Aylesford Paper Mills, 24 hours a day, seven days a week. Five Douglas Tugmasters were bought for the task followed by a further five in 1959. No.153 was in the first batch.

Left: Wigan Garage rebuilt an old Douglas Tugmaster with a fifth wheel coupling for site shunting named the 'Phoenix'. In the background is Seddon no.141 and three Ford D600s.

Below: Another more adventurous of Wigan's builds was 'The Beast' built from Foden no.233 - 631 SKM after its S21 cab was wrecked in an accident. Not the prettiest of vehicles, it succeeded 'Phoenix' as a shunt vehicle. Depot Engineer Jimmy Myler, in jacket and tie, appears in the right of both pictures.

Gravesend Garage was inherited when the Imperial Paper Mills fleet was taken over in 1961 and served a rigid fleet - no trailers. Another garage already existed four miles up the road at Empire Paper Mill and during the mid Sixties, the garage at Gravesend was closed and the needs of the North Kent fleet were catered for at Greenhithe. In 1970, technician Graham Day was seconded to Greenhithe, being appointed Depot Engineer in 1971. A review was carried out to determine the best solution for the dispersed fleet in the area which highlighted the time wasted and the cost of constantly shuttling between the two sites. The main fleet was located at Gravesend rather than Greenhithe.

At Gravesend, a space existed between the old garage and a drivers' mess room/ locker room. An extension was proposed, approved and built which included an additional pit and higher access doors. With the enhanced facility, all work with the exception of major accident

For Wigan Garage, mention has already been made in Chapter Three of Les Marsh, it's first Engineer. When Les left, a replacement, name no longer recollected, took over for a very short period. He was followed by Jimmy Myler, later to be appointed Area Maintenance Engineer in 1969. Phil Green took over on Jimmy's retirement in May 1987.

A competent Wigan Garage was not to be outdone by the Aylesford and Thatcham vehicle building exploits. Their first example of home built vehicles was a site shunting tractor based on a former Douglas Tugmaster brought up from Aylesford. It was rebuilt and it's Scammell auto coupling replaced by a fifth wheel.

It was named 'Phoenix' but whether it arose from ashes is not known! The second contribution was a much more robust tractor for site shunting based on Foden S21 no.233 - 631 SKM. The original cab, wrecked in an accident, was replaced by a half cab and the resulting vehicle was appropriately named 'The Beast.' The paint finish left a little to be desired and probably caused raised eyebrows in some quarters but it was nevertheless a very functional vehicle.

and paint jobs which were sent to Aylesford, could now be undertaken. This included engine, gearbox and axle rebuilds and the reflooring of trailers. The Greenhithe premises were vacated and leased to a Reed Transport subcontractor, P.A.D. Transport. When the Imperial Paper Mills site finally closed in 1985, the remaining fleet retreated to Greenhithe and it's garage again occupied. This is further mentioned in Chapter Fifteen.

The other workshop to be mentioned was at Darwen. It was sited close to Hollins Paper Mill and benefited from steam heating from the Mill. This was a plus especially in winter. The downside was that it was built on a slope. It had a roller shutter door at the top of the slope, a small wicket door at the bottom. It was a feat of driving especially in winter to reverse trailers into the garage as the hill was off Hollins Road and had a very bad camber all the way down - not for the faint hearted! As it was near to the Mill's waste and pulp yard, if the wind blew in the wrong direction, the garage was filled with debris. When it rained hard, the water didn't go down the drain but straight through the garage. There was a major problem when it snowed.

Within was the first Manager's and Traffic Office built on a platform above the working area, an ideal position from which to address the troops. Included, as well as spares, antifreeze and oils, was the sheet and equipment store and a brew-oil (colloquial mid Lancastrian for a place where tea is made, hardly a tearoom!). It had one pit and a light hoist. It did have one other characteristic. The warmth from the heating encouraged a virulent breeding colony of cockroaches which rapidly scurried into hiding when the lights went on. No pest controller ever succeeded in beating these intruders! Initially, former Hollins Paper Mill Engineer Bill Hilton, five fitters and a storekeeper were employed. At a later date, John Catterall was appointed Engineer, leaving the Company in May 1985. Thereafter, Darwen Garage was managed from Wigan Garage.

By 1989, the Darwen fleet had reduced to eight and the decision was taken to close the garage in February and consolidate all maintenance and repairs at the larger Wigan garage. Despite the physical disadvantages,

everyone had a considerable affection for the old garage.

Before this Chapter is complete, there needs to be mentioned the Mobile Vehicle Inspector. Jim Sullivan's name has already been mentioned. Jim joined Aylesford Garage as a fitter in 1962. The mid Sixties saw pressure on the road haulage industry to clean up it's act with regard to maintenance standards. The Transport Act of 1968 was on the horizon. Concerned about raising it's own standards, the Company appointed Jim as its Vehicle Inspector in 1966 and for the next 17 years he lived out of a suitcase and with a white Ford Escort van changed every two years. He had the authority to stop a Reed Transport or other Reed Group vehicle anywhere at any time for inspection and, if necessary, take it off the road. Jim was not the most popular of employees when he turned up in a depot, often unexpected. "Stop em is here" would be the message around the Traffic Office, a nightmare when the depot was down to it's last empty trailer and stopped by Jim with defects. Nevertheless, Jim's role was vital and helped greatly to improve standards, reduce GV9s and raise the Company image out on the road.

Jim relocated to Thatcham and usually managed to return to that depot for Friday afternoon. Aylesford was invariably a Monday call and Wigan once a month whilst Corrugated Cases factories running their own fleets were also included within his sphere of operation. Edinburgh was visited every six months, Shirley near Solihull was quarterly and so on. Jim also became the Company scavenger for parts from breakers. One episode was recalled when RT was introducing the early Scanias into the fleet. Spares were in short supply and Jim managed to find 18 or 20 brake shoes at a Manchester area breakers. They would be relined and put into stock until needed. He returned to Thatcham with a rather overloaded Escort van but almost home, spotting a police presence at Chieveley Services, was forced to hide up for over an hour until the coast was clear! Long after the fleet had changed to 5th wheel, Aylesford Paper Mills was desperate for some Scammell type trailers for internal work. With his contacts, Jim found eight or ten at a breakers in Wokingham, ex Courage, which were duly purchased and shipped to Aylesford.

Inevitably, Jim regularly found himself involved with breakdowns day and night and at major accidents arranging transhipments and vehicle recovery. In all, he covered around 35000 miles each year. With the cutbacks of the eighties, Jim left the Company in April 1983 with a redundancy package but he had played a vital role in keeping the fleets, RT and Group, safely on the road.

Left: A Tugmaster of different cab design at Aylesford. Douglas have been building towing vehicles since 1947.

Chapter Eight

Hayes, Kings Langley and Watford

The significance of these places will be progressively disclosed. From late 1961 into 1962, the Reed Corrugated Cases production at Brentford was transferred to Thatcham and the factory on the Great West Road was closed. It's fleet of vehicles was transferred into Reed Transport. However, Thatcham was in the opposite direction to Brentford's main customers; Heinz and United Biscuits in NW10, A.E.Wilmer and Roses Lime in Hemel Hempstead, Nestles in Hayes, Middlesex and Beechams in Brentford. To serve these customers from a greater distance would have meant an increased fleet and an ever present risk of traffic delays along the old A4.

The Company decided to open a sub depot using the yard of J.H.Moore in Pump Lane, Hayes, Middlesex. Three Brentford drivers, George Gurney, Jim Kennedy and Johnnie Lane, transferred on 2nd July 1962 to be based at Hayes. Three Atkinson FC/Scammell tractors and nine trailers were sourced out of the Thatcham fleet with the flexibility of being A Licenced rather than C Licenced as the Brentford fleet had been. This fleet was controlled from Thatcham with George Gurney as Foreman, telephoning for the next day's instructions each afternoon. Thatcham night men shunted between six and nine loaded trailers to Hayes each night. Always included were two loads for Wilmer in Hemel Hempstead which were George's responsibility. The Hayes based drivers would reload empty pallets for RCC, pulp from Becketts at Kingston and wastepaper from merchants for Colthrop Board Mills to be shunted back to Thatcham each night.

With two large customers in Hemel Hempstead, the next move came with the renting of part of the yard of E.J.Masters Haulage in Railway Terrace, Kings Langley. Three trailers were based there and so loads for Wilmer and Roses Lime could be shunted closer to their premises

Thompson & Norris Ltd factory at Great West Road, Brentford was eventually to become part of Reed Corrugated Cases. In this 1955 view, driver Jack Howlett is seen standing beside his Bedford van in the new owner's livery. Jack is mentioned in Bob Murphy's reminiscences of the time detailed in this chapter.

for delivery by Thatcham or Hayes based tractors as second jobs. A further move occurred on 2nd September 1963, when Frank Pruce joined the Hayes operation as a night driver. Frank's first job was to run to Thatcham, changeover and deliver to Heinz in NW10. Then to return to Thatcham and collect a second trailer loaded for the next day. This tight operation was controlled by Thatcham Traffic Manager Tom Howe, an ex TRTS/BRS/C&C driver himself. Having a Hayes based night driver also provided the opportunity to service the three tractors at night between the first and second changeovers - unless of course a major defect was found and then the Thatcham Night Foreman Reg Taylor would substitute a tractor, if possible, not specifically allocated.

In 1967, the Roses Lime contract was lost by RCC and the Kings Langley operation ceased. By the end of 1968, the Hayes operation had been switched to 5th wheel tractors and trailers with greater flexibility within the overall fleet.

So where did Watford fit in? Reed's printers in Watford - Odhams Press - generated baled waste paper known as PAMs (periodicals and magazines) which was destined for St Annes Board Mill and Avonbank Wastepaper, both in Bristol. The Company had four 12 ton flat-platform fifth-wheel trailers based at Odhams which were loaded by their own shunter. Trailers could now be shunted at night to Watford. There were also regular loads of waste cardboard from Wilmer back to Colthrop. With RCC loads for Hemel Hempstead and three or four loads daily from Colthrop to Nabisco at Welwyn Garden City, Watford became an important hub for Thatcham Depot. For example, George Gurney would deliver one load direct from Hayes, dropping back into Watford to deliver two more loads and accumulating return load trailers for the night return runs. The whole

Left: Unique in the fleet was Albion 'Claymore' underfloor engined box van 965 JHX. It was new to Thompson & Norris at Brentford and came to Thatcham in 1962 on relocation of that business. It is pictured at Brentford with its driver Jack Howlett. It became fleet no.814 and was withdrawn in 1964.

Hayes/Watford changeover operation was supplemented by day vehicles as required. All this was in pre M4 days. The Hayes operation continued well until 1972 when J.H.Moore decided to reduce the size of the Pump Lane premises by offering part of it for redevelopment and this included the compound used by RT.

The operation was moved to N.M.T. Storage at the rear of what is now Heston Services on the M4 and it was business as usual. By early 1975, the N.M.T. rental had spiralled and with the M4 now open between Theale and London, this operation from Heston ceased and deliveries were made direct from Thatcham with west London now only one and a half hours away. Two of the remaining three Hayes/Heston drivers took redundancy, Frank Pruce retired.

In its time, this tightly controlled operation was an asset to Thatcham Depot and enabled an excellent service to be provided to the Reed Corrugated Cases main customers despite the extra mileage incurred as a result of the factory transfer.

Before the Brentford related story closes, it is an appropriate time to include a contribution from one of the

Left: This handsome Commer pantechnicon was new in 1961. With it's Middlesex registration 7292 MM, it was probably ordered for the Brentford factory but diverted to Aylesford as no.121.

Right: 154 TKP, a BMC 10-ton artic arrived in May 1962. As part of the 'C' Licence fleet it had an 8xx number and was normally engaged on Reed Corrugated Cases work. Thatcham's Matador recovery unit is in the background in this June 1967 view.

Far right: Rear view of a former RCC Brentford BMC FFK clearly showing the Scammell coupling mechanism.

Above: For increased work from Reed Corrugated Cases a number of BMC high cube box vans were acquired from 1962. The body of no.813 - 104 TKN, an Austin FFK140 purchased in the May of that year, had a capacity of 1250 cubic feet. It is pictured here in August 1967 in RCC two-tone livery.

ex Brentford drivers, Bob Murphy:

"I joined T&N (Thompson & Norris) as a driver in Jan 1950. The vehicle I drove was a Guy Chieftain (? Albion). T&N also had two three-wheeled artics - Scarabs were they called? - that were on continuous deliveries to Heinz at Harlesden, Bedford three-tonners and a little later Bedford artics. Alf Athew and Jack Howlett drove a lorry and trailer.

In those days lorries and trailers had to have two drivers. Joe Jones was Despatch Foreman when I joined T&N and Despatch Foremen were responsible for Transport also. I guess 50% of transport was on outside contractors, Joe Moore and Acton Transport doing

mainly local work, Hoyle Transport of Manchester, Mayfield Transport of Southend, Silver Roadways did some distance work. We also had a daily supply of railway containers.

In the latter days of Brentford, Reed Transport became involved. They were based in London. The T&N livery was green and white and when Albert E.Reed bought us out, I seem to recall that we went to Oxford and Cambridge blue".

Bob went on to work in the Planning Dept of the Thatcham factory before retiring. To add to Bob's reminiscences, the rail container operation involved the loading of containers for some deliveries, collected by the GWR road fleet. The mention of Reed Transport involvement almost certainly relates to the hire of the two Austin fixed artics, nos 43 and 44, of the Perkins & Glover fleet. See note 6 of Appendix 3.

The colour scheme of Oxford and Cambridge blue referred to were the dark blue and light blue of the original RCC livery, continued by Reed Transport for the dedicated Corrugated Cases fleets.

Left above: Ex Reed Corrugated Cases, Brentford tractor no.801 - 85 UMP is recovered on a snowy day back to Thatcham after an accident.

Below: A view of the 'Nissen' huts loading area at Reed Corrugated Cases, Thatcham with five Atkinson 'Silver Knights' in a variety of livery styles. The picture dates from around 1965.

Chapter Nine

Hauling Bombs for Uncle Sam

With the takeover of Cropper & Colthrop Transport in 1960 came a contract with the United States Air Force. The contract had commenced in the late 1950s and was to transport bombs (minus their detonators) from the USAF base at Welford in Berkshire, which had opened during the Second World War in 1943, to other USAF bases at Brize Norton, Fairford, Alconbury, Bentwaters, Mildenhall, Lakenheath, Bruntingthorpe and Wethersfield. The contract gave the USAF the opportunity to phone up before 4.30pm and request any number of vehicles for their use the next morning. The average number requested would be between three and six. The vehicles used were Foden S20 eight wheelers or Austin/Scammell tractors with 10ton trailers. Later, into the Sixties, the Atkinson 5LW tractors were used.

Specific eight wheelers and 27ft single axle trailers were allocated for the contract, being adequate for the nine-ton loads. These had cleats welded to the side raves into which slatted side and tailboards each about 4ft in height were slotted. They were made by Thatcham's Garage carpenter, Bob Edwards.

Because of the short notice given by the USAF of their next day requirements, it was often necessary for late night tran-shipping by fork truck driver Charlie Charles to make enough rigids and trailers with cleats available.

No special training was required for this operation but certain rules had to be complied with. Each vehicle had to be equipped with a fire extinguisher and were required to travel in convoy. A mate, or 'shotgun' as the Americans called him, was required initially on every vehicle but was later relaxed to the front, middle and rear vehicles of the convoy. Finding 'second' men at short notice stretched resources. Charlie Charles, shunters Tom Limpus and Reg Black, Garage painter Percy Pontin and recovery driver Alec Gourley usually found that they had been 'volunteered' as mates.

All cigarettes, matches and combustible items were confiscated on entry to the loading dump at Welford and, while the vehicles were being loaded by the USAF staff, drivers and mates were taken to a safe haven to be given tea and a cigarette. On completion of loading and having pulled clear of the bomb dump, the drivers were given back their cigarettes, etc and then given a specified route to be followed for their consignment destinations. Once the drivers were on the road, they were not checked and chose a route they knew and which suited them the best. The only rule observed was that they travelled in convoy.

Tony Gliddon recalls that one day six vehicles loaded up for Wethersfield. The route given to them was via Rickmansworth, Watford, Hertford and on to Bishops Stortford - a slow and tortuous route even today. Doug Barrett was leading the convoy and, once clear of the gates at Welford, soon stopped to inform the others that he was not going by the designated route but would go via the A4 and Chiswick and then round the North Circular, saying it was up to the others which way they chose. All six decided to follow Doug in convoy. If they had been found out, one cannot speculate on what the Authorities would have said about six loads of bombs travelling in and then around London! On arrival at the destination, they were again stripped of all combustible items and then while the vehicles were being unloaded by the USAF staff, the drivers and mates were sent to a designated area for tea and a smoke.

Derek Appleby recalls one occasion in the mid sixties when four vehicles arrived at the gatehouse at Alconbury and the convoy was told that they would not be allowed to go any further and that USAF staff would drive the vehicles to the bomb dump for unloading. The drivers and mates were taken to the canteen for a cup of coffee and to wait for the return of their empty vehicles. The next time

No.793 - PBL 820 was one of a batch of seven Austin BMC/Scammell tractor units delivered to Thatcham in 1957. This vehicle was driver Tony Gliddon's mount in the story of the twelve vehicle convoy hauling expired ammunition to Milford Haven detailed in this chapter.

they saw their vehicles was some two hours later when they looked out of the canteen window to see the Americans racing all four empty Atkinsons down the runway towards the gatehouse. Other movements included empty aluminium long range fuel tanks which were fitted underneath the wings of aircraft to increase their range. These went to the same destinations as the bombs and were transported in long slatted crates.

In 1962 or 1963, a one-off movement of out of date ammunition, again loaded in crates and destined for Milford Haven, involved twelve vehicles. To achieve this, some of the elderly ex C&C Albion Chieftains of 1955/1956 vintage were required to accompany the newer Austins and Atkinsons with Scammell coupling 27ft trailers. Side and tailboards were not required for this movement but fire extinguishers were a definite requirement.

A mate was required on every third vehicle and, because of the size of the convoy, it was decided to send a fitter in case of a breakdown. The fitter concerned was John Tilling, who recalls taking his box of tools and also had to act as mate to Pat Oswald. The only problem that occurred was a puncture on one of the trailers but as they were twin wheeled and already in Carmarthen and with only forty miles to go, John took the decision to carry on regardless to their destination.

It was in Carmarthen that the RAF was supposed to meet the convoy to escort them to their destination but for some reason they did not turn up. It is presumed, but has never been confirmed, that while negotiating the one way system in Carmarthen, the convoy went down one road while the escorts came up the other road, passing each other in the one way system. The convoy, knowing the way, continued on their own.

On arrival at Milford Haven Docks at around 7.00pm, the ammunition was unloaded by 'handball' by the RAF onto a US freighter for an unknown destination, all twelve vehicles being unloaded by 8.00pm. All drivers and mates were then put up for the night in the Seaman's Mission in Milford Haven where they were reprimanded for being noisy. They had not realised that there were fishermen staying who were trying to get an early night in order to be up at four o'clock to catch the early morning tide.

Tony Gliddon, who was on this journey in his 1957 Austin no 793 - PBL 820, recalls that they all returned empty to Thatcham and that John Tilling, the fitter, realizing that the Austin was faster than the Albions and Atkinsons and wanting to get home as quickly as he could, rode back as passenger with Tony.

This contract with the USAF ended in 1969.

Right: OBL 502 was one of several magnificent Foden S20 cabbed eight-wheelers allocated to Thatcham, this example being new in 1957. It could carry a 15 ton payload and had a Gardner 6LW engine. Vehicles of this type (with cleats fitted to the side raves) were employed on the ammunition contract. No.785 is seen outside the Thatcham Traffic Office in 1966.

Chapter Ten

The Seventies and Some Contraction

After a decade of expansion, the Seventies were to be a mixture of gains and losses. There were pockets of expansion but the UK was entering a period of recession and this was to have an adverse effect on the paper making industry. Perhaps the term consolidation might better describe this period.

1970 began with Reed Transport responsible for the transport needs of nine paper mills. Their annual production figures were as follows:

Aylesford Paper Mills		
including Brookgate	13 machines	361,000 tons
Colthrop Board Mills	3 machines	125,000 tons
Darwen and Lower Darwen		
Paper Mills	6 machines	60,000 tons
Empire Paper Mills	3 machines	45,000 tons
Hollins Paper Mill	3 machines	50,000 tons
Imperial Paper Mills	6 machines	150,000 tons
Sun Paper Mill	2 machines	40,000 tons
Tovil & Bridge		
Paper Mills	7 machines	65,000 tons
Total Production		896,000 tons

Three smaller mills at Penicuik, Retford and Sawston, were not included. Add to this significant combined tonnage the high volume of raw materials moved by road into these mills - wastepaper, pulp, machinery, machine clothing - and the distribution from the three largest Corrugated Cases factories - Aylesford, Thatcham and Wigan - and an outside observer might consider that Reed Transport's position was comfortable and well settled for the future. Nothing was to be farther from the truth. By the middle of the decade, the situation was far from comfortable as will be shown a little later in this Chapter.

Mention has already been made in Chapter Six of Reed's freight forwarding

company, Pioneer Shipping & Forwarding Company Limited. Based in Reed House, Piccadilly, London, it had originally been formed out of the old Reed Central Buying organisation in 1964. With a staff of 35, it was incurring considerable annual losses. It was decided to place the company under the responsibility of Reed Transport. A restructuring programme was undertaken, reducing the staff level to 14. The operation moved into spare offices at London Depot, 38 Great Suffolk Street and by 1971 had become profitable. It's Manager was Harry Whetcombe.

The company's principal activities included a charter shipping operation from the USA of linerboard shipments on behalf of Great Southern Paper Company of Stamford, Georgia, through the port of Panama City on the Gulf to the UK and mainland Europe. The vessels used were from the Lykes Line SEABEE system where 500ton barges were floated out from the stern of the mother vessel and by using a stern lifting system. A photograph has been included showing the stern view of the 'Almeria Lykes' with a tug manoeuvering a barge into or out of the vessel. Great Southern was a major supplier of linerboard not only to the Reed Corrugated Cases factories but also to many competitors. The barges were brought into the various docks and wharves along the River Thames including the jetty of Imperial Paper Mills at Gravesend and Deep Water Wharf at Erith. This

Right: A view of the Lykes Line vessel 'Almeria Lykes' on the River Thames with a barge being manoeuvred into or out of the stern. A previous ship to carry the name was involved in the Malta convoys of World War Two and succeeded in shooting down two aircraft. It sank after being torpedoed on 13th August 1942.

Left: The jetty of Imperial Paper Mills at Gravesend on the River Thames was used to handle linerboard from the USA out of Lykes SEABEE barges on behalf of sister company Pioneer Shipping & Forwarding Co for delivery throughout the UK. The jetty's three Stothert & Pitt cranes tower above one Reed's Scania units - no.237 - and another haulier's Volvo F86 six wheeler.

Below: No.76 was one of 19 AEC AV505 engined Mercurys purchased between 1969 and 1971 The vehicle being captured on camera by Roger Kenney in a Lancashire street whilst its driver takes a break digesting the contents of his newspaper.

was perfect traffic for Reed Transport and a close relationship quickly developed with it's new sister company. Pioneer also had both an import agency and an export forwarding agency, handling Worldwide a multitude of raw materials, finished product, machinery and spare parts for Reed Companies. It also was responsible for marine and other related insurance covers on behalf of Group Companies.

The company certainly was a paper specialist but with Darwen Depot now formed, it was to take on the distribution of a rather different paper product with it's own idiosyncracies - wallpaper base and then the paintable wallpapers. From it's creation in mid 1969, Darwen delivered wallpaper base from Hollins Paper Mill to the WPM staining branches, the largest two being in the town of Darwen - Relief Decorations at Queens Mill and C & J. Potter at Belgrave Mills.

Relief Decorations manufactured embossed white papers, Potter the printed patterned papers. Both presented logistical problems. Queens Mill was next door to

Hollins but the 'back end' required vehicles to use a tortuous route through narrow back streets strewn with cars which necessitated police intervention on occasions.

Belgrave Mills was at the top of the town and delivery required the reversing of small trailers up a pronounced gradient. The area was prone to congestion and a nightmare in bad weather. Unfamiliar hauliers attempting to deliver on long trailers could not reverse into the bays. The year 1972 saw the involvement with the finished product from the two mills.

The loading at Queens Mill was primitive and a story in itself. 30ft flat trailers were used for 'handball' loading

Right: A weekend photograph of the Darwen Depot fleet at home. Ten of it's eleven Foden S40s, two older S21s, a Ford and two AEC Mercurys on parade with Hollins Cottage affectionately called 'The Farmhouse' in the background.

Below: No.911 - BKT 194K was one of eleven Foden S40s supplied to Darwen Depot in 1972. This one is photographed at the Alex Cowan Paper Mill at Penicuik about to leave to return to Darwen with the night trunk load of smalls deliveries for London Depot to distribute. The driver standing to attention is Bill Porter.

off a chute to the rear of the trailer, one box at a time. This involved a day shunter with some assistance. The two main destinations were Halesowen and Nottingham, served by nightly tramp runs, the night drivers repeating the 'handball' routine. A highly pilferable product, all 'returns' were immediately placed in a spare office in the depot until the paperwork could be thoroughly checked. The job was inefficient and not profitable.

With the increase in demand for paintable wallpapers and the growth of DIY sheds, it was clear that Queens Mill could no longer cope with primitive handling methods but lacked the room to reorganise. There was no room to palletise. In 1975, a warehouse was leased at Clayton le Moors, with a later move to Altham near Accrington. New 40ft trailers were provided for this operation. Full loads were now palletised but the 'handball' practice was still necessary in the move to the warehouses. Some small consignments were still despatched direct to customers from Queens Mill. By the

mid 1970s, 40ft curtainsiders were introduced in Relief Decorations livery. By the end of the Seventies, the distribution was moved to Lostock with a five loads a day shuttle from Darwen, supplemented when necessary. There were also direct deliveries from Hollins into Lostock.

In parallel with the wallcoverings business, the paint distribution from Crown Paints was taken on from 1972 but although briefly mentioned in Chapter Six, this operation has been described in detail later, in Chapter Twelve. There was another offshoot of the WPM business which began in 1973. 15ton loads of cloth in 1cwt bundles were delivered from Dawes in Nelson to the WPM Company Sandersons at Uxbridge. Not the favourite of jobs, this was also 'handball' and a very good way for drivers to lose weight. Drivers termed the bundles 'dead pigs' and it must be admitted that on occasions, this job was used as punishment. The business continued until the early Eighties. Latterly, subcontractors were used.

At the beginning of this Chapter, mention is made in the production figures of a mill at Penicuik. In 1966, a paper merchant and fine papers manufacturer, Alex Cowan, was purchased by Reed. The merchanting side eventually merged with Spicers, already owned by Reed, in 1967 to form Spicer - Cowan. The company operated a sizeable fleet throughout the UK which never became a part of Reed Transport although new vehicles were sourced by RT as part of it's Group purchasing role. The two mills owned by Alex Cowan in Penicuik, in the Esk Valley south of Edinburgh, transferred into the Reed Paper & Board Division to join the other mills. A small fleet was operated from Penicuik which retained it's

Left: Seen at Hollins Paper Mill at Darwen. No.926 - TKM 214N was one of two Scania L110 tractors for the Darwen fleet in 1974. The white radiator is less conspicuous than earlier Scanias with the panel carrying the Scania name finished in green and not white.

Left below: Ford D800 rigid, probably no.186 - UKN 526H dating from 1970 pictured in Aylesford Depot well sheeted and roped ready for the road.

It is appropriate at this stage to describe the situation of the parent Company with the changes which were to take place and which were to directly affect RT in due course. But first the legacy from the Sixties. The UK paper industry's prospects were bound up by international politics of the time. The UK failed to enter the EEC in 1963 and 1967 due largely to France's veto. Economic growth was at a halt. The UK was a part of EFTA. A new Labour Government had introduced a temporary 15% import surcharge in late 1964 but in January 1965, a further 10% EFTA tariff was removed, thus largely cancelling out the surcharge. In 1967 the surcharge was removed and the final elements of EFTA tariffs eliminated. There was a flow of imported paper into the UK as a consequence. The Scandinavian producers then increased the price of pulp but not their paper prices. During 1968 and 1969, paper consumption increased in the UK, home production was increased but not as fast as imports. Prices were static despite pulp cost increases.

As from 1st April 1970, IPC (International Publishing Corporation) was merged with Reed Group and on 29th July that year, the new enlarged Company became Reed International. That part of the new Company most involved with RT, i.e. the Paper Mills, Corrugated Cases, Fields, Reed Medway Sacks and RT itself, became a part of the Main Division, Reed Group. WPM including Crown, became another main division, Reed Decorative Products. In due course, a further main division was created in October 1971, Reed Building Products, of which customer Key Terrain was a principal part.

Back to Reed Group. At it's formation, it had a 17% market share of UK's paper and board production; 12% of consumption. It held 25% of the UK corrugated cases market, 23% of multi-wall sacks and 11.5% of cartons. In the year 1971/72, Aylesford Paper Mills' return on capital dropped to zero and the prospects for the two mills with the highest capital investment, Aylesford Paper Mills and Imperial Paper Mills, were poor if the market conditions continued. During the winter of 1970/71, it emerged that

independence throughout. However, Darwen Depot enjoyed a close business relationship with Alex Cowan. The mills had a sizeable business in the London area with the need to distribute small consignments of fine paper to printers and merchants. Darwen from about 1970 provided a daily service collecting full trailer loads of 'smalls' from Penicuik, returning to Darwen each afternoon for trunking overnight with a changeover with London Depot. London would then distribute the next day. Darwen relied on loads of reels to RCC at Edinburgh from Sun Paper Mill, starting the cycle on a Sunday after a local job, to be at Penicuik for Monday midday. London was never short of Lancashire loads from Aylesford or Gravesend to feed it's leg of the operation. This was a marvellous service able to deliver over 400 miles into Central London in less than 24 hours. In 1976 the Mills closed and this successful operation and happy relationship came to an end.

a project was underway involving Reed and Bowater with the idea that their pulp and paper operations should merge. However, in March 1971 it was announced that 'mutually agreeable terms' could not be arranged. Had the merger occurred, the path forward for RT may have been very different as Bowater also had a sizeable transport operation.

The Company's largest customer, Aylesford Paper Mills, entered the Seventies with 13 machines in production. The combined capacity was about 6840 tons each week. With the effect of events of the previous ten years described above and the failure of the Reed/Bowater merger project, in 1971 APM was forced to close five machines with a potential loss of 1870 tons each week, 27% of it's total.

Elsewhere at Thatcham, Colthrop had already closed a machine in 1966 and a second one was closed in 1971. Thereafter, only cartonboard was to be produced. During the Seventies, machines at Imperial Paper Mills were progressively closed. In the north, Darwen Paper Mill was closed in 1972 although it's salle (room) at Balle Street used for slitting sheets of paper continued in use and survived well into the Eighties. A 24 hours / seven days a week shuttle between Balle Street and Lower Darwen Paper Mill continued to operate.

An interesting development came in 1973. Aylesford Depot by now had grown to 85 vehicles employing about 140 people. It was proving to be too large for efficient control and operation. The customer base was such that it required both maximum weight vehicles for paper deliveries and maximum cubes for lightweight deliveries of corrugated cases. There was a natural split of traffic and so it was decided to create a new and autonomous Depot, adjacent to Aylesford Depot to be known as New Hythe Depot. Thereafter, Aylesford was to concentrate on the needs of the Paper Mills, Reed Medway Sacks and non Group customer Kimberly Clark. New Hythe Depot took responsibility for the local Reed Corrugated Cases factory and another Reed company, Key Terrain, a producer of pitch fibre drainage pipes, later plastic building products. George Blackman was appointed it's Depot Manager, moving from Tilbury. His place was taken by Dennis Morgan.

George did have his own unique philosophy towards managing. Whilst

Dennis was understudying George's job at Tilbury prior to taking over, he noticed that the Office mail always arrived during the afternoon. It was never opened on arrival by George but set aside until the next morning. When Dennis asked one day if George was going to open the mail, the reply was "we don't want to take any problems home with us, do we?"

By now, with Tilbury and now New Hythe, the number of operating bases had reached eight.

In the year 1973/74, Reed Transport handled 1,989,000 tonnes of traffic, achieved a trading profit of £214,000, operated a fleet of 246 vehicles with 600 trailers and employed 575 people. Sister company, Pioneer, made a profit of £58,700 and employed 15 people.

The UK generally was in recession during this period. The Company struggled on trying to keep it's head above water but in March 1975 the fleet was reduced by 25 vehicles, 43 people were made redundant and a further reduction of 20 people was made by natural wastage. This was a sad period in the Company's history.

Len Woods retired as Northern Area Manager in the North West in 1975. Chris Halliwell had been appointed Darwen Depot Manager in 1974. There were other Depot Management changes. Dennis Morgan took over at Wigan Depot in April 1974 when Bill Bailey left the Company. Gordon Pease succeeded Dennis at Tilbury.

By this time, the Tilbury based fleet had risen to five Scanias together with a berth shunting operation with a total of 20 trailers to facilitate preloading. Gordon had previously been the Chargehand / Shunter at Empire Paper Mills and before that, a driver at Gravesend. He was on the move again when, in September 1976 he was seconded to Thatcham Depot before being appointed Thatcham Depot Manager on 1st February 1977. Thatcham Depot had a succession of Managers prior to

Right: For the Reed Corrugated Cases Aylesford fleet, following the Ford D600s of 1968/69, came the bigger bhp DA2114s from 1974, no.107 - GKP 648N being an example. Driver Terry Martin is seen here talking with his boss, New Hythe Depot Manager George Blackman.

Right: The first Volvos entered the fleet in 1974 of which no.67 - TKO 301N was one of sixteen F88s recorded. The retention of the black radiator grille compares with the white treatment given to other makes of the era. Len Jones is seen roping up a load of mixed size reels on a wet day at the Aylesford Depot. Main roping was over the flysheet, not the correct method particularly in wet weather.

this period. After the retirement of Tommy Cantwell, John Telford took over followed by John Henderson when John T left. John H was originally at Aylesford but later moved to London. When John H transferred to Group Company J.&J. Maybank, Mike Griffiths joined the Company and on his departure, Chris Halliwell held the reins for a while. Ian Beaumont doubled up as Manager for London and Tilbury.

In 1976, the Company returned to Tovil & Bridge Mills in Maidstone with the opening of a sub depot to Aylesford Depot located in Bridge Mill. This move resulted in responsibility for the total mills operation. Two tractors were involved in the internal mills movements on days, one on nights. The shuttle over to the various Aylesford factories involved two tractors on

days, one on nights. For example, between 50 and 60 loads each week were delivered to Kimberly Clark.

Initially, Leyland and Seddon tractors taken over were used, but soon there was a progressive flow of ERF, Scania and Volvo tractors on to the operation, relegated from Aylesford Depot general work. An attempt has been made at Appendix 9 to identify those vehicles operated by Tovil & Bridge Mills between 1959 and 1976, including those at the time of this second takeover. Five

Left: It looks as if the driver of Scania no 54 - FKP 340V may have left the engine running whilst he checks if his next trailer is loaded. Taken outside the Top Bay of Tovil Mill in Maidstone, this 1980 LB81 is likely to be on the Tovil to Aylesford shuttle. The Mill closed in late 1982 and a modern housing development has since been built on the site.

Left: No.710 - AKK 460T is a 1978 Ford DA2114 with a full liveried RCC curtainside trailer. Note the extendable ladder mounted on the back of the cab to aid the safe sheeting of the flat platform trailers. It is seen here in this Phil Moth picture heading west down the M4 destined for Thatcham.

Left below: A pair of Ford 'D' Series 12-ton capacity artics, nos. 740 and 744 - JKL 757N and MKR 992P respectively, from the batch that arrived to replace the Bedford TKs in 1975/76. They are pictured on the wash-down area. Their drivers Pete Maisey (left) and Ivan Richardson (right) stand by no.740.

drivers transferred from the mills employment - Sid Brenton, Alan Down and Michael Bodkin followed six months later by John Caudwell and Keith Parks. John Grierson (of Daily Mirror fame) was appointed as Supervisor for the sub depot which remained open until late 1982 when the mills finally closed.

Not mentioned earlier, a small factory at Aylesford, a part of Reed Corrugated Cases which manufactured paper tubes and in fact was known as the Tube Factory, operated it's own small fleet of vehicles. Independent and very protective of it's own fleet, the transport operation became the responsibility of Reed Transport. Four, possibly five, Ford D series tractors with trailers together with one D800 rigid and their drivers were transferred into New Hythe Depot in 1976. Some of the vehicles' details are at Appendix 16.

During the mid 1970s, traffic flows throughout the network fluctuated almost from day to day. In 1975 the Company put it's toe in the water of continental operations. Earlier, mention has been made of the acquisition at Thatcham of the carton manufacturer, Cropper, by Reed way back in 1956. In the early 1960s, Reed had brought all it's cartonmaking activities under the name of Reed Cartons.

In 1964 Reed purchased another carton manufacturing company - Field, Sons & Company Limited with a factory in Bradford. A company of high reputation and quality product, the name of Field was retained by Reed and made responsible for the existing Reed Cartons operations. Thus the factory at Thatcham was once again renamed. Field was developing a mainland Europe market especially in Holland and was particularly interested in the Field name appearing on it's delivery vehicles. Reed Transport rebuilt a tandem axle flat platform trailer into a TIR specification tilt trailer in Field livery and deliveries commenced to Ammerzoden in Holland. There was also regular export traffic from Tovil & Bridge Mills to Duffel in Belgium. Aylesford Paper Mills was selling into northern France and another Aylesford Company, Key Terrain, had a large customer in Roubaix near Lille. Field gained other customers in Holland. Eventually, three TIR trailers had been added to the fleet. The other two, appropriately, carried the Reed International name.

The total operation was shared between Thatcham and Aylesford Depots. The original Thatcham team was made up of Doug Barrett, David Buxey, John Dixon, Colin Dumelow and Pat Oswald with 1974 MANs nos 758, 759, 760, 757 and 762. Later, a sixth driver, Ed Murray, joined the team with 1973 Scania no.728. So keen was Ed to become involved that he built his own

Above: TKO 303N, a MAN 16.232 tractor purchased for European work is pictured here coupled to tilt trailer no.1298 at Aylesford when new in September 1974.

Left: MAN 16.232 artic no.759 - TKO 978N, new in September 1974 and allocated to Dave Buxey was used on continental work. It is pictured here loaded with reels for Belgium.

Below: New in June 1978, Volvo F10 no.94 - XKL 539S, one of eight examples purchased in 1978 is seen coupled to TIR trailer 1299A outside Aylesford Head Office.

fold down bed into the day cabbed no.728. The Aylesford team comprised three drivers - Mick Cook and Len Andrews with Volvo F88s nos 74 and 75 and Cyril Long, with a Scania 110. All were given the necessary training particularly with regard to documentation and, at that time, Customs procedures. Back loading was precarious but a Reed Company in Holland, Sphinx Tiles at Maastricht, began to import into the UK. In need of a warehouse facility, Reed Transport created space in it's Depot at Thatcham which had a small storage area and provided an Office for Sphinx staff.

Full loads of palletised tiles from Maastricht straight back into Thatcham became the best backload source for this small operation. A Reed paper mill in Holland, at Eerbeek near Arnhem also provided the occasional return load back to a Reed Corrugated Cases factory. The remainder of the backloading needs were sourced from other operators and freight forwarders, rarely what would be described as prime traffic. Sea routes were either Dover to Calais or Zeebrugge or occasionally Felixstowe to Zeebrugge. The operation ceased in early 1979 but the Company had been able to demonstrate to it's customers that at least it had the capability to operate outside of the UK. A few stories from this operation have been included in Chapter Eighteen.

The direct running with Aylesford and Thatcham vehicles was only a small part of RTs involvement with freight forwarding in the true sense. Since the early 1970s, RT had increasingly provided a freight forwarding service for it's Group domestic customers despite sister company Pioneer Shipping also offering a similar service. In due time, RT absorbed all the export forwarding business which, at it's peak in the late 1970s/early 1980s, had grown to around 7000 loads per annum. This included all grades of paper and also wastepaper together with cartonboard, cartons and the occasional load of corrugated cases; in fact any product produced by Reed Companies. The Freight Forwarding Department was based in Head Office rather than a Depot and was an adjunct to the administration function which also handled all vehicle licensing and insurance processes. Ron Moore was the Traffic Manager responsible for all these activities during this period.

The year 1977/1978 recorded 1,739,000 tonnes handled - down by 12.5% against 1973/1974, a fleet of 202 vehicles excluding shunt and ancillary vehicles and 490 employees.

There were management changes effective on 1st March 1978. John Marsh had left the Company, Ken Lewis being appointed Southern Area Manager in his place. Ken Sackett took over as Aylesford Depot Manager. George Blackman had retired and Harry Chittenden took over as New Hythe Depot Manager. For the previous six months, Harry had been Equipment Supervisor in the South East to help counter the abuse and losses (and the resulting costs) of vehicle equipment - sheets, ropes, scotchboards and wedges. This included visiting the wastepaper collection and discharge points where items were frequently 'lost', left behind or damaged. Prior to that, Harry had been New Hythe's Depot Supervisor. Bill Dale retired at the end of 1978 and was succeeded by Ron Adkins as Managing Director as from 1st January 1979. Ron's appointment must have been a baptism of fire as the next episode of the Company's history is recounted.

Above: No.81 - TKO 564R, a Seddon Atkinson T38C290 tractor entered the Reed Transport fleet in June 1977. It was a precursor to eight T36C250 examples being purchased in the Autumn of that year; four each for Darwen and Aylesford depots.

The Seventies cannot be left behind without the mention of the 1978/1979 Winter of Discontent, in particular the Lorry Drivers' Strike as part of the industrial unrest of that winter and the effect it had on Reed Transport. It had been the policy of transport unions since 1976 to campaign for £65 for 40 hours on the top weight vehicles. This had been resisted by many employers and, coupled with the Government's pay policy of 5%, contributed to the haulage strike. The Company had however settled on £65 for 40 hours on 26th September 1977 for 18/21 ton vehicles. The hourly rate for overtime remained at £1.375 per hour (£55) but when the Stage l and Stage ll (from the Government pay freeze) payments of £10 per week were added, the total pay was indeed £65. When the crisis began to take a grip on the Country, Reed Transport was already in negotiations to actually improve on the £65. The effect of this was that when the strike began, RT drivers were allowed to work normally, although discouraged to cross picket lines. Most subcontractors were on strike, but some worked if they were paying the new rate.

The effectiveness of the strike was mixed in different parts of the Country. It's length varied in different areas. For instance, in parts of the south, the strike lasted three to four weeks. In the north west and Scotland, it lasted up to ten weeks. It all happened during a period of intense cold weather and snow. During this period, anyone who had previously argued against Reed owning an 'in-house' haulage company kept a low profile. Although very much restricted in capacity, RT kept Group production going in most factories, by providing raw materials when needed and moving the maximum finished product with the resources available. This was achieved over seven days periods as the rest legislation had been relaxed for weekends. The operations were run very much like military campaigns with deliveries made where there were no pickets throughout the days and nights.

Every trailer was loaded and communications were of a high order, enabling depots to deliver loads whenever they were able. As the strike progressed, particularly in the north, local RT managers were able to go to local Union Committees to plead for exemption papers to allow very small hauliers to operate. This helped the situation greatly as, for example in certain parts of Merseyside, pickets were out on arterial roads. Towards the end of the strike, the striking drivers were becoming demoralised and it was not unusual for RT managers to treat pickets to breakfast or 'teas all round' on the snowy picket line.

The Continental operation ended during the strike when the domestic needs were the priority and never recommenced. Ironically, the last runs carried out by Thatcham with Colin Dumelow and Ed Murray were empty out on a Friday to the mill at Eerbeek to collect desperately needed loads of starch for Group customers, starved as a consequence of the strike. Out of hours by Saturday night, they were relieved at Dover.

The period of the strike had showed the Company at it's best. Through sheer determination, guile and professionalism, it kept the machines of the parent Company working. Reed Transport had remained on

good terms with the unions throughout as well as with the striking drivers. Union permits were neither necessary nor accepted by the Company. This co-operation had been essential and had paid off because the goodwill and relationships continued after the strike had ended.

In late 1979, the Company returned to an involvement with company cars when it was asked to take over responsibility for the sourcing, administration and disposal of 1000 fleet cars on a 'fee per car per year' basis. John Marsh returned to the Company as Projects Manager after an absence of 21 months, the initial project being the management of this car fleet.

As at 31st December 1979, the trailer fleet comprised 154 single axles, 49 tandem axle single wheels and 332 tandem axles - a total of 535. The equivalent figures for vehicles are no longer available but a month later, as at 28th January 1980, the fleet comprised 205 vehicles - 15 rigids, 68 19/22ton gvw, 19 24/25ton gvw and 103 32ton gvw. There were also 20 shunt and 26 ancillary vehicles including small vans.

Below: No.81 - PKE 772R, a Scania LB81 tractor, first went on the road in August 1976 being allocated to Aylesford. It is seen the following year on the route of the A1 in north London having made its way up the Holloway Road and passing 'The Lion' before bearing right onto Archway Road with a load of mixed reels.

Chapter Eleven

Vehicle Costing and Programming

Somewhere within this History there needed to be described those two most important processes - vehicle costing and vehicle programming. The middle was as appropriate a place as any to include this aspect of Company procedure.

In the ideal haulage world, each vehicle would have had it's own profit and loss account. This was fine all the time a Company operated rigids from a single base. But Reed Transport, from the late fifties, was moving rapidly into full articulation, with loaded trailers continually being hauled by two or more different tractors until the completion of delivery and regularly by tractors belonging to more than one Depot. There had to be a practical workable method of vehicle costing which could be believed and accepted by the senior management and the operational staff. Each vehicle was allocated to a group. The group number was simple to understand and administer. Each Depot had a number:

Aylesford	1
Gravesend	2
Thatcham	3
Wigan	4
Darwen	5
New Hythe	6
London	7
Tilbury	8

Each type of vehicle or operation was also given a number:

Contract Hire	0
Van	1
4-wheel rigid	2
RCC tractor/trailer	3
(applicable to the early 16ton gvw fleets)	
Local hire	4
12 tonner (20/21ton gvw)	5
15 tonner (24/25ton gvw)	6
20 tonner (30/32ton gvw)	7
Night trunker	8
Tilbury/Ayles shuttle	9
(Aylesford Depot Scania 6x2s only)	

Thus, the Thatcham based 20 tonners were in group 37, the Gravesend 15 tonners in group 26 and so on. Fixed costs were easy to allocate per group. The allocation of overheads was more difficult. Should a 20 tonner because of it's greater earning and profit potential carry a greater proportion of a depot's overheads than a small rigid? Then there was a question of central (Head Office) overheads. This was done by depot on the basis of 50% numbers of employees and 50% income with an allocation against the subcontracting activity of a Depot. Variable costs were not so easy to allocate because there was a greater reliance on operational or maintenance staff correctly coding fuel and tyre issues and maintenance costs.

Most importantly, care was needed when allocating the weekly pay cost including expenses such as subsistence, overnight parking and tolls. Drivers were switched between vehicle groups perhaps midweek and administratively this needed a close dialogue between the operational and the administration staff. The depot results were published 12 times per year based on Reed accounting periods, i.e. 4-4-5 weeks. At least the results were not based on a calendar month which would have been a nightmare with mid week cutoffs.

The group results per depot could never have been 100% accurate but were probably close to 95%. Some groups included 10, 15, 20 or more vehicles so vehicle per day costs, income and profit/loss were based on group averages. Taking all aspects into account, it was a good system and lasted for many years. Even in the early days of computerisation, the group formula was still used.

Above: Thatcham Driver A.Whatley's payslip in August 1960. Take home pay - incl. allowances - £14.10s.2d for 56 hours work.

The Weekly Planning Traffic Sheet (WPTS) was to endure the test of time. No document had greater longevity. When Ron Adkins moved down from London Depot to Aylesford in 1956, he brought with him his own design of vehicle planning sheet. A facsimile is reproduced below. Measuring about 20in x 28in and used in conjunction with a larger base sheet, it became the standard document throughout the Company. Both sheets were printed on a thick paper and could stand the many alterations daily by the HB pencil and rubber! This was pre computerisation.

As will be seen from the facsimile, there were seven main vertical columns to run from Saturday to Friday each week, each new sheet being built up on each Friday morning for the Saturday, Sunday, Monday and beyond programming. As mentioned in Chapter Three, the term 'programming' was used rather than 'planning.'

The base sheet had the fleet numbers and registration numbers listed down the left hand side, occasionally changed when vehicles were changed. On the WPTS itself, there were 20 horizontal sections, each of three lines so up to 20 vehicles per sheet could be accommodated. At times this left insufficient room for all the manoeuvres or deliveries on a particular day but the traffic staff were sufficiently inventive to adapt.

Within each of the seven main columns, the left hand column took the driver's name and start time, the small middle column took a simple code denoting the customer or activity whilst the main column was used to describe the load, line by line if necessary for multi deliveries. For articulated vehicles, the trailer number was included within brackets to the right of the main column. Timed deliveries had the required delivery time added, using the right hand column if appropriate. Other notations were added, for example an 'N' if the load was to be nightloaded the night before.

Thus, a typical day's entry for Aylesford Depot might have been:

97	R.Young	A	20 x 58 Mirror Holborn (360)	8.30
389	6.0	Ex RTL	(362) Mirror Holborn	10.30
EKP		L	Waste Maybank, SE7 (A) (362)	

This was interpreted as follows:

"Driver Bob Young on fleet no 97 (Foden S20 tractor) starting at 6.00am delivered a load of 20 reels size 58in (width) from Aylesford Paper Mills to the Daily Mirror at Holborn EC1 at 8.30am on trailer no 360 (There was more than one Mirror printing house). His second job was to deliver trailer no 362

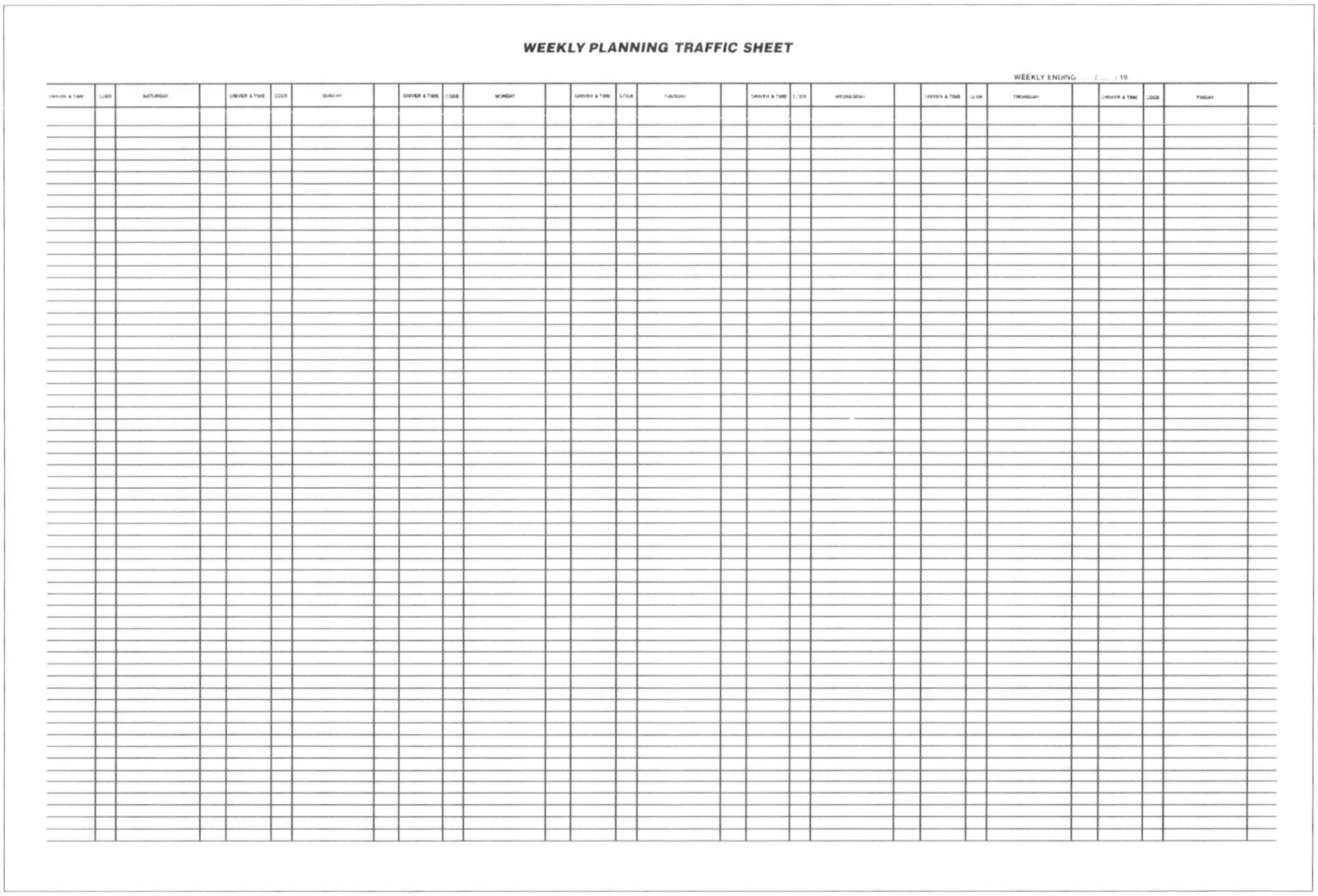

WEEKLY PLANNING TRAFFIC SHEET

WEEKLY ENDING ...... / ...... / 19

DRIVER & TIME	CODE	SATURDAY	DRIVER & TIME	CODE	SUNDAY	DRIVER & TIME	CODE	MONDAY	DRIVER & TIME	CODE	TUESDAY	DRIVER & TIME	CODE	WEDNESDAY	DRIVER & TIME	CODE	THURSDAY	DRIVER & TIME	CODE	FRIDAY	

out of London Depot also to Holborn for 10.30am, the trailer having been shunted overnight from Aylesford to London Depot. His third job was to load (backload) wastepaper from J.&J.Maybank at Charlton, London SE7 back to Aylesford Paper Mills".

This was a system which was easy to apply and easy to follow. Everyone could 'read' the sheet, depot staff, foremen, shunters and drivers alike.

One very important aspect of the WPTS was that it was the basis for invoicing. Thus using the previous example, the clerk would invoice Aylesford Paper Mills for the first load and Maybank for the third load, the codes 'A' and 'L' being the 'to be charged' prompts, striking a line through each entry as he or she did so. The second load would have been picked up elsewhere on the WPTS as an entry against the night driver, thus:

    A   20 x 58in   Mirror Holborn (362) to RTL
    Ex RTL   (364)   Empty to Aylesford

Other customer codes used, by no means the total, were as follows:

    CBM   Colthrop Board Mills
    IPM   Imperial Paper Mills
    SUN   Sun Paper Mills
    RCC   Reed Corrugated Cases
    L   Always related to a backload which had to
           be invoiced by the Depot moving the load.

Where a vehicle backloaded from another depot, the entry was indicated thus:

    Ex RTT (366) Gillingham

- the backload being provided by Thatcham Depot on trailer no 366 to Gillingham, Thatcham being responsible for the invoicing and the allocation of the income to the correct vehicle group and not the depot that moved the load. Clear?

A load from a Reed Corrugated Cases branch, charged on the basis of price per load with a premium for two or more deliveries, might look on the WPTS thus:

    RCC   15T   London EC2, E14,   E4   (453)

In the days before 40ft/12m trailers, a load on a 33ft trailer would be indicated as nominal 15T, a 30ft trailer as 12T, a 24ft trailer as 10T and a rigid as 7T or 8T. Thus the clerk responsible for invoicing would know to add a premium for the second and third deliveries. Two deliveries in E14 rather than one would have read:

    RCC 15T   London EC2, E14 2, E4   (453)

A return load of pallets would be shown thus:

    L   Pallets   Ex (customer's name) E4 (RCC) (453)

- as the return of pallets was a chargeable movement.

One benefit of the WPTS was that each sheet could be rolled up and stored for future reference, for years. These were important archives where later reference was needed for, say, vehicle accidents, personal accidents or goods-in-transit insurance purposes. It has to be said that as each successive week's sheet was added, by the time it was considered sensible by a Traffic Office to file away the older sheets from several months previously, the stack of sheets could have grown to a one inch depth and was heavy!

Inevitably, there developed many variations to this well proven system to cope with individual depot needs. This sheet stood the test of time and was used well into SCA days, often alongside the inter depot computer system which was to be introduced during the 1990s.

Left: Thatcham Traffic Office staff in October 1966. Seen left to right are: David Flitton, Bernard 'Scatty' Attwood (Vehicle Foreman), Mike Pearce (Traffic Manager) and Dick 'Spearo' Haines.

Above: Aylesford's Traffic Office in 1975 with Ken Sackett studying the fleet's operations on the Weekly Planning Traffic Sheets of that week. Alan Adrian is the Traffic Clerk alongside.

Below: A view of the Thatcham staff on the occasion of Beryl Aust's leaving presentation in 1960. Pictured (left to right) are: Reg Hart, Harry Rosier, George McBain, Roy Burgess, Tommy Cantwell, Sidney Ashman, Cecil Bosley, Jack Cannon, Dick Haines, Beryl Aust, Harry Alder, Peter Smith and Albert Barrett.

Above: MD Bill Dale (right) pictured with George Blackman on his retirement in 1978. Mrs Blackman with a bouquet. George was ex Imperial Paper Mills, the Gravesend Foreman, Tilbury Supervisor and finally New Hythe Depot. Bill Dale himself retired soon after being superceded by Ron Adkins.

Right:
The month of November 1966 saw the retirement of three long serving Thatcham staff members. (left to right) Bob Abbs, Dick 'Spearo' Haines and Joe Tanner.

Left below: Eric Fowler and Stuart Wise in the Traffic Office at Thatcham in February 1975.

Below: Thatcham traffic office staff Tom Howe (left) and David Flitton as photographed by Steve Wimbush on the 8th September 1965. An Atkinson tractor passes outside.

Chapter Twelve

Not only Paper and Packaging But.....

Certainly the main activities of the Company were serving the Paper Mills and Corrugated Cases factories. Non Group customers aside, Reed also owned companies in other industries. The Building Products Division was one such group. One of it's constituents based on the Aylesford site was Key Terrain Ltd, formerly Key Engineering Co Ltd. An early product manufactured at Aylesford was pitch fibre drainage pipe made from wastepaper and pitch. These pipes were distributed throughout the UK and abroad. Later, the Company produced a vast range of plastic pipes, guttering, facias and fittings for the building industry.

Until 1969, the distribution was mainly on flat platform vehicles with the pipes loaded both across and lengthways. This required special equipment in the form of timber bases with metal end caps and holes drilled to take upright stanchions. This equipment was made by the Aylesford Workshops - almost an endless production process. Sets were supplied to subcontractors for example, on a "return or you pay" basis. The administration involved was endless and many hundreds of sets of equipment were in circulation.

In 1969, it was agreed to provide a new fleet of seven four-wheel flat platform rigids in full Key Terrain livery on contract hire. The livery was red with white lettering. This was very much a multi delivery operation throughout the UK with empty return running. Most of the deliveries were to builders merchants. The vehicles were Ford D800s with 24ft bodies and numbered K1 to K7 and all entered service in 1969. They were a part of the Aylesford Depot fleet but in 1973 the Key Terrain business became the responsibility of the new New Hythe Depot. This customer was sold by Reed at a later date, becoming Caradon Terrain Ltd.

Two Ford DA2014 tractors were introduced in 1973, one numbered K9 which was in the red livery whilst K10 appeared in the rather drab Sherwood Green of Caradon Terrain. Both operated with 33ft 6in single axle flat platform trailers, modified with high 8ft headboards and with sockets along the raves in which to mount the pipe stanchions. At about the same time, the two Ford D800 boxvans provided for Reed Corrugated Cases - one was number 156 - were transferred to the contract, repainted in red livery and green livery respectively and renumbered K8 and K11. All the above vehicles are listed in Appendix 17.

In 1977, the original rigid fleet, K1 to K7, was renewed with six Leyland Clydesdale rigids and two Ford D1311 rigid boxvans, K12/14 to 20. K13 was

Right: Key Terrain was part of Reed Paper Group.
To show their products to potential customers this 37ft long BMC artic demonstration vehicle was used to tour the country.
It was adaptable for display in three different forms depending on space and length of stay.
The unit had originally been purchased to promote the packaging division of the Reed Paper Group - see image in Chapter Six, page 62. Further use would be made of the trailer when it was adapted to serve as office accomodation at 46 Berth, Tilbury.

Left: No.206 - RKK 170G was one of three Bedford KM rigids bought in 1969 for Aylesford Depot. It is seen here with a tidy load of pitch fibre pipes from Key Terrain. One of the Foden S21s, no.230 - 306 SKK is seen in the background.

Left below: Not all Key Terrain loads were tidy, however. This photograph shows a typical 'Camel's Hump' load fortunately not requiring full sheeting.

Right: K2, one of seven Ford D800s purchased in 1969 to provide a new fleet of seven 24ft flat platform rigids in full Key Terrain livery of red with white lettering on Contract Hire. New Hythe depot was given the responsibility for the vehicles.

Right below: A Leyland Clydesdale, numbered K8 - VKK 288X, one of a batch of six purchased in 1981 designed to work with 18 Ray Smith 26ft 6in framed demountable bodies - one of which stands alongside.

operations and renumbered K10. Later, in 1986, a further two curtainside bodies were added, K68/69. Additions to the vehicles were two Leyland Freighters in 1985, numbered K12 and K14, followed in 1988 by two more examples, K15 and K16. Reuse of fleet numbers was endemic. K11 was reused, this time for an ERF B Series tractor reallocated from Thatcham. Formerly no.763 it was painted in the Caradon green livery and used for yard shunting. The fleet from 1977 is listed in Appendix 19.

Coincidentally, almost all of Reed Transport's business had been derived from the 'Five Ps'. Paper, packaging and pipes have been well covered. Plastics were a part of Key Terrain / Caradon Terrain's business but later plastics were to become an even greater part of the activities from Darwen Depot. Add to that the fifth 'P' - paint also from Darwen and the pattern has been completed.

Reed International moved into plastic packaging with the purchase of Superfos at Oakham in 1983 and later followed by Smith's Containers at Raunds and Rushden. Distribution was handled by various independent hauliers from that area including Arthur Spriggs, P.C

avoided! All were painted in the Sherwood Green livery. The curtainsiders had grey curtains. Two additional vehicles, Boxer K21 and Clydesdale K22 - later renumbered K9 - joined in 1979 and 1980.

A review of loading practices at the factory resulted in the next renewal in 1981 being more Clydesdales but with Ray Smith 26ft 6in framed demountable bodies. K1 to K8 entered service with 18 bodies. There were 14 flat platform bodies K50 to K63 and four with curtainside bodies, K64 to K67. At the same time the earlier K18 was retained, converted by Ray Smith for dropbody

Howard and Emmens. A study was undertaken by Reed Transport but failed to make any inroads into that business in the East Midlands. Subsequently, the businesses were renamed Reed Plastic Containers.

In late 1991, RPC announced the opening of a new factory at Blackburn but it wasn't until 1992 as SCA Transport that the Company was successful in obtaining the business. The factory was just two miles from Darwen Depot. Thus began the involvement in the fourth 'P', albeit as the Company in it's new guise. Now for number five.

Already mentioned briefly in Chapters Six and Ten, the distribution of paint for Crown Paints in Darwen began in 1972 alongside Crown's own fleet. A young Traffic Clerk, Chris Halliwell, had joined the Company in October 1969 and was located within the Crown factory. But Chris already had experience of working inside Crown with his previous employer, BRS Blackburn. Under BRS, there was a direct telephone link between the Walpamur loading bay and the BRS Office. In those days, the loading was almost entirely 'handball' with a multiplicity of tin sizes usually in cardboard trays but also drums and cardboard carboys. There were other products including powders, putty, fillers, display materials and sundry decorative materials.

To load paint correctly was an art. It was a driver's

worst nightmare to have a spillage. RT established it's office within the 'picking' area with the clerk and a shunter. By now there was a move towards some palletisation. Crown's own fleet delivered to shops and small customers and developed their own heavy fleet to deliver to their Regional Distribution Centres (RDCs) at Bristol, Glasgow, Halesowen, Nottingham and Uxbridge, previously Perivale. All additional traffic was passed to RT. As with wallcoverings, the Seventies saw a growth in DIY generally and the DIY sheds in particular.

The traffic surplus to the Crown's 'own' fleet was covered by a combination of fixed trunks

(more in Chapter Nineteen), regular set piece Direct Delivery Services (DDS) and 'overs'- any excess demand in any direction. DDS runs included the south west - Bristol, Exeter, Plymouth, Taunton and Truro, the south - Basingstoke, Bournemouth, Portsmouth and Southampton, the south east - Ashford, Brighton, Canterbury, Maidstone and exports to Portslade, the east - Chelmsford, Colchester, Ipswich, Norwich and Wymondham, and Wales - Cardiff, Carmarthen, Chepstow, Newport and Swansea. Industrial paint in 45 gallon drums for the steelworks at Gorseinon and Shotton was almost daily. Progressively, 'handball'

gave way to total palletisation.

In 1985, the business increased with Crown's purchase of Berger and Cuprinol. In due course, the RDCs were rationalised down to three, at Bristol, Rugby and Uxbridge. Throughout the history and into the SCA days, the Company maintained an office within Crown and Depot staff could expect to receive next day orders up to 9.00pm and a 24hour callout was not unknown. The level of service was renowned for it's total commitment and reliability. So the so called 'Five Ps' probably accounted for at least 95% of the Company's business.

Above and left: The next fleet for Key Terrain were Leyland Freighters with Ray Smith demountable bodies. K14 - B998 XKN, new in 1985, shows off it's original livery. Key Terrain later became Caradon Terrain and so K14 took on a new livery.

Chapter Thirteen

The Importance of Waste Paper

For any haulage company operating primarily with rates schedules and on the basis of spot hire or payment by load rather than mileage or per week in a form of contracts, the maximisation of two-way loading was vital. Reed Transport was no exception. Baled wastepaper was to become it's principal backload throughout the network.

Fortunately for the Company, it's main paper mills customers were using less and less imported woodpulp and increasing tonnages of recycleable wastepaper. At Aylesford for example, pulp mainly arrived by barge from Rochester; wastepaper was to come in by road and from the four corners of England. For an example of the increased useage of wastepaper, newsprint machine no.13 at Aylesford had a capacity approaching 90,000 tons per year. When opened in 1957, it used 100% pulp. In 1968, 20% of it's raw material was wastepaper and in 1982 it was using 100% wastepaper. Reed was a pioneer in the process of de-inking - the extraction of printing ink from waste newspapers and magazines.

By an agreement completed in August 1964, Reed acquired a 50% interest in the wastepaper merchant J.& J. Maybank Ltd based in Charlton, London SE7 and also Portsmouth. This Company took over the responsibility of sourcing all grades of wastepaper for the various Reed Mills and also had many non Reed customers. It was vital that RT became a major supplier of transport for this raw material especially as the demand for this commodity was to dramatically increase throughout the Seventies and Eighties.

RT's involvement with Maybank increased progressively but it must be said that significant flows of baled wastepaper were sourced from areas where the Company had little operational coverage.

Maybank acquired or opened a network of branches throughout the UK and retained the freedom to use other hauliers where Reed Transport could not provide the required level of service. In addition to Charlton and Portsmouth, the branch network was progressively extended to Basingstoke, Bedford, Bury, Caldicot, Cambridge, Colchester, Gateshead, Glasgow, Lowestoft, Maidstone, Newhaven, Oxford, Poole and West Bromwich. An Associated Company was based in Leicester. Maybank also sourced wastepaper from many merchants and other wastepaper groups. This business presented a phenomenal opportunity for Reed Transport, albeit at very keen rates.

In addition to this, Reed Corrugated Cases factories produced baled wastepaper from the trimmings from cases manufacture. All factories required a stand trailer to be progressively loaded throughout the day and night. Changeovers had to be exactly timed; an early changeover would result in an underweight load whilst a delayed changeover could halt production processes in a factory where there was no room for stacking baled waste. The larger factories such as Aylesford, Hartlepool, Thatcham and Wigan produced one load a day whilst the smaller factories produced perhaps three loads per week. The usual destination was East Mill at Aylesford. This produced excellent opportunities for depot to depot night running. Other destinations included non Group Mills and occasionally the smaller east coast ports for export.

Wastepaper transport was not always straightforward. In times of shortage of supply, loads were vitally urgent often arriving at a mill dangerously low on stock. Conversely, at times when supply greatly exceeded mill demand, strict weekly quotas were applied to branches. A 200 tons quota for one week meant exactly just that.

OKN 664G, an AEC TG4R Mandator tractor went on the road in August 1968 being numbered no.70 and allocated to Aylesford depot, one of thirteen such examples purchased in that year. The unit is pictured here well-laden with waste paper - the lack of a flysheet and bulk of its load provide the clues to the cargo being carried.

Reed TRANSPORT

Transport provided to collect 190 tons was not acceptable. If a branch took a gamble and tried to exceed a quota, say with an extra load, then the mill would invariably reject the load and it would remain on wheels until the next Monday morning. If the haulier missed a delivery within the quota week then there was real trouble!

For a period of around eight months during 1978 and 1979 one of Wigan's Traffic Clerks, Stan Ellison, was based at Maybank's Bury branch in the dual role of Co-ordinator between the branch and RT and to study the total transport needs of the branch. Much later, during the late Eighties, an extensive project was undertaken resulting in the total responsibility for all baled tonneages from all branches

Above: TKO 979N, a MAN 16.232 20-ton artic new on 1st October 1974 is pictured here in this photo taken by Phil Moth heading home down the M4 near Reading when comparatively new sometime in 1975. Driver Ted Whatley is at the helm.

Left: Two Volvo F10s when new in April 1978 to Wigan Depot. Nos. 989 and 990 - XKL 537S and 538S respectively. They are parked at Maybank's branch at Bury having loaded baled wastepaper. XKL 538S had been placed in service without it's fleet number. Note the absence of the white band below the windscreens.

Below: No.84 - F589 KKK, an ERF E14 32TT 6x2 tractor joined the Reed Transport fleet in June 1989 being allocated to Aylesford depot. This picture, dating from 1990, reveals the unit outside the premises of Poole Wastepaper Company ready to head home. Brian Stephenson was it's driver.

being passed to RT. For a period, responsibility was taken over at the rate of one Branch each fortnight.

In 1990, the Company diversified into tipper trailers when three were purchased to operate a daily shuttle between Bury branch and non Group customer Shotton Paper Mill, delivering loose newspapers and magazines. The trailers were Wilcox bodied on Fromant chassis with independent donkey engines and therefore useable behind any tractor. The operation was the responsibility of Darwen Depot.

In summary, the wastepaper business developed into and remained a vitally important part of the Company's operation. It was more than merely 'back load' traffic. It was prime traffic demanding a high level of service and played the most significant role in reducing empty running and in creating profitable night shunting and trunking operations.

Chapter Fourteen

'Double Bottoms'

This chapter heading sounds too much like a condition applied to overweight transport people! In May 1976, 'Commercial Motor' invited Reed Transport to participate in an "in-service" trial of a double bottom combination. Not to be confused with today's terminology - roadtrain, the double bottom combination involved a tractor coupled to a 23ft single-axle semi trailer coupled to a second similar trailer by way of a single axle drawbar dolly unit. An articulated roadtrain would be a better description today. The trial was to serve two purposes:

a) "to assess the potential of the doubles for typical in-service use."

b) "to gather sufficient data so that the safety aspects of doubles operation can be fully evaluated."

Assistant Technical Editor of 'CM' at the time, Trevor Longcroft in a letter dated 26th May 1976 to Ron Adkins, General Manager, went on "I should like to obtain sufficient favourable data to encourage further tests, but at more realistic speeds."

Volvo supplied an F88 tractor, MHS 53P whilst Crane Fruehauf supplied the two trailers. Volvo also made available F86 tractors for use at either end. The overall length of the doubles outfit was 18 metres. The trial week was set to commence Monday 9th August 1976. The starting point was the premises of Odhams Press at Watford, a Reed International owned Company, the end of the run Reed Transport's Depot at Goose Green, Wigan. Both terminals were within two miles of the Motorway. The DoE had agreed to issue an order authorising the use of this special combination. It was to be limited to 30 mph on normal roads, 40 mph on motorway. The gvw was of course limited at 32 tons (Imperial) and with an unladen weight totalling 13.7 tonnes, a maximum payload of only 18.8 tonnes was possible. The operation was carried out under the control of Aylesford Depot with driver Peter Allen. Prior to the trial, Peter and his Depot Manager Ken Lewis, went to Fort Dunlop's skid pan to become acquainted with the outfit. Test drivers were the first to handle the vehicle.

A copy of the Order of the Secretary of State for the Environment dated 29th July 1976, still in the possession of Peter Allen, has been included in Appendix 20 and confirms the strict terms for the operation and the route to be adhered to. For the first run on 9th August, the northbound load comprised reels of paper for Warrington

on one trailer and Nelson on the other. The outfit had been assembled at Watford on the previous Saturday. Southbound was soap powder from Lever Bros for two SPD Depots. Two round trips were run during that week, Monday up and Tuesday back, Wednesday occupied tipping out in the south from Watford, reloading and reassembling, Thursday up and Friday back. The main conclusions from the trial were firstly from the safety view that a limit of 40mph would cause driver fatigue and boredom, whilst from the economics view a payload of under 19 tonnes and the impractical two separate 23ft platforms, were too restrictive if applied to Reed Transport's type of operation.

Above: The Volvo supplied F88 and the Crane Fruehauf trailers loaded at Odhams Press, ready for a run to Wigan.

The trial was fully documented in 'Commercial Motor' published on 24th September 1976 under the heading "I'll have a double" by Technical Editor Graham Montgomerie. Thirty three years on, copies of the 'CM' will be hard to find. Thus by kind permission of 'Commercial Motor', part of the article has been reproduced.

"Due to the extensive resurfacing (or should I say rebuilding?) being carried out on M6 at the moment, much of this section is down to two lanes. In this region the overhead signs indicate that trucks should keep in the nearside lane with both lanes being restricted to a maximum of 50 mph. The amount of bunching we caused and the resultant tail-back of commercial traffic had to be seen to be believed. After two or three minutes like this we had a police car alongside urging us to get a move-on which posed a rather tricky problem. I was driving at this point and in the document tray of the Volvo was the special authorisation from the DoE with it's proviso that we did not exceed 40 mph. And now I had a very irate constable alongside politely suggesting that I should put my foot down! Luckily we returned to three lanes almost immediately so the problem solved itself because I must admit that I wasn't sure which to adhere to - the DoE's ruling or the instructions of the police".

It was agreed to run a further trial about a month later, this time at 50 mph on the motorway. These runs were to concentrate on advertising and filming for the participants. Peter Allen recalls that on the second run

back, Graham Montgomerie was passenger and leading the trial. They agreed to put the outfit through it's paces and between Daventry and Northampton, Peter confessed with a grin, that a speed of 80 mph was sustained for a short while!

The various Constabularies on the route had been notified in advance, but this hadn't filtered down to the Motorway patrols, who had been continually stopping the vehicle through the two trial weeks and making due enquiries. On this occasion the Warwickshire patrol lost the speeding vehicle but their Northamptonshire colleagues spotted the outfit

southbound as they were patrolling in the opposite direction. They reached the next exit to return southbound in pursuit. By the time the patrol caught up with them they had slowed down but without a tachograph had no way of proving the rather excessive burst of speed. Peter described the outfit as "extremely stable".

At the Commercial Motor Show at Earls Court that autumn, film footage was continually being shown on the Volvo, Crane Fruehauf and Lockheed stands. A very short feature was included on the BBC's 'Tomorrow's World' programme. Several photographs have been included. At about the same time, a similar trial was carried out in France using a left-hand drive F88.

Today with 41 tonnes gross, 15.5 metres and 56 mph, the actions in the Seventies to find solutions to move bulk freight between motorway terminals for subsequent redistribution within urban areas are interesting to reflect upon. Would articulated roadtrains offer greater flexibility than the present rigid and drawbar combinations now in common use? Perhaps? The trial took place at the time of the Dyke Report. Would the ability to 'divide' an otherwise heavy load into two separate deliverable parts solve for instance the access problems caused by weak bridges? Whatever the Industry's views are today, Reed Transport played a small but important role in 1976 in the exploration of alternatives.

Left: This picture shows the dolly link to the leading trailer with driver Peter Allen who drove the combination on the trial.

Below: The F88 headed outfit with its southbound load of Lever Bros. soap powder eventually destined for two SPD depots.

Chapter Fifteen

The Eighties with Looming Uncertainty

At the start of the Eighties, RT had seven depots and two sub depots - Tilbury and Tovil. Ron Adkins continued as Managing Director. The Country was split operationally into two with Ken Lewis as Southern Area Manager and Chris Halliwell as his Northern counterpart. Depot Managers were Ken Sackett at Aylesford, Jack Saunders Gravesend, Gordon Pease Thatcham, Dennis Morgan Wigan, Colin Smith Darwen, Harry Chittenden New Hythe and Ian Beaumont London and Tilbury. Roy Burgess, originally from Thatcham, was appointed Financial Director as from 6th October 1981.

The one certain aspect in life is change and there was no exception to that rule to be spared for Reed Transport. By July 1980, the Tilbury fleet had reduced to two 20 tonners and one shunt unit on the Berth. Then this decade was to see the premises of the two main roots of the Company disappear. London Depot - 38 Great Suffolk Street, Southwark, SE1 - had reached the end of it's viable existence. The customer base had changed together with the paper product mix and therefore the mode of operation as the natural and progressive outcome no longer required a depot in central London. The landlord, British Railways, was demanding a significant increase to renew the lease. The only conclusion was to close the depot which took effect on 3rd April 1981. The remaining drivers and staff were made redundant and the vehicles returned to Aylesford for reallocation. Ian Beaumont remained in the Company as a relief Manager and on the sudden death of Jack Saunders in 1982, took over at Gravesend. The memories remained, however, of an impressive fleet at it's peak in the 1950s amid the railway arches and cobbles still resounding to the sounds of an earlier

London. The second 'disappearance' was to come a little later.

During 1981, after an extensive study of operating costs versus revenue generated, the decision was taken to cease night trunk operations between Aylesford and Wigan and Thatcham and Wigan. Several drivers were declared redundant and the eight Wigan Volvo F10s nos 987 to 992/996 and 997 were transferred to Aylesford. They were renumbered, see Appendix 19, note 7. This was to help counter the psychological emotions of the time, the taking out of Wigan of all heavies. Thereafter, Wigan became a corrugated cases only fleet with lightweight vehicles.

The 1980s saw more Mill closures. Tovil Mill was finally closed in late 1982 and thus the starting base for Albert Reed's dream of a wholly owned paper mill had gone forever. Today, modern housing developments stand on the sites of the former Tovil and Bridge Paper Mills. One part of the development does carry the name of Albert Reed Gardens and at the top of Tovil Hill there stands a pub called 'The Royal Paper Mill'.

The year 1983 was to see more cutbacks. On 24th May, it was announced that 56 out of 199 jobs at Aylesford were to go. On 30th June, a further announcement was made concerning Thatcham, where 21 out of 68 jobs were to be lost. In May 1985, Colthrop's South Mill was closed and seven 20 tonners were taken out of the Thatcham fleet with consequential redundancies. There was a further blow inflicted when, by 1984, the final machines at Imperial Paper Mills had been shut. All was not immediately lost, however. As space in the reel stockrooms became available in line with machine closures, so RT was able to attract the Reed Canada reels of newsprint direct from the

32-ton gross MAN 16:280 no.771 - SKN 730X loaded, fully sheeted and roped with 20 tons of reels. The red triangular 'Inflammable' sticker on the front bumper was required when used on the Darwen, Lancashire trunk due to the southbound load being paint from the Crown Paint Factory located in Darwen.

Left: A nice group standing at Greenhithe Depot with the garage in the background. ERF B Series from 1977, no.88 - VKP 140S and no.92 - WKN 273S both of which started life at Aylesford are pictured together with Scania LB81 no.218 - FKP 333V.

Below: The new Depot in Colthrop Lane that was constructed in 1984.

'Reed Voyager' across the Imperial quayside on the River Thames and into the vacated areas. Some early tonnages were put into outside warehouses including Noblett & Underwood at Northfleet, W.E. Hasleden in Strood and Marriots in Gravesend. In addition, the quayside facility was used for the unloading of the SEABEE system barges as described in Chapter Ten. Photographs have been included of this 'across the quay' operation, both of newsprint and linerboard.

The onward deliveries to the printing houses, particularly to the Daily Telegraph, was a lifeline for the Gravesend fleet during this difficult period. Two fork truck drivers, Alan Davis, mentioned later in this chapter, and one other had been recruited for this operation from January 1983. The Reed Canada operation started a few weeks later.

In 1985, Reed had sold the whole site for redevelopment and so Gravesend Depot was finally closed. Fortunately, a small workshops with offices remained at nearby Empire Paper Mills at Greenhithe, rented out for many years to a Reed Transport subcontractor, P.A.D. Transport. By now the Gravesend fleet had reduced to thirteen 20 tonners with three shunt units, one of which was based at Empire Paper Mills. The relocation to Greenhithe in September 1985 resulted in a further reduction to six 20 tonners and the one shunt unit at Empire.

There were during this period many depot Management changes. Aylesford's Manager Ken Sackett opted for redundancy and so Len Parsons took over that depot until his retirement in 1986. Colin Smith left the Company in March 1984. By now, the Darwen operation had shrunk with the Mill closures and, with Chris Halliwell based at Darwen, the post of Assistant Depot Manager was created, to be filled by Stan Ellison,

a traffic clerk from Wigan. Roland Simey was recruited to replace Len Parsons at Aylesford but left in 1988 to be replaced by another outside recruit, Phil Younger. Harry Chittenden was next to retire, in November 1987. Tim Munt was recruited to take over at New Hythe. Two appointments during this period were John Marsh to Business Development Manager in July 1985 and Graham Day from Buyer to Fleet Engineer in February 1986.

The parent Company needed to maximise the benefit from the disposal of surplus land at various locations. At Thatcham, Reed Transport's fleet had reduced considerably from it's original 88 vehicles acquired from Cropper & Colthrop. Most of the trailers dedicated to the Corrugated Cases factory were parked at that factory anyway. A surplus piece of land on the opposite side of Colthrop Lane was made available and a new depot and workshops was built with a tarmaced parking area with fuelling installation alongside. The new depot was opened on 10th September 1984. In 1985, the rambling old depot with it's rabbit warren of offices, workshop and warehouse was demolished and the land sold for hi-tech development. The TRTS legend in the form of buildings had disappeared but again the memories of the Company roots lived on.

Early 1986 saw the first 38 tonner enter the fleet at

Right: No.237 - SKR 493H, one of the three Scania LBS110 6x2s after being cut down to 4x2 pictured on shunting duties on Imperial Paper Mills' jetty loading Reed Canada newsprint from the hold of 'Reed Voyager'.

Below: An image from previous times, unloading pulp onto lighters at Rochester. They would be brought up the River Medway by tug to Aylesford Paper Mills' East Mill Wharf.

Left, below and left below: Evolution of dockside unloading procedures. When a ship is not at sea it is not earning, methods such as these have reduced berth time from days to hours. Kraft linerboard for the corrugated cases industry and unitised bales of pulp destined for paper mills being transferred from hold to quayside by suction using on-board cargo handling equipment.

Aylesford, an ex demonstrator ERF C Series no 66 - C703 ULE. It's driver was Peter Wallace. Also, in late 1986, the last 32 tonner was purchased for Gravesend, no 220 - D849 KKN. For details see Appendix 19 whilst Chapter Twenty covers the subject of vehicle specifications.

The Company was always an ardent member and supporter of the FTA and it's predecessor, the TRTA, rather than the RHA. During 1985, the Company was one of several which contributed to the FTA's 'fighting fund' against the London Boroughs Transport Scheme, which sought to control the entry of HGVs into central London outside of normal working hours. The opposition failed and the permit scheme was introduced in January 1986, creating initially an administrative nightmare and the need for all permit authorised vehicles to carry an LBTS plate.

Above: C703 ULE an ERF 38 tonner with Cummins turbocharged engine was new on 21st November 1985 to Aylesford Depot being the first 38 tonner to enter the fleet. It is seen here posed for the camera of Stuart Wise at Thatcham in June 1986. Note it's LBTS plate.

Left: Leyland Roadtrain no.772 - HEU 860X, seen here at Thatcham, was allocated to Gordon Fogarty. Regular delivery locations included Burts of Portishead, Bristol and also Vernon Packaging, Northampton where palleted loads of board from Colthrop Board Mill would be delivered.

Below: XKL 533S, an ERF B Series 250 tractor was orginally allocated to London depot when purchased in February 1978 but with the closure of the Great Suffolk Street premises in 1981 was reallocated to Thatcham and renumbered from 154 to 767. The unit was photographed by Phil Moth around that time.

Right: This Leyland, no.798 - C807 BKN, was new into service in September 1985 and allocated to Bernard Smith. The view at its home depot dates from 1990.

Below: E253 UKP a 12-ton Leyland Cruiser was new on 1st December 1987 and delivered in plain white livery for special deliveries from RCC coupled to a similarly painted trailer. Some customers, for commercial reasons, specified that deliveries to their premises had to be undertaken with vehicles that did not carry any markings. The tractor is pictured at the new Colthrop Lane depot in July 1990.

Above: Leyland Clydesdale rigids had been bought for the Reed fleet since 1977 but 1981 saw the type's artic tractor counterpart enter the fleet including four destined for Thatcham including no.787 - SKN 724X. It is pictured here in RCC livery alongside no.784 - GKP 590V a Ford D2418TR tractor acquired in the Spring of 1980.

Left: Another RCC liveried unit. No.134 - C313 GKR, was a Leyland Cruiser 16-17 tractor purchased in July 1986 along with twelve others in that year; four - including no.134 - allocated to New Hythe depot.

Probably the brightest part of the business during this difficult and emotional period was the development of APM Storage Services at Aylesford, culminating in warehousing capacity of about 450,000 sq ft. Of that, 130,000 sq ft was bonded particularly for the Canadian Daishowa newsprint. As machines at Aylesford had been closed and removed, the vacated buildings were refurbished particularly the floors and, together with the surplus paper stock rooms, became ideal buildings for warehousing activities. Paper was the speciality product and customers included many competitors of Reed and later SCA. Even soft drinks were welcomed into this new venture.

Sister Company Pioneer Shipping was handling a significant volume of imports through Felixstowe. In May 1987, RT opened an office in Trelawny House, at the port to work in conjunction with Pioneer's local agent, Grange Shipping. Frank Grossmith from Gravesend Depot was appointed to the role and relocated. The office remained open until the end of 1990. No vehicles were based at Felixstowe.

A significant milestone was reached in the late Eighties which was to have a far reaching effect on Reed Transport and other Reed Companies, most of whom were it's customers. Reed International decided to divest itself of all it's manufacturing interests to concentrate on it's more lucrative publishing businesses world wide. A management buyout was put together headed by the Canadian born Reed Director, Peter Williams. The new company, Reedpack Limited, was formed on 16th July 1988 and included those Mills remaining in the UK and Holland, the Corrugated Cases factories - and Reed Transport. The Company had survived in name and with all it's former Reed International customers intact. Reedpack was to survive for just two years.

One customer which had not been included in the Reedpack purchases was the Reed Canada newsprint mill. The Japanese paper group Daishowa purchased this company from Reed International but it was to remain a customer of Reed Transport and into SCA ownership. With Imperial Paper Mills closed and demolished so the use of the Thamesside jetty and warehousing facilities for the Canadian newsprint imports was gone. Reed Transport was able to persuade Daishowa to ship into Sheerness Dock and use the APM Storage Services facilities at Aylesford instead. At the peak of this operation and with a strong market for the Daishowa newsprint, when the 'Reed Voyager', now renamed the 'Daishowa Voyager', docked at Sheerness, within two to three days 300 to 400 loads had been shuttled into Aylesford for storage and later onward delivery to the printing houses. This became a tightly run logistical operation with Southern Area Manager Ken Lewis and Storage Services Manager Fred Sheriff playing the key roles together.

There remained a close and friendly relationship with the ex Reed, now Daishowa staff in Canada built upon a superb service at every stage of the operation. This proved invaluable when, under SCA ownership, the main storage facilities were lost and Ken was able to persuade Daishowa to ship into 44 Berth Tilbury, the SCA terminal and thus the Company as SCA Transport retained this important customer and it's business. By this time, Daishowa considered SCA to be a major newsprint competitor and was very wary about a close relationship with anything connected with SCA. Service excellence triumphed in the end.

As to Pioneer Shipping, this had progressively reduced in size and operation. In September 1989, it's Manager Tony Gee who had succeeded Harry Whetcombe, retired. The remaining two staff moved into the Head Office at Aylesford, soon after to reduce to one. The name eventually disappeared under SCA ownership.

It had been Reedpack's dream to build a new hightech newsprint machine at Aylesford, a project study started by Reed International's Reed Paper & Board Division. The capital needed was more than Reedpack could realise and was one of the reasons for SCA's interest in the Company. Reed had it's many years of experience of the technology of deinking and recycling of newspapers and magazines as a main attraction. Whoever was to finally build the new machine and all the infrastructure

Left: The high reach clamps of the Hyster trucks were an essential asset in maximising the storage capacity at APM Storage Services.

Right: E141 AKN, an ERF E14 six-wheel 38-tonne gvw tractor unit is pictured at Thatcham in 1991 with Inka Kirby, the depot's first lady driver, at the helm.

Below: Another view of no.779 - E141 AKN, later repainted in the blue livery and name of the subsidiary shipping company, Pioneer. Note the Colthrop Board Mills liveried curtainsider.

Right below: No.86 - G865 SKE, an Aylesford based ERF 38 tonner coupled to a Tautliner trailer, both finished in a new experimental livery as described later in Chapter 20. The vehicle was new in January 1990 and was photographed by Derek Appleby at Thatcham Depot in the May of that year.

Office and Traffic Office on the top floor with a clear view out over the vehicle compound. Drivers' facilities were on the lower floor. The move to the new depot was in 1991. New Hythe Depot was able to remain in it's same location but with an altered entrance and the new access road was built. In a land swap arrangement, the ex Reed Company, by now Caradon Terrain, took over the old depot building and the remaining parking area.

The next and final milestone in the Company's history came on 20th July 1990 when SCA purchased Reedpack. For the first few months, very little was heard of SCA within Reed Transport, hardly surprising as it was the smallest company and not exactly involved in the core business of papermaking and packaging!

needed, would have a problem of access and Reed Transport's Aylesford Depot stood in the middle of the only practical route to the new Mill site. The Depot was to move for a third time on the Aylesford site, back to East Mill and to a rather strange looking two storey building on stilts overlooking the by now redundant pulp yard of East Mill, Aylesford Paper Mills.

The crane gantry structure had been demolished long ago and the site had the benefit of concreted hard standing, ideal as a vehicle and trailer compound. This was security fenced and a fuel installation was located within the perimeter. The building had been empty for a long time and had been used as a laboratory after it's abandonment as the Mill's Yard Department Office. It was refurbished with the Manager's

There was one early move towards SCA with a series of meetings with SCA Transforest Terminal at 44 Berth, Tilbury, mentioned briefly earlier. By now, some of the large London printing houses were building new premises and equipping themselves to unload vehicles by automated systems. SCA from it's mills in Sweden was a major supplier with newsprint shipped through 44 Berth. Agreement was reached to supply a tractor unit with three curtainside trailers in full SCA Graphic Papers livery for this operation. As described later in Chapter Twenty, the Foden tractor was the only 4x2 38 tonner ever purchased, necessary to enable an extra reel to be carried with the lower unladen weight countering the additional weight of the PCL Rolaload system trailers. The vehicle was on the Greenhithe Depot strength but based at Tilbury with driver Alan Davis, mentioned earlier.

The first few months of SCA ownership was a worrying period of uncertainty for the Company. Reed Transport was placed within the Packaging Group of SCA which included the Mills and Corrugated Cases factories. It became known to the Senior Management but kept a secret within the Company that SCA was seeking a buyer for the Company. Three companies are believed to have been approached and certainly one took sufficient interest for a Director to pay a visit to the Head Office at Aylesford, perhaps out of curiosity.

This process took place during the Spring of 1991 and afterwards seemed a less than enthusiastic exercise. In fairness, SCA's Packaging Business Group had greater problems with it's hands with the sell off of parts of it's acquisition it didn't want and the integration of the rest into it's own structures. Finally, SCA Packaging's President Colin Williams, based in Brussels, telephoned Ron Adkins to welcome formally Reed Transport into SCA. Reed Transport changed it's name to SCA Transport on 15th August 1991 and became a wholly owned subsidiary of a giant Swedish owned company. The statistics from that date are no longer available but as SCA Transport at the end of February 1992, six months after the change, the Company had 240 employees and 121 vehicles.

Under Reed ownership, the Financial Year ran from April to March whilst SCA traded on a calendar year. Thus, under SCA ownership from July 1990, although still trading as Reed Transport, the Company produced it's Directors' Report and Accounts for the nine months period from April to December 1990. The turnover was reported as £10.75 million with a profit before taxation of £573,000. For the full financial year 1991, the turnover was £13.172 million with a profit before taxation of £652,000, a far cry from the Company's turnover in 1947 of £43,000.

Despite the earlier cutbacks, the Company passed into SCA ownership lean and profitable, ready to face the many new challenges that Swedish ownership would present.

Left: Foden S104 no.225 - H959 AKL was the only 4x2 38 tonne gvw tractor. It was purchased for operations out of SCA's 44 Berth, Tilbury Terminal and was the only vehicle to be painted in SCA livery prior to Reed Transport being confirmed as a welcome part of SCA rather than being sold. The three trailers it operated with were PCL Rolaload trailers for automated unloading of end-on loaded newsprint reels.

Chapter Sixteen

Reed Transport People

Good people are a company's greatest asset. Road transport seems to be one of those industries which engenders loyalty and enthusiasm from it's employees especially when the going gets rough, at a time when other industries suffer low morale and despondency. True transport people with diesel in their blood revel in the daily challenge. Reed Transport was fortunate in having a wealth of such people.

In 1959 the Company signed it's first National Agreement with the T.&G.W.U. which was hereafter recognised as the sole negotiating body for weekly paid employees. Until 1970, the weekly wage levels were in two scales - London Area for Aylesford, London and Gravesend and Outside London Area for Thatcham, Wigan and Darwen. An increase was payable to all hourly employees after two years service.

Effective from 29th June 1970, the two scales were negotiated out and the differential of about 1.8% was gone. Also on that date, the increase for new employees came into effect after one year. The weekly wage was based on a 50 hours guaranteed week in the form of 5x10 hour days, overtime being paid after eight hours. All drivers and technicians were supplied with overalls.

The next landmark for drivers' pay came in 1975 when the 10 hour day was reduced to nine and a half hours, 47½ hours Monday to Friday, on which the upstanding weekly wage was based. There was a strong belief that drivers' hours were too long and the Company took the initiative for the reduction.

The advent of the HGV Licence brought the need for a driver training programme. An Aylesford Depot Supervisor, Len Parsons, became the first person in Kent to take and pass an HGV Class 1 Driving Test to be quickly followed by a second, Dennis Morgan, Dennis being the first driver in Kent. After Motec Training, both did a spell of driver instruction and many young trainee drivers, initially employed as Yardhands, owed their achievement of HGV Licences to these two colleagues. Eventually all of the larger depots had their own qualified driving instructors.

Dennis Morgan has recalled an amusing episode during driver training. Dennis and another Aylesford driver, Alec Sancto, were being instructed by Len Parsons. He had placed two cones in a position where, to pass between, there was about one and a half inches clearance either side. Dennis and Alec were each challenged to drive between without touching the cones. This they both achieved. For a bit of fun, they then challenged Len to do the same. As Len drove away to position his vehicle for the run, Dennis and Alec moved the cones in slightly. The inevitable happened.

Len Parsons subsequently became Depot Manager at Gravesend and later Personnel Manager for the Company. Dennis Morgan took over from George Blackman the running of the office at Tilbury in 1973 followed by his appointment as Wigan Depot Manager

Above: Driver training at Aylesford. New recruits were known as Yard Hands. Foreman Ron Ayers is instructing the new intake in the auto coupling procedures whilst long serving driver Sid Geering in the cab looks on. Sid was one of the drivers who transferred with the Tovil & Bridge fleet in 1959, his latter years at Aylesford spent as a day shunter preloading trailers.
The recruits are Charlie Hedge looking closely at the coupling, Malcolm Thompson closest to the camera. Their colleague's name is not recalled.

from April 1974. Wherever possible, promotions were made from within with staff relocated at company expense when necessary. At this point it must be recorded that at the end of the Seventies, five of the seven Depot Managers had risen through the Company from being drivers, a sixth had been a foreman, previously an engineer.

Driving training has already been mentioned but other training was vital, particularly relating to the handling of reels of paper. Today, most reels are carried 'on end' in curtainsiders with unloading by clamp truck. Until the

Left: Ron Ayers instructing the three Yardhands in sheeting and roping, particularly the cross roping at the front of a load of three high reels of paper

Right: No.189 - RKR 915 was one of nineteen six and eight wheeled AEC Mammoth Majors taken over from Imperial Paper Mills in 1961. It is seen here competing in a Maidstone round of the National LDoY competition. An interesting facet in it's history is that it was originally built as a six wheeler being returned to AEC at a later date for modification and upgrading. Behind, one of Express Dairies AEC MkV eightwheel tankers awaits its turn for the test.
Photo: A Hustwitt (c) NA3T

early Nineties, reels were usually carried on flat platform trailers 'on the roll' with scotchboards tied back and front and wedges for each reel in between. Where reels were loaded 'two high', invariably the driver had to 'break down' the upper tier, a potentially dangerous process for the inexperienced, often with reels weighing in excess of one ton. Reels were then rolled to the rear and onto a bank, such was the usual practice in earlier times.

Another option particularly with newsprint reels perhaps weighing 15 cwt was to load 'three high' with the top tier in rope slings. Drivers needed to ensure that slings were in the right position and when the overhead crane came into action were standing well clear once the sling was in the hook.

New drivers were never allowed to deliver reels until they had been properly inducted by an instructor or long serving driver. There was also the added skill needed to sheet and rope flat platform trailers often with 'camel's hump' loads. There was a further complication with the use of over-ropes. These were ropes attached to the top of the headboards of both rigids and trailers and then, on a 'two high' load of the larger diameter reels, pulled up and over the front reel of the upper tier, down onto the bottom row so that the next and subsequent reels on the upper tier sandwiched the ropes which were then attached to two tie bars on the rear of the body. The theory was that in the event of sudden and violent braking of the vehicle, the risk of the top reel or reels being catapulted forward off the load and onto the cab was drastically reduced. Much later this practice was discontinued as customers began to complain about the indentations made into the reels by the sandwiched ropes.

As trailers increased in length, so the amount of tarpaulin increased. The standard sheets on a 40ft trailer were two of size 23ft x 29ft, each with one flap and then a flysheet. The procedure was to rope over the mainsheets and then top with the flysheet - no easy feat on a windy day. The theory was that the flysheet would flap slightly in transit and rainwater would be shaken off. Just like pitching a tent. Human nature being what it is, the procedure generally was ignored and the main roping was over the flysheet after placement thereby defeating the whole object of a flapping flysheet to help keep off the rain. Many photographs illustrate this malpractice.

Reed Transport was an enthusiastic supporter of the Lorry Driver Of the Year Competition. For a period it ran it's own 'in-house' LDoY Competitions at Aylesford. Photographs are included of some of these events.

In June 1963, John Baggaley, a reporter from 'Motor Transport', attended one such event and an article "How to run a driver contest" appeared in it's 21st June 1963 edition. There were 46 entrants with drivers from all five depots as well as from other Reed companies. Gravesend Depot Manager Len Woods was the compere. The event was held over a Saturday and Sunday and included other activities such as football matches and fun items for children. There were four classes of vehicles:

Light rigids
    Class winner Stan Ashcroft - Wigan Depot
Medium articulated vehicles
    Class winner Tony Gliddon - Thatcham Depot
Heavy articulated vehicles
    Class winner Tommy Tanner - Thatcham Depot
Heavy rigids
    Class winner David Hoose - Wigan Depot

Below: A LDoY competitor, the post obscures the fleet no.174. EKL 312C was an Austin FJK160 new in 1965, the driver of which was Gilbert Wood, later to become Safety & Training Manager for the Company. The venue was Lockmeadow, Maidstone with the old Market buildings in the background, now long demolished to make way for a new market hall with adjoining cinema and dining facilities. Photo: A Hustwitt (c) NA3T

Left below: Another competitor was this Austin 5K/FED3 no.27 XKT 479, one of the fleet taken over from London Paper Mills in 1961. Lockmeadow, Maidstone was alongside the River Medway. The historic building on the opposite bank as the background is the Archbishop's Palace dating back to 14th century, a former private residence for Archbishops of Canterbury.
Photo: A Hustwitt (c) NA3T

Right: The Company ran it's own Lorry Driver of the Year competitions, this one at Aylesford Depot with Foden no.17 - XKL 320 being put through it's paces. By now, this much photographed Foden has had it's side panelling removed. The brick building in the background to the left is the 2-bay vehicle wash with the Depot's diesel tank to the right. Note the FV1600 Humber radio communications vehicle provided by the Army for the public address system.

Above: 504 SKK with Tony Gliddon at the wheel photographed on Saturday 13th October 1962 negotiating test no.4 at the Thatcham Depot Driving Competition. The closely watching Ron Tanner was acting in the capacity of a Marshall. No.734 along with it's stablemate no.741 were eventually cut down to 4x2 tractors.

Right above: Twenty eight year old Tony Gliddon won three of the four classes in the Reed Transport Thatcham's driving competition on Saturday 13th October 1962. The competition was held in accordance with the regulations of the National Driving Competition and there were 65 entrants.

Below: The occasion is a combined RoSPA awards / Wigan LDoY competition in January 1970. Driver Joe Boulton holds the cup aloft whilst Depot Manager Tommy Atkins stands to the left. The cup holder to the rear is Les Gaskell, the daytime Depot Foreman. Others pictured include Bill Bailey, Stan Ellison, Night Foreman Jimmy Darbishire and Depot Engineer Jimmy Myler.

The overall winner as Reed Transport's Lorry Driver of the Year was Tom Tanner with Stan Ashcroft as runner up and Tony Gliddon in third place. Certainly, an earlier event had taken place in 1961 with Alf Mackrill of Thatcham Depot the overall winner and presumably there was an event in 1962 also. In addition to the Aylesford event, Thatcham and Wigan Depots also held their own local competitions.

The National Lorry Driver of the Year Competition had one of it's regional events staged, conveniently, in Maidstone and the Company was always well represented. Several photographs have been included. One Aylesford driver, Len Parsons, won the TRTA Cup in the National Final in 1961.

The Company was not only an enthusiastic supporter of the LDoY Competitions but also at Aylesford co-hosted an annual 'Be a Better Driver' Rally for car owning Reed employees. The other co-hosts were Cobdown Car Club, a club open to employee membership and the Reed Group Safety Department. The second such rally held in 1960 included questions on the Highway Code, a 30 mile road section, width assessment, parking and three-point turns. It was reported that 60 employees competed in this particular Rally.

Every encouragement was given to staff to improve their personal and professional skills. The Company participated in many Group run training courses and seminars appropriate for all levels of staff - Senior Management, Depot Management, Supervisors and so on. Safety training always played a significant part in the training programmes.

All employees, weekly and monthly paid, enjoyed the

benefits of working for a large manufacturing group - generous holidays with pay, a very good pension scheme, initially non-contributory and later contributory, and personal accident cover. These benefits were far in advance of the norm within the general haulage industry particularly during the early days of Reed Transport. Drivers interviewed for a new job were astonished to learn that a pension scheme came with the job. Long service was commonplace, previous service accrued with Perkins & Glover and Cropper & Colthrop for example being counted. Thirty years plus service was quite a regular occurrence and forty years not uncommon. Long service with the experiences and skills thus gained was one of the Company's strengths. There were close family relationships - fathers and sons, brothers, uncles and nephews and at least one grandfather and grandson, although not at the same time.

There is no doubt that the combined cost of the upstanding weekly wage, the Company contribution to the Pension Scheme and Personal Accident Cover, even the supply of overalls and safety footwear, when related to operating cost, set the Company at a disadvantage when competing in the general haulage market against hauliers with lower 'people' costs, probably by about 15%. Similarly, Group customers who continually sought out the most competitive prices for their transport, made no allowance for this corporate cost when rates reviews were up for negotiation.

Contrary to the view within some quarters of the haulage industry that Reed Transport had it's main business handed down on a plate, the Company had a continual struggle to retain and increase it's Group business in terms of competitive prices whilst producing a financially healthy balance sheet year on year with a return on the capital invested acceptable to the parent Company. In no way is this intended to suggest that Reed Transport's senior management were reluctant to submit to the paying of a relatively generous package to it's employees but it illustrates the pressure within the Company at all times to be super efficient with all of it's operations in order to fund those costs. The financial results thus achieved were a tribute to it's people.

Above: Chapter 20, page 144 tells of Wigan driver Bill Parr winning the Volvo national fuel consumption economy test. Shortly afterwards, Sir Alex Jarrett, Chairman of Reed International at the time, was paying a visit to the Reed Corrugated Cases factory at Wigan and had been made aware of Bill becoming Volvo's national winner. The photo taken on 21st August 1978 at Wigan features Sir Alex at the wheel of the Volvo, Bill in the middle and with Lady Jarrett in the passenger seat looking on.

Right: One of the most familiar backgrounds for any photograph, London's Tower Bridge. This is probably the last picture taken of London Depot drivers at a time when it's fleet was down to about four heavies. The Depot finally closed on 3rd April 1981. This would have been a Reed International safety related presentation as Safety & Training Manager Gilbert Wood is holding the plaque. Left to right are Manager Ian Beaumont, 'Lofty' Grist, 'Taffy' Harris, Dick Gregory and Ted Groom. The Scania is probably no.221 - SKK 660M.

Left above: A group of Wigan drivers on a Saturday in about 1973 against a background of Scania 110s and Ford D600s. Depot Manager Bill Bailey handing a notice to Drivers' Representative Bill Parr concerning the future of heavies at Wigan. Northern Area Manager Len Woods stands behind Bill Bailey.

Left: Heroism recognised in 1973. Darwen Depot drivers on the occasion of the presentation of a watch to night trunk driver Jimmy Holmes. Jimmy had not long started his run to the Strensham changeover when, near Leyland, he witnessed a terrible accident when a car hit a wall and burst into flames. Jimmy dialled 999 and rescued a young girl from the car. Her boyfriend died. Jimmy also received a Certificate for Heroism from the local Mayor. The venue is the Crown Club in Darwen. Northern Area Manager Len Woods is behind Jimmy slightly to the left with Safety & Training Manager Gilbert Wood, folded arms, is pictured further left.

Left: A group of Gravesend drivers at a Safe Driving Awards presentation around 1970. The venue was the Terminus pub in Gravesend, now long since gone. Back row left to right: Len Strickland, Keith Hogwood, Dave Osborne, Stuart Hogwood, Len Parsons (Depot Manager), Derek Shaw, Mike Lawrie-Johns and Johnnie Green. Front row left to right: Sid Whittaker, John Hewitt, Ken Cheshire, Tony Huntley, Len Lyons and Ernie Lewis. Sid Whittaker contributed two stories for chapter 17.

Below: Aylesford Depot drivers at a RoSPA Safe Driving Awards presentation. The venue is the Cobdown Sports Pavilion at Aylesford. The author is pictured extreme right, arms folded. MD Bill Dale is pictured in front of the flag post with Ron Adkins to his right.

Above: A Thatcham Depot summer trip to Southsea in the early 1960s, courtesy of a Reliance Motor Services of Newbury's Burlingham Seagull bodied AEC.

Below: Thatcham Depot football team circa 1967 Back row - left to right: Name not recalled, Bill Hawkins, John Ives, Colin Dumelow, Ed Murray, Peter Guilford. Front row - left to right: Pat Oswald, Sam Scutter, Tommy Tanner, name not recalled, Maurice Singleton.

Left: This photograph was taken in August 1958 outside Tovil Working Mens' Club. All were employees of Tovil & Bridge Mills and include many drivers and fitters who would later transfer to Reed Transport at different times. Names are as follows: Back row - left to right: Bill Wright, Maurice Patey, Lloyd Sunnucks, Derek Smith*, Ken Parks, Fred Stafford, Dougie Gilks*, Archie Mungeam*, Cyril Cogger, Reg Wooding, Len Trowell, Keith Patey, Doug Arnold* Middle row - left to right: Robert Fitzsimmonds*, Gordon Cooper*, Bill Whyman, Jack South, Dick Whittington*, George Ransome, Dan Marsden MD, Fred King, Bonnie Francis*, Bill Lomas, Harry Chittenden*, Ken Wratten*, Sid Geering* Norman Edwards *. Front row - left to right: Joe Fischer, Charlie Brooks*, Jack Smith, Frank Brown*, Charlie Weeks*, Les Chambers, David Hughes*, Charlie King*, Ernie Stannett*. Those marked with* joined RT in late 1959, 18 in total. The 19th, Ron Packham was on holiday and missed the photo call. All are listed in chapter 4, page 37. Harry Chittenden and Ken Wratten have contributed material to the book.

Above: Taken in Reed Transport's Board Room and MDs Office on the occasion of Foreman Ron Ayers' retirement. This photograph is significant as it includes many Aylesford Depot employees who have a mention within this History. Left to right are Harry Chittenden, Ken Sackett, Ernie Brooks, Bert Norley, Ron Ayers, Peter Allen, Doug Arnold, Alan Stephens, George Lewis, George Martin, Len Parsons, Johnny Bull and Ted Brooker.

Above: Thatcham's Harry Gibbs pictured in 1967 refuelling no.183 - HKJ 230D, an Atkinson FC fitted with Cummins 180 engine. Harry was a steamer driver with TRTS, then through BRS and Cropper & Colthrop to Reed Transport. Harry became the Depot fuel pump attendant.

Right: Bill Cook is seen in this Steve Wimbush picture preparing his artic outfit powered by ERF LV tractor no.30 - KKK 340E for his last trip on the night trunk from Thatcham to Aylesford on 27th August 1969. Another long serving employee, he retired the following day.

Above: Harry Alder retired in 1969 after 42 years service. He is seen being presented with his retirement gift by Alan Glover, Managing Director of Reed Transport Ltd. Harry joined TRTS in 1927 as a steamer driver, then through BRS and Cropper & Colthrop to Reed Transport. He became Foreman and later a member of the Administrative staff.

Far left: Ron Adkins joined P&G in 1949, taking up the Aylesford Depot Manager post in 1956. By October 1967 he was responsible for Aylesford and Gravesend. By the summer of 1968 he was General Manager and appointed MD on 1st January 1979 when Bill Dale retired. This picture dates from that time. Ron himself retired on 30th September 1991 as RT settled down as SCA Transport.

Left: Roy Burgess took over as Financial Director in October 1981 having moved from Thatcham to take up the post. He is pictured at the time of his retirement in September 1991. He was succeeded in the role by Steve Smith. Roy originally joined Containers Ltd, Thatcham in 1949 later transferring to Cropper & Colthrop Transport.

Chapter Seventeen

A Funny Thing Happened on the Way to..........

Stories abound from within the Company of mishaps or events, both humorous and serious. Here are a few for your enjoyment as retold by those employees involved:

Tony Gliddon was a Thatcham driver, later to come into the Traffic Office as a Traffic Clerk. This story from 1968 relates to a job from the Atomic Energy Research Establishment at Harwell, not far from Thatcham, as told by Tony.

"One Friday we took three 20 ton trailers out to Harwell to be loaded over the weekend by AERE staff to go to Drigg on the following Monday morning. The load was to be a bed load of 45 gallon drums stood on end containing low level radioactive waste and weighing just under 20 tons. On the Monday morning Jimmy Jackson, John Dumelow and myself took three ERF tractor units powered by Cummins 180 engines to Harwell, arriving there nice and early for the long haul to Drigg. No motorway for this journey in the Sixties and very few bypasses for towns and villages either.

Then it all went wrong. Some bright spark, a member of the AERE staff, suddenly realised the drums had not been checked for leaks prior to being loaded. Therefore he was not going to release them. Needless to say a huge row broke out between various members of AERE staff; nothing we could do but sit and wait whilst the storm raged on. We had no say in the matter.

After a while it was decided to offload the outer rows of drums on all three trailers so that the two inner rows could be lifted by forktruck, checked for leaks, then the other drums could be checked and reloaded. By the time they had completed this operation it was late morning. Finally we were given the OK to proceed to Drigg. We quickly threw a flysheet over each load, roped down and prepared to leave.

At this point Jimmy and John went into discussion about how far we were going to get with the legal amount of driving time we had left for that working day. After a short while it was decided Sandbach in Cheshire just off the A50 was about as far as we were going to get so Jimmy made his way to the phone box and booked three beds for the night at a pub he knew in Sandbach, a regular stop especially for drivers of

ERF and Foden vehicles as both factories which manufactured these makes of vehicle were both close by.

On arrival at Sandbach we parked the vehicles on the town centre car park along with other lorries that were there for the night, locked up and made for the pub. Everything was fine now except that we were half a day adrift on journey time. The publican showed us to our rooms, then we washed and cleaned up and went down for our evening meal.

Around eight o'clock two local police officers came into the pub. The biggest one of the two (and he was big) with three stripes on his arm bellowed 'are the three Reed Transport drivers in here'.

'Er yes' we replied wondering what the hell the problem was. Perhaps we should have left our side lights on or something.

'Get your keys and go back to your vehicles now', he snapped. We got our keys and went back to the lorries. When we got there he was waiting for us, hands on hips, face as red as a beetroot.

'What on earth do you think you are doing' he said. 'Three loads of radioactive material parked in the middle of town'. Him with the three stripes on his arm had spotted the radio active stickers on the drums which were showing just below the flysheets.

'What's actually in the drums' he asked.

'R A waste' we said, 'that's all we knew and that was the truth'.

'And how much does each load weigh' he asked.

'About 20 tons' I said.

'God Almighty, you mean to tell me there's 60 tons of this stuff parked here'.

'Yea, about that' I said getting a bit fed up with his uptight attitude.

'Well, you can't park it here; get it moved NOW'.

'OK', I said, 'so where do you suggest we move it to'. I was getting angry now. We had had enough problems for one day.

'I don't know' he said. 'That's your problem but you are not parking it here. Just get it moved NOW'.

I could hear Jimmy and John chewing something over and after a few minutes John said 'follow us'. They had decided that because we were driving ERFs we would try our luck at the local ERF factory. Jimmy led the way. On arrival at ERF main gate Jimmy stopped and had a word with the night watchman. I saw him point to a large concrete parking area. Jimmy put his hand up and proceeded in through the gate, John and I followed. We parked up in a neat line three abreast. Jimmy uncoupled his tractor unit. John and I jumped in with Jimmy and we travelled back to Sandbach town centre and parked up and made our way back to the pub for a well earned pint. Later we went to bed, bloody glad that day was over. Next morning we were up early, had breakfast and said thankyou to the landlord. He wished us good luck and a safe journey, Jimmy ferried us back to the ERF factory, Jimmy coupled up to his trailer and we set off for Drigg.

The weather was warm and sunny as we made our way up through the Lake District. Later in the afternoon we arrived at Drigg, we were offloaded fairly quickly and then made our way back to Whitehaven for the night, confident we had a lot better day on Tuesday than we had on Monday. In the evening we went to a club in the town and had a few beers. This was more like it!".

Footnote: Tony Gliddon would have been driving 707 - GKM 893D, Jimmy 'Jock' Jackson 722 - GKO 239D and John Dumelow 30 - KKK 340E, all with 33ft tandem axle trailers.

Above: Tony Gliddon's no.707 - GKM 893D, the Thatcham based ERF is in urgent need of a new bumper to tidy up it's appearance.

Another Thatcham driver, Derek Appleby, has remembered when he carried a load of heavy water!

"Back in the early Sixties, I was driving an AEC eight-wheeler EDP 438 (no 747), not normally mine but the regular driver Charlie Warren was away on holiday. I just got back into the depot when the Vehicle Foreman Bernard Attwood came up and said 'fill up and report to the Atomic Weapons Research Centre at Aldermaston for a load of heavy water' -

a new one on me. So I filled up, checked the oil and water and away I went to Aldermaston.

When I arrived at the gate I was checked in by the MoD Police and taken to the loading bay where there were dozens of 40-gallon oil drums, these I learned were what we were to carry. These drums were filled with concrete except for a hole in the middle about 12 inches long and about six inches wide and the heavy water was in this. After filling, the drum was welded up.

After being loaded, I was taken to the washroom where I had to wash my hands and then put them through a Geiger counter to see if they were clean - no radioactive stuff on them. But no such luck. I had to wash them again and again until they were clean. It was only then that they let me go. I took the load back to the depot. The next day there were four lorries under escort by MoD Police. We were escorted to a Navy yard in Gosport where we were unloaded by crane onto a Navy boat, destination unknown. We then returned to Thatcham Depot empty".

The following tale came via Chris Halliwell:
"In the late Seventies, one damp Saturday morning, a union meeting had been held in Wigan Depot in the old portakabin. As it was breaking up, Bert Marshall who was the Foreman did his customary practice of emptying the large steel kettle of it's contents out of the portakabin window so that he could make a fresh brew. Within a minute Driver Charlie Higson entered to collect his notes for his load, his face, hair and shoulders covered in tea leaves and looking extremely angry. At that point Bert went over to Charlie, waving his notes mystically, looked him directly in the face and said 'don't tell me Charlie, you're going on a long journey!' All the drivers exploded into laughter, including Charlie. Suffice to say, Bert was careful in future".

Not every time John Grierson delivered to the Daily Mirror at Holborn did the delivery go sweetly. See Chapter Three. John has related one occasion when things went slightly adrift, literally!
"One Saturday morning in August 1969, I was planned to deliver one load direct to the Mirror from Aylesford starting at five o'clock in the morning. Then to go across to Vauxhall Bridge park to change trailers and deliver a second load across to the Mirror which had been shunted up the night before. The staff at the Mirror on a Saturday used to have 'job and knock' as they called it, which meant once all the deliveries had come in from Aylesford and the other suppliers, they could go home.

They had every incentive to get the job done quickly. On this particular morning the reels had been cleared when the gang leader shouted 'pullout, Reedy'. I was only half way through tying the back scotchboard across the fly sheet and main sheet to the trailer. I had not completed this job when I pulled around the corner to the office where the staff used to sit and have a smoke and a cup of tea. In doing this, the rope on the offside of the vehicle got caught under the wheel and catapulted the scotchboard through the office window. They came running out of the office like a load of little rabbits and never returned whilst I was present".

In Chapter Eleven, to illustrate how vehicles were programmed each day, an example using Foden no.97 with Driver R.Young has been shown. This was not a mythical driver/vehicle combination - Bob Young was the one time driver of no.97.

A group of retired Aylesford Depot drivers meet regularly for a lunchtime drink on every fourth Wednesday to reminisce about the old times and generally to put the World to right.

One story dating back probably forty years related to their late pipe smoking colleague Bob Young, a driver not associated with much humour but nevertheless much revered by all who worked with him. Bob was, as in the Chapter Eleven example, on a 'one up and one out from London Depot' to the Daily Mirror at Holborn. During the unloading of Bob's first load and working on the platform, he bent over and his beloved pipe fell from his top pocket to be crushed into fragments by the approaching 15 cwt reel. That was bad enough but on Bob's return later with his second load, again bending forward, his tin of tobacco fell from his pocket into the path of a descending reel, again to be crushed beyond use. Not humorous from Bob's point of view but a story still in the minds of his colleagues after such a long time. Bob, on relating this sorry tale, would not have shown so much as a glimmer of a smile but no doubt his audience at the time would have been much amused.

Ken Wratten has already been mentioned as one of the drivers who transferred from Tovil & Bridge Mills to Aylesford Depot. His vehicle was one of the Albion HD57 six-wheel rigids - SKM 412 which became RTs no.4. One incident in his early RT days has been recalled:

"I arrived with a load of reels at Odhams Press in Long Acre, London WC2 - my first visit. Unsure where to position my vehicle for offloading, I parked on the double yellows, leaving no.4 unlocked. I went into Odhams to seek guidance. I came out only to see a police constable driving the Albion away. I went back into Odhams for help from someone in authority. Eventually a senior Odhams person made contact with a police superintendent and after quite a row I was able to retrieve no.4 from the pound without penalty".

As a footnote for Albion enthusiasts, Ken recalls the rather unique door key, about two inches long with a notch at the end which mated with a lug within the cab door. Had he used the key, it would have foiled the PC's attempt to remove no.4!

In 1960, the Company inherited from Cropper & Colthrop a mobile Coles crane based on an ex RAF Thornycroft Amazon six-wheel chassis, EMO 683, originally dating from 1942, see Appendix 7. This short story comes from it's regular 'crew' member, Ron Mulford.

"Sometime during the mid Fifties, I was on my way with EMO 683 to a disused airstrip at Challow. The job entailed lifting a redundant fuel tank off it's base and onto a vehicle supplied by Amey from Wootton near Oxford. A mate was required and on this occasion it was Jack Marsh. While descending Chain Hill on the outskirts of Wantage, I realised that the footbrake was not holding us back sufficiently to be able to stop the Amazon at the bottom of the hill where I knew there was a T junction complete with 'stop' sign.

I had both my hands through the steering wheel pulling hard on the handbrake to maintain some sort of control. I shouted to my mate Jack that we would not be able to stop at the bottom. Jack was by now already a whiter shade of pale. On rounding the bend near the bottom of the hill, I spotted a policeman who had arrived on the scene to check that the 'stop' sign was in working order. Then to my amazement, the officer stopped in his tracks when he spotted the unusual sight of the mobile crane approaching, then stepped back in surprise and duly held up any oncoming traffic, before proceeding to wave us through the junction. The officer was totally unaware of our predicament and completely oblivious to the lack of brakes on the ageing Thornycroft."

One night in the mid Sixties, Aylesford drivers Peter Allen and Ray Martin were returning from their trunk changeovers with Wigan using the A5. Peter stopped at around Hinckley with Ray pulling up in front. Immediately before pulling away, someone jumped on to Ray's trailer and with the benefit of a low load, settled down in the middle for a free ride. Ray was totally

Left: Thornycroft EMO 683, the subject of Ron Mulford's story.

unaware of what had happened. Peter as the witness following behind, failed to attract Ray's attention and when they stopped again at St Albans, the hitcher leapt off and disappeared. As they again pulled away, the character reappeared out of the dark and again leapt on the trailer. This time, Ray had seen what had happened. The next stop was outside Barnet Police Station but again the intruder escaped but Peter and Ray did report the incident. Someone certainly had a free ride!

One day, Gravesend driver Sid Whittaker was delivering newsprint to the Farnham Herald, a four-wheeler job. Sid was on the platform assisting in the unloading when he saw a youngster grab a bag from a parked car nearby. Doing his 'good citizen' act, Sid jumped from the platform, grabbed the young man and marched him into the premises. The only problem was that the young man was the son of the Guv'nor and had left his school bag in his father's car by mistake! Nevertheless, Sid was praised for his vigilance but suffered much embarrassment over the incident.

On another occasion, Sid was returning down the Holloway Road past the Archway in one of the former Imperial AEC six-wheelers. A Rolls Royce was attempting to overtake despite an oncoming flow from the opposite direction. The car became squeezed between Sid's AEC and another lorry in the other direction. To Sid's horror, he watched the offside front wheelnuts of the AEC score down the nearside of the 'Roller' which was being driven by a lady. Sid well recalls the language uttered by this 'lady' which would have made any lorry driver blush at the time. Fortunately, witnesses were at hand and Sid was exonerated of all blame. Sid later became a Traffic Clerk at Gravesend and transferred to Greenhithe when the Depot relocated.

Another funny story from Thatcham's Tony Gliddon recalls the occasion when he and Lionel Lyford stayed overnight in Norwich, having both delivered to RAF

Woodbridge from Welford on behalf of the US Air Force. Sitting at the breakfast table, Lionel picked up a bottle of tomato ketchup, shook it vigorously, the top came off and the contents were shot over a canary in a cage behind him. Needless to say, in Tony's words, "they quickly ate their breakfast and scarpered before anyone noticed".

More appropriately recorded here are two humorous comments from the Aylesford Traffic Office, courtesy of Alan Jones, Jonah to his mates, well known for his dry sense of humour. In that depot, morning starts before 5.00am were extremely rare so when Depot Manager Ken Sackett asked Alan to start at 4.00am, the reply was that "4.00am was for policemen and prostitutes." Alan, of course, did as he was asked.

From Aylesford, deliveries to the RCC factory at Lydbrook was regular traffic, perhaps three per day. Alan's pictorial description of the Lydbrook run was "humps, bumps and mutton", alluding to the grazing of sheep within the unfenced Forest of Dean.

To end, here is the account of the occasion when Alan Jones was risen, literally, to dizzy heights.

A regular Aylesford run was to envelope manufacturer Samuel Jones in Camberwell, SE5. The warehouse was alongside a creek feeding into the River Thames. Drivers were required to reverse down an alley at right angles to the creek. On this occasion, in the early Sixties, Alan had Foden eight-wheeler no.242 - 164 AKM. It was raining and he was on top of the three-high load of reels, rolling the sheet back one at a time to keep the paper dry.

The top tier was always unloaded by crane using rope slings. The crane driver couldn't see the vehicles and drivers and was always guided by a second man who had a direct view of both. This was the period when drivers were issued with green serge overcoats as a part of their uniforms, most welcome during the era of non existent or inadequate cab heating. Alan was wearing his coat. Somehow, unbeknown to Alan, the bottom of the coat became sandwiched between the inside of the sling and the reel. He signalled that the reel was ready to be lifted to the second man who signalled on to the crane driver to lift. To Alan's horror, he was hoisted up with the reel, swung out over the creek and into the upper floor. He returned down two flights of stairs to his Foden, shaken but otherwise unscathed.

Left: In May 1967 two of Thatcham's ERFs were charged with conveying oversized loads from Culham Laboratory in Berkshire to Southampton Docks. The second 18ft abnormal load in the convoy was driven by Jock Jackson and is seen negotiating the narrow streets of Whitchurch, Hants which in those days formed the A34 trunk road. What cannot be seen in this picture is a length of guttering down pipe accidentally 'collected' when passing the 'Swan' at Newtown. It survived the trip to Southampton but it's not clear whether it made it across the Atlantic!

Chapter Eighteen

.......But Not Every Day was a Good Day!

No matter how much effort went into training at all levels, accidents inevitably occurred. Some were bad. The Company sadly had fatalities; thankfully very few. There were also mechanical failures particularly on the early vehicles. There were instances when an element of luck was on the side of the Company or the driver. A few have come to light and are recorded to illustrate particularly the hazards of the earlier days.

George Smith joined the Company at Aylesford on 8th January 1956 and was allocated the ex BRS Bedford O/Scammell artic no.210 which had a payload of 10 tons. Two stories related to this vehicle have been told by George.

"One morning pulling up Farningham Hill A20, a con rod came through the engine block - what a noise. The Workshops came out with a spare unit and the breakdown vehicle. We changed units and I continued on with the journey and 210 was towed back to Aylesford. On another occasion, I loaded in the BRS Warrington Depot one Saturday morning with soap powder for SPD Aylesford and continued part way home, continuing on my way Sunday morning when I arrived at Bert's Cafe, Swanley for a cup of tea. I checked round the vehicle, when I kicked the front offside tyre to my surprise the track rod dropped to the ground. It had worked loose from the track end knuckle joint. I often wondered what would have happened if that happened when travelling in traffic".

George's next vehicle was Foden two-stroke eight-wheeler no.220 - LYP 184 which had been transferred to

A Thatcham Commer HDY tractor, no.712 - 622 LKN, looking rather mangled after an accident.

the A Licence fleet from the Perkins & Glover fleet, originally no 17.

"Two-Twenty was loaded with paper sacks for a small drop in York and the main part for ICI Redcar. I came through a small village called Rusarp, ten miles south of Redcar having delivered the small drop in York. On the north side of Rusarp was a very steep hill. Halfway up the hill was a warning notice for all heavy vehicles to stop and engage crawler gear which I attempted to do. When I applied the brakes, the pedal went down to the floorboard. I pumped the pedal without success. I tried the handbrake which did not help. In the meantime, the vehicle had started to roll back. I realised I could not allow the vehicle to go down the hill into the village. I noticed on my offside that there was a wide grass verge and a thick stone walled farm building. I locked the steering round to allow the vehicle to roll into the wall. I hit the wall and the vehicle rocked to a standstill. I got out to check what damage had been done.

Fortunately, the load of paper sacks had been loaded over the rear of the vehicle which acted as a buffer. There was no damage to the wall or vehicle. I then checked under the vehicle for brake fluid leaks but found none. On further checks I found the brake on the nearside of the trailing back axle at fault. On raising the back plate, bits and pieces - distance pieces and nuts and bolts - fell out. I rang Aylesford Workshops and was instructed to ring Fodens at Darlington for assistance. When I related what had happened, they informed me that the automatic brake adjustor had collapsed and if I kept pumping the foot brake, the brakes would come

Reed TRANSPORT

Left: This photograph of wrecked Maudslay Maharanee no.21 - HGK 928 show the fragile build of the cabs in 1947.

Left below: Another wrecked Maudslay Maharanee was no.22 - HYR 196 also of 1947 vintage. It is shown still coupled to it's single axle fixed semi-trailer.

back, which did happen. Also it would be safe to continue to Redcar and report to Darlington the next morning for repairs".

Retired Thatcham driver Derek Appleby has contributed this tale of a particularly foggy day.

"I left the yard at 06.30 one morning in November during the very early Sixties and the fog was very thick. I was driving a seven-ton four-wheel Guy Otter rigid with three drops for London. I got onto the A4 outside the depot and thought this is going to be a b**t**d! For a start the single windscreen wiper was working but leaving a black mark where it started and finished. I was now in a stream of traffic going slow, watching for lights of vehicles coming the other way. I got through Reading and it was now getting light so that helped. I travelled on to The Square Deal Cafe at Knowl Hill (which is still there) and stopped for breakfast (no motorway in those days). I got talking to a driver from London who worked for Milehams Transport of Purfleet and he said that it was bad all the way through.

After breakfast, I went on to my first drop that was in Hayes, Middlesex - sweet cartons for Callard &

Left: On the night of 'Maundy Thursday' 23rd March 1967, Len Digweed set out from Colthrop with the Wigan trunk, driving Atkinson FC 6LX 20 ton unit no.705 - EKN 571C first registered on 7th October 1965. Unfortunately he got no further than Chapel Street, Thatcham when he was involved in a serious accident ending up demolishing a Reed Company house next to 'The Wheatsheaf' public house. Fortunately Driver Digweed was only slightly hurt as he managed to abandon the vehicle before impact. This picture reveals the situation the following morning, a Good Friday.

124

Right: Foden no.743 - 310 SKK was later to come to grief when in the charge of driver Ephraim Perry it failed to negotiate the roundabout at the A4/A34 at Speedhamland, Newbury in May 1969. In this view the Foden based mobile crane is about to start clearing up.

Right below: Foden FG no.746 - 829 RKT, was first registered on 9th November 1961. Fitted with a Gardner 6LX engine and the S21 'Mickey Mouse' cab, it is pictured here having run into trouble whilst unloading its load of waste paper.

Bowser ex Reed Cartons in Thatcham. I got there but still no let up in the fog. The chap who unloaded me gave me some sweets saying 'chew on these'. So having cleaned my windscreen, I drove off to my second drop at Wembley round the back of the Ace Cafe on the North Circular Road.

The delivery was two pumps from Pulsometer Pumps of Reading. I unloaded these and as time was getting on I had to find digs so I phoned the Union Jack Club in Waterloo. 'Yes they had a bed', so I crept round the North Circular Road and when I came to turn into Edgware Road there were policemen with torches showing you where the turning was! It was now dark and the next thing I had to do was find somewhere to park.

Down the road a bit I met a youngster of about twelve years of age who says 'Want somewhere to park, Mister?' So I say Yes and he replied 'Cost you 2/6 but no one will touch it'. So I follow his lamp and he guides me down a side road and I pay him, get out my case, lock up and head for the nearest Underground station. I walkdown Edgware Road and I then think 'what was the name of the street I'm parked in' so I had to walk back and look, so back I went. I then found a station and made my way to Waterloo.

On reaching my digs, I had a shower and went down to my dinner. I then decided to have a look outside. I walked through the doors but could not see across the road so I retired to bed for a good night's kip. The next morning after breakfast I went outside and the fog had cleared a bit so I went back to my lorry and checked everything was OK. I then proceeded to Barking with my third and last delivery, which was board ex Colthrop Board Mill for their customer, Remploy. After tipping this load, I phoned the London

Depot and I was told to go back empty to Thatcham. The fog had lifted slightly more, making the journey back much easier than the day before".

In Chapter Ten, mention has been made of the Company's operations to the Continent. The following stories have been contributed from the drivers involved.

On one trip, Thatcham drivers Ed Murray and Colin Dumelow were returning home loaded with reels from the Reed Mill at Eerbeek near Arnhem. Ed's Scania no.728 became stuck in high range but, determined to make his ferry booking, Ed nursed the Scania back to Calais. Luckily Ed was directed onto the bottom deck which was on the level and ended up parked in the centre lane right at the bow end.

Whilst having a meal, Ed was amused to hear all the

other drivers talking about how quickly they wanted to disembark on arrival at Dover. He knew from his position that he was to be the first one off the ferry. He also knew that being stuck in high range he would not be able to make it, but dared not to let out his secret. On arrival at Dover, all engines were started up ready for the all clear to make a quick embarkation including Ed who then had to pretend that his problem had just occurred. He would never have been allowed onto the ferry if the crew had been aware of his plight earlier. After the inevitable delay to everyone aboard, two Port Authority Tugmasters pulled Ed clear off the ferry. A fitter from Aylesford was sent down and a new micro switch fitted to rectify the problem.

Another example of nursing back to Dover concerned Thatcham driver Pat Oswald in the lead with Dave Buxey following, both with flat platform trailers loaded with tiles from Maastricht. Dave heard an almighty bang and then saw a piece of one of his trailer tyres go flying through the air in front of him and land with another bang on Pat's cab roof, scaring him almost to death in the process. These were the days when trailers were fitted with remoulds, a practice later abandoned in favour of new tyres. They made it back to Dover before calling out a tyre company.

On one occasion Pat Oswald, through an Agent, was fixed up with a load of cases of Cinzano Bianco from Raffles in Paris for delivery to Gloucester. The customer was Stowells of Chelsea. On arrival at Dover Customs, Pat was accused of smuggling because 20 extra cases had been loaded onto his tilt trailer which were not on the documentation. This was a new product to be given away as a promotion, free to major customers. Customs demanded that extra duty was payable and that the cases should have been included on the documents.

Both Raffles and Stowells refused to pay the extra duty saying it was not worth it as the product was to be given away. Raffles were not prepared to take the cases back and so they were confiscated by Customs. When Pat enquired what they would do with it he was told that 'they would tip it down the drain'. Eventually the load was released and at the Gloucester delivery point Pat had another delay. Soon a lady Customs Officer arrived, checked the seal, inspected the trailer from a ladder placed at the rear to ensure no roof holes, convinced herself that no tampering had occurred and the load was given the all clear.

Aylesford's Mick Cook has recalled the importance of checking export documents before leaving the UK. There was an occasion when he and Len Andrews each loaded 22 pallets of paper for delivery to The Hague. Shipping from Calais to Zeebrugge, Mick spotted that their T Forms were made out for 44 pallets each, not 22. They finally cleared Zeebrugge soon after midnight and would normally have taken their rest. They decided to risk the T Forms and cross into Holland at the quiet time, the middle of the night.

They presented their documents at the Wuustwezel customs point and, with no inspection, were stamped

Above and right: This type of mishap with free standing trailers being unloaded by less than experienced truck and crane drivers resulted in new safety rules being written by the Company and involving the placement of stabilisers (right) forward of the landing legs.

through. Unable to find a suitable parking area, they drove through to the customer's premises at The Hague, arriving at around 3.00am. This does demonstrate the flexibility which all those drivers concerned with the operation exercised but, of course, this was at a considerable cost with regard to pay.

Mick's worst experience on this operation came when he was returning home from Calais when the ferry was caught in a force 12 gale in the Channel which resulted in the sailing taking over 13 hours before berthing at Dover.

Fortunately, Reed Transport's areas of business rarely resulted in loading and unloading delays. There were, of course, isolated instances but they were few and far between. The principal involvement with dock work was

Left and left below: The New Hythe Depot driver of Ford D600 no.21 - PKN 315G with trailer 423N took a right turn out of the entrance to Aylesford and New Hythe Depots somewhat aggressively and whoops! Fortunately the straightening operation was a well tried and proven process as these three pictures show. The bottom view reveals the board and ropes essential for a successful conclusion.

at 46 Berth Tilbury and the Company benefited from it's own infrastructure allowing trailers to be pre-loaded.

There was one delay, however, which surely beat all records, recorded with some humour by Thatcham driver Derek Appleby. It is centred around a job for the US Air Force, the business described in Chapter Nine.

"Back in the Sixties, four drivers with two mates driving early Austin and Atkinson Scammell coupling units with 27ft trailers were detailed to report to the USAF Station at Welford. We arrived at the gatehouse and reported to the Sergeant of the Guard for four loads of ammunitions destined for Felixstowe Docks.

After being relieved of our cigarettes and matches (counted how many in packet - we had been before!), we were then escorted to a bunker where we were told to park. We got loaded and then sheeted and roped the loads. We were then escorted back to the car park near the gatehouse and an officer (with more salad on his chest than I'd had for dinner) wanted to see our fire extinguishers and gave us a talk on what to do and not to do. We collected our delivery notes and cigs and set off with Arthur Whatley in the lead (can't think who was his mate), then next was Pat Oswald (no mate), then Ray Phillips with Blackie Reg as mate, then yours truly as tail end Charlie.

On arrival at Felixstowe we found the US Army Port Control and went to book in leaving the mates to look after the lorries. When we handed in our notes the Sgt told us the boat the loads were going on would not dock until a week today, today being Tuesday. This cocked things up a bit so Arthur phones our Thatcham Traffic Office and is told to phone back in one hour. After he came off the phone he told us 'we have to stay with the loads'.

We then told the US we had to stay until the

boat docks. This pleased them as now they had to find us a place to park the loaded trailers. After about an hour we had to take them to a British Army base within the docks. So away we go and with a US escort get to the army base where we are shown where to park. We leave two units and four trailers, put all our gear in two units and drive to our digs, which are just off the seafront.

Each morning we drive to the docks and check in the US Port Control on the boat's estimated time of arrival, then into the canteen within the dock complex for tea. We also phoned Thatcham everyday and on Friday morning, now four days after arrival, we were told we could come home for the weekend. We made some enquiries and found a van driver willing to give us a lift to London. We were dropped off along the Embankment and hitched a lift to Thatcham. On arrival at the depot to collect our pay, Arthur and myself were told we would be going back to Felixstowe on Sunday afternoon, ready for Monday morning.

On Sunday we were given a firm's car to deliver to London Depot and then we took a taxi to Liverpool Street Station to catch the train to Ipswich and then another taxi to Felixstowe. The two mates were to be left at Thatcham and Ray and Pat will travel up on Monday. The four of us booked our digs in Felixstowe every day. We kept in touch with the US Port Control and also Thatcham every day. This went on until Thursday when the boat arrived and we were able to deliver our loads. This pleased us and the British Army lads as they had guarded the loads day and night since our arrival, ten days ago".

Derek went on to describe the return loading from Canary Wharf back to Fields at Thatcham and the end of this saga. Certainly one for RT's Book of Records!

These next two stories could well have been included in

Chapter Seventeen and come from Aylesford driver Sid Vaughan, an inveterate joke teller, mainly of the more dubious kind. He became well known for getting blocked in - literally.

Sometime in the early 1980s, he arrived with a high curtainsider at a Kimberly Clark customer in Leicester with a load of rolls of tissue wadding. Sid duly reversed into the customer's premises and around a corner away from his vision of the entrance. It proved to be a long unload with a part load of returns then to be loaded - four hours in all.

Sid had noticed a team of builders assembled when he arrived. What he didn't expect to find as he turned the corner to approach the entrance/exit to leave was an archway which was being built with the shuttering already in place to take the brickwork. There was no way the curtainsider would pass beneath. The conversation with the Irish builders can be imagined but went something like this.

"What's this, candid camera? Is it real?"

To which the not unexpected reply was

"Not my problem, mate."

Sid phoned in to Aylesford Depot speaking with Ken Sackett and explained his plight.

"There is this wall and archway blocking my exit."

Ken's not surprising response, knowing Sid's sense of humour, was

"Stop b.....ing about."

It was the builders' problem of course. The shuttering was taken down and Sid made his delayed departure for home.

Then, about three weeks later, Sid arrived at Metropolitan Paper Works in Bow, London E3 with an 8.00am delivery of reels of paper from Aylesford. The customer had asked for the delivery a day early for good reason. Once empty, Sid approached the entrance/exit to depart only to find the Gas Board had arrived a day early and dug a trench in the road.

Sid again phoned Ken Sackett at Aylesford Depot and started to explain the problem. Ken's reaction was

"Not another wall!"

Sid's response was

"No, just a hole!"

Eventually with the help of the customer, steel plates were laid and Sid departed for London Depot for his next job. Sid was never allowed to forget these two occasions when history repeated itself within three weeks. Funny or just another two bad days?

Left: This Aylesford Depot Volvo F10 caught fire at Reed Corrugated Cases factory at Histon after the changeover of the baled waste trailer. Another bad day for it's driver Sid Vaughan! No.44 - XKL 538S, was formerly Wigan's no.990.

Chapter Nineteen

Night Services

The continual pursuit of opportunities for night operations is paramount to any road haulier. The ability to utilise expensive assets over a 24 hour period, rather than having them stand idle after a day's work, is a dream of any transport company. Reed Transport was no exception. It's night activities could be separated into three categories - long distance trunking, short distance inter depot shuttles and night deliveries to specific customers on a regular basis.

The predominant flows of long distance traffic within the Company were always between the south and the north west and it was on this basis that night trunk services from the southern depots were developed. Wigan was always to be the northern terminal, ideally situated less than two miles off junction 25 of the M6. Darwen Depot, as well as being established later - in 1965 - was farther north and also being less accessible from the M6, was never a focal point for night trunking to Kent. Even if the M65 had existed from the late 1960s, then the extra distance part-icularly to Kent would not have allowed the situation to be any different.

A Darwen to London service did operate success-fully from about 1970 to 1976, as mentioned earlier in Chapter Ten and between 1969 and 1983 a changeover with Thatcham operated, covered later in this Chapter. In any case, as will be later mentioned, the source of many southbound loads was to become Warrington, from Lever Bros and J.Crosfield, and Warrington was relatively close to Wigan Depot. Also Lever Bros at Port Sunlight, also nearer to Wigan. Varying levels of site shunters were provided at Lever Bros and Crosfields during the long duration of the business relationship, including night coverage for a period.

On Monday 2nd November 1959, the M1 was opened - in the words of the Press at the time - 'between St Albans and Birmingham'. The haulage industry now had the

Aylesford Depot's no.80 - 127 BKO, an Austin 5K/FED/T3 Scammell tractor heads north with its load of newsprint.

benefit of 72 miles of motorway, the A5 could be avoided and the journey time to and from the north west was reduced. Wigan Depot had opened in February 1960 and it is believed that a night trunk service began operating from Aylesford to Wigan in about April of that year. Certainly by June/July, a night trunk service was operating using the 1959 intake of Leyland Comets. For a short while before, Austin 5K/FED3s may have been used.

There were no halfway changeovers and the Aylesford drivers went through to Wigan, returning the next night. As far as can be recalled, two drivers did three round trips starting on Sunday night and two worked Monday to Saturday with three round trips. The night drivers were Eric Lowrey and Joe Westaway as one pair, Johnny Howard and Johnny Jell the second pair. Limited to 12 ton payloads, typical northbound loads would be newsprint for Bolton Evening News or Rochdale Observer. South-bound would be machine parts and machine clothing for the Mills.

At about the same time, one Foden eight-wheeler per night would run from London through to Wigan, again pre-sumably starting the week's run on Sunday night. The Fodens were two of the renumbered two-strokes nos 216, 217 and 218 transferred from Perkins & Glover C Licence fleet as A Licence replacements. In the event of a delay in tipping out at the southern end in time for reloading and return to SE1, the third Foden could be substituted. The London based drivers involved included Bill Brown, Ron Haddon, Chris Mallett and the trunk driver whose surname was possibly Collins?

Typical northbound loads would be reels of wallpaper base from Empire Paper Mills at Greenhithe to destinations such as Oldham, Radcliffe or, at worst, Holmes Chapel. Later the one and only Leyland Octopus no.226 and Foden no.241 were transferred to London Depot for this operation. Eventually, the use of rigids on

Left: Between 1956 and 1964 many Austin tractors were purchased. It looks from the picture that no.80's route north took in the newly opened M1.

Left: Unloading at the premises of the old Bolton Evening News. Now part of the Crompton Place shopping arcade.

Left and left below: On another occasion Austin/Scammell no.211 - 565 AKK is captured entering Wigan after the night run north. This vehicle was one of the early replacements for the ex BRS fleet. Later, Leyland Comets would be assigned to this task. (left below) Unsheeting in preparation for unloading at the premises of the Bolton Evening News.

Above and right top: Overmanning was endemic in 'The Print' in the early post war years. Six men plus the driver to unload was excessive. These two images clearly demonstrate the primitive unloading method where reels were barred down and turned for rolling off the trailer.

this service proved to be too problematic and nos 226 and 241 were returned to Aylesford in exchange for two Leyland Comet tractors. No.226 was given back to it's original driver, George Smith, in exchange for one of the Comets. A story from George follows later in this chapter.

By November 1960, Wigan Depot was able to provide drivers for changeovers with Aylesford using 'Bobs Cafe' on the A45 at Stretton-on-Dunsmore. For trunk drivers, this meant a Monday to Friday night operation with a shared Saturday night perhaps once a month. This quickly built up to seven changeovers each weekday night with Aylesford. From each direction there were five eight-wheelers including the two AEC Mammoth Majors nos 225 and 227 and eight Foden S18s and S20s including nos 214, 215, 220 and 224. The other two pairs were two Foden tractors nos 92 and 95 and two Leyland Comet/Scammell tractors. These vehicles can be found in Appendices 6 and 17. One of the Wigan trunkers of that time, Bill Parr, has recalled that "the two AEC Mammoth Majors were the most powerful and fastest vehicles made at this time. They had six-speed overdrive gearboxes and were fitted with the AV760 - 11.3 litres engines of 226bhp, this in comparison to Foden two-stroke 4.8 litres - 117bhp and the Gardner engined ones (6LW) of 8.4 litres and 112bhp. It was like getting on a race horse after being on a donkey!"

Prior to November 1960, in fact in the May of that year, two Foden six-wheel rigids were transferred from the South to Wigan and a three times a week round trip night service started operating to the Reed Corrugated Cases factory at Histon with paper from Sun Paper Mills down, returning with baled waste trimmings for Sun. One driver started on a Sunday night working to Friday, the second from Monday to Saturday and staying over at Histon whilst their vehicles were turned around. The original trunkers were Maurice Gray and Albert Peace.

As the Foden S21 tractors entered the fleet in 1961 and 1962, so the Aylesford to Wigan service saw the rigids progressively withdrawn, replaced by full articulation. The preference was always to employ permanent night trunk drivers rather than forever switching between days and nights, although this was necessary to cover holidays and sickness. The regular trunkers during the 1960s included Tommy Knight, Albert Malyan, George Martin, George Smith and Frank Spohr, followed later by Doug Beard, David Elcombe, Bernard Knight and several others. Apologies for names missed. The day shunters were also a fairly constant team. Nicknames and banter were always a mark of a well spirited haulage company (thank goodness) and RT was no exception. In fact, a several pages appendix could have been devoted to nicknames only. Remember the TV Western series 'Bonanza' and the High Chaparral? The Ponderosa was, of course, Aylesford Depot. So the day shunters became 'Hoss' - Harry Chittenden, 'Little Joe' - Bob Axford and 'Adam' - Charlie King. The 'trunks' traffic clerk, Ken Sackett, had to be Ben Cartwright!

At the height of the operation, 16 trunks left Wigan for the South nightly - Aylesford 9, Gravesend 3, London 1

Above: No.218 was one of three Foden eight wheelers transferred from the C Licence fleet to the A Licence fleet to be used nightly between London and Wigan. This atmospheric picture of the Foden FE6/15 S18 with its Wigan-based shunter in the Manchester area was taken by Roger Kenney.

Below: Foden S21 no.222 - 456 NKP, new to Aylesford in April 1961, ready for the 'off' with a three-high load of reels.

and Thatcham 3. It has been suggested that only Suttons of St Helens exceeded RT in numbers of trunks per night from the area. Wigan trunkers included Fred Ashcroft, Bill Darbishire, Neil Derby, Alf Ferguson, Ronnie Fernley, Tommy Gallagher, Sid Harvey, Frank Hogan, David Hoose, John Howard, Norman Hunt, Ted Marsh, Bill Moss, George Percival, Bill Unsworth and Roy Watt.

In 1960 or 1961, the BBC produced a documentary based on the night trunk operation from Wigan which was shown on National TV. The original plan was to film from the cab of one of the AEC Mammoth Major eight-wheelers but it was found to be too small. One of the Atkinson 5LW tractors was chosen with Bill Darbishire - 'Wigan Bill' - as the driver. Unfortunately, enquiries to the BBC have failed to gain any further information about this film.

Northbound loads were predominately reels of paper for the Lancashire corrugated cases and paper bag manufacturers, including RCC at Wigan, and also the printing houses. Southbound loads were generally soap powder from Lever Bros for SPD Depots - Aylesford (the best), Redhill and Lancing (second best), Widford and Wapping (less attractive). Other loads would be chemicals from J. Crosfield, the continuing flow of paper machine parts, machine rolls and machine clothing for the Mills and a growing number of wastepaper loads.

After the S21 era, so came the 20 tonners - the ERF LV 64CUs, Scania 110s and Volvo F88s, then F10s. The southbound traffic of soap powder did bring it's own

problems particularly for Aylesford Depot. The return to Wigan of the necessary corner boards was not a problem but the pallets were. Almost all of Aylesford's northbound loads were large diameter reels of paper loaded two high or the smaller diameter to three high. It was a precarious job after sheeting up to lift 20 or more pallets onto the top of a load without injury to the shunters and without damage to the sheets and, as a consequence, the paper. It was equally a nightmare offloading at the Wigan end.

Wigan's Depot Manager Jim Atkinson achieved anecdotal notoriety for his regular appearance on the bridge over the M6 at Lymm, still wearing his pyjamas, checking the running times of his beloved Wigan trunk fleet returning in the early hours to the depot! As mentioned in Chapter Three, Jim collapsed and died in his office on 1st December 1967.

Night trunk services between the south and Wigan were developed based upon initiatives by the southern depots particularly to provide a next morning delivery service for their customers. The success in backloading from the north was largely due to Jim's enthusiasm and expertise. He wasn't always the most approachable of people but he had the respect of those who worked with him in the early days.

The other main Aylesford night activity was with London, or rather the other way around. Between three and four London based drivers were employed each weekday night shuttling loads between Aylesford and

Left: The Reed Corrugated Cases factory in Warrington Road, Goose Green, Wigan. Reed Transport's Wigan depot is located to the left in the picture and left of the main site road that leads off the dual carriageway of the A49.

London, each covering three round trips. London bound loads were especially newsprint, magazine paper and paper for the many paper bag manufacturers. There were occasional return loads back to Aylesford of reel centres for reuse and wastepaper. During the period of the 1960s and 1970s there was a variety of night deliveries from Aylesford, not long term regularity but always a bonus to boost vehicle utilisation. These included magazine paper for Odhams Press and Sun Printers, both at Watford and corrugated cases for Key Glass at Harlow. There were also shuttles between Aylesford and Gravesend, a regular flow being newsprint for Fleetway Printers at Gravesend.

It was Thatcham Depot which probably developed the greater variety of night operations than any other depot. At it's peak in the late Seventies, up to eight drivers were on the road at night. The two main customers, Colthrop Board Mills and Reed Corrugated Cases, both produced significant and regular flows to their major customers and it was on this reliable base that the night operations were developed. The years quoted in the following summary of Thatcham's night services are from memories of those involved and may be slightly out.

The North West featured prominently from Thatcham. Between 1962 and 1965, every night six nights a week, a Thatcham driver would leave for the 220 miles journey through to Sun Paper Mills at Feniscowles near Blackburn. This was a three driver team, one working Sunday to Friday, a second Monday to Saturday, each doing three round trips, whilst the third shunted on days. The regular drivers were Doug Barrett, Tom Tanner and Tony Gliddon, who rotated within the three week cycle. The 1960 Commer TS3 tractors were used. Northbound loads were baled waste from RCC Thatcham or St Annes Board Mill at Bristol; return loads were reels back for southern customers. A Sun Paper Mills driver shunted at the North end. Digs were a bus ride away in Blackburn.

With Wigan Depot now capable of providing drivers for changeovers, Thatcham ran up to three trunks per night with Wigan up to 1981. Loads north were plentiful - board for Stockport, Manchester and Liverpool customers and corrugated cases for United Glass at St Helens and Skelmersdale. Southbound loads were mainly soap powder from Lever Bros for SPD at Reading, Redhill and Lancing and another customer at Eynsham. Changeovers varied and were at the 'Lincoln Farm Cafe' at Stonebridge, 'Blue Boar Cafe' at Dunchurch, 'Sunnyside Cafe' at Wychbold (still there but no longer a cafe) and Strensham Services on the M5. Often, a short run to Heston, see Chapter Eight, was made before the run up to Stonebridge or Wychbold. The regular drivers included Bob Bird, Len Digweed, Henry King and William Keen. The whole range of Thatcham vehicles were used - Commers and S21s in the early days, 20 ton ERFs, Atkinsons, Scanias and MANs in later years.

Left: Atkinson Gardner 5LW tractor no.61 - 8507 KM dating from 1963 is seen loading in Aylesford Paper Mills with driver Johnny Reader barring a second tier reel into place.

The other north west link was with Darwen from 1969 to 1983, with changeovers again at Stonebridge or Dunchurch. Northbound loads were board for destinations such as Great Harwood, Bacup, Rossendale, Leeds, Halifax and Bradford. Southbound loads were of wallpaper base for Christchurch or paint for Gosport. In the mid Seventies, a night delivery was needed by WPM at Fishponds, Bristol. The changeover was moved to Strensham Services and Thatcham driver Tom Tanner ran back direct to Bristol, positioned the trailer for offloading and, with an empty trailer already left at Bristol, returned to Thatcham. The Bristol delivery ceased in the late Seventies but WPM at Uxbridge then required a night delivery and a similar adjustment was made to the service. Other drivers involved on this run were William Keen and Michael Palmer. The service often ran on a Saturday night. Again, the full range of heavies were used.

Darwen Depot's business with Crown Paints has already been described in Chapter Twelve except for it's vital night services. During the Seventies, the depot would have at varying periods up to three trunks with Gravesend for Uxbridge, two with H.G. Taylor of Mendlesham for Chelmsford and night tramps to Glasgow and other destinations as the needs required. It's service with Thatcham has already been mentioned.

Between 1972 and 1980, a north east service was operated with friendly hauliers. A changeover with Stiller Transport, then of Darlington, operated until 1974 with a swap at Leicester Forest Services or, if the Stiller driver was running late, at Trowell Services on the M1. Northbound loads were board for Killingworth or Gateshead whilst southbound was steel for Winchester often on trombone trailers or urea for Micheldever in 30ft tipper trailers, the sides collapsible down to flat trailers for the return trip. Terry Hartnett and Tom Tanner were the regular drivers, using Scanias or Foden S40s. From 1975, the service operated with Elddis Transport of Consett using the same changeover points. Southbound loads were usually for Andover. The same drivers were involved, with the later ERFs and MANs used.

From 1964 to 1970, the Birmingham area was served with an overnight run to the Reed Corrugated Cases factory at Shirley. Loads were mainly for four customers, RCC themselves and at Chasetown, Oldbury and Birmingham. An outbased driver shunted and reloaded with wastepaper from West Bromwich, Stechford, Tyseley or Birmingham. The Shirley based tractor was S20 no.798 - RJB 326. The night driver was Frank Cheal with an S21 which was left at Shirley when no.798 was due it's service.

Chapter Eight has already described one particular shuttle operation to west London but between 1962 and 1966 there was a daily flow of cases from RCC to British Nylon Spinners at Brockworth, Gloucester. Two trailer

Above: By present day operating standards and conditions, the Austin FFK tractor would not be associated with intensive night and day operations. During the late 50s / early 60s, at least 60 FED3 and FFK Austin tractors passed through the fleet. One of the daily operations were night shuttles from Thatcham to the top of Birdlip Hill with loaded trailers to be shunted into British Nylon Spinners at Brockworth the next day. No.766 - 7751 KP was new in April 1964 and preceded the Atkinson 5LW tractors on that run. Tom Mansky with arms folded was the regular day driver seen here at the Birdlip Hill changeover point. The trailer was one of the forerunners of the curtainsider, body built by RT and known as a pallet carrier, and is described in Chapter Seven.

loads were shuttled each night to a former Army camp at the top of Birdlip Hill, just past the 'Air Balloon' pub on the Cheltenham road. Day drivers delivering to Brockworth then doubled back for one or both loads. Drivers included Tony Gliddon and Bob Bird with Atkinson 5LW/Scammell tractors.

Finally, there were the round trips each night to the south eastern depots. To Aylesford from 1960 there were two runs to Aylesford each night with reels for the corrugated cases factories at Aylesford and Tovil, printed cartons for Kimberly Clark at Aylesford or board for Maidstone. Back loads were for RCC Thatcham, news-print for Newbury, Bournemouth, Poole, Gloucester and Bristol and occasionally paper sacks for Chinnor, Oxford.

Bob Bird particularly remembers these latter loads as the paper sacks were in loose bundles (before palletisation) and with settlement needed at least two stops to tighten the ropes. This was of course pre M25 and the route was through west London. Drivers from 1967 were William Cook, Richard Copping and Henry King. Michael Palmer took over from Henry in 1983 and was still on the Thatcham - Aylesford night run as SCA.

For a period from 1988 to 1990, an average of one load of wastepaper per week, preloaded on a trailer from the Sava Centre at Theale, was delivered direct to the wastepaper plant at Aylesford Paper Mills. More recently, the service reduced to one per night with wastepaper from RCC Thatcham direct to Aylesford Paper Mills and reels back from Aylesford Paper Mills to RCC Thatcham.

Between 1966 and 1977, there were one or two loads nightly to Gravesend, usually board for Erith or Gillingham and west bound loads of wallpaper base for WPM at Gosport and Shand Kydd at Christchurch or paper for Purnells at Paulton and Standard Cheque at Midsomer Norton. Drivers were Jock Watt, Michael Hill (from 1975) and Derek Owen.

Initially, Foden eight-wheelers were used until 1968 and thereafter S21s until the 20 tonners arrived. The operation switched to Greenhithe when Gravesend closed. Thatcham generated many deliveries for London and so frequent shuttles up to Great Suffolk Street were operated with backloads of wastepaper from the many merchants in London back to Colthrop Board Mills. Drivers included Bob Maddison, Tom Mansky, Bob Bromfield, Roy Hawkins and Michael Palmer. Services continued until the depot closed in April 1981.

In Chapter Six, mention has been made of trailer parking facilities at Vauxhall Bridge and later Potters Fields. Thatcham Depot made full use of those facilities as the cramped conditions in London Depot limited the direct runs into the Depot. The extent of the Thatcham night operations demanded a full time night foreman, Reg Taylor, on duty from 10.00pm until 6.00am. When Reg retired, Johnnie Dumelow took over the job. The demand for night drivers resulted in a rota system of day drivers to 'fill in' when needed, not a popular move but a necessary one.

The Winter of 1962/1963 was particularly harsh. It snowed hard on Boxing Day and continued for weeks into the New Year. The Reed in-house quarterly magazine for employees, 'Papyrus', in it's Spring 1963 edition included a feature entitled "The Great Freeze Up", covering Reed Transport's operations during this extremely difficult period. After an introduction, the feature goes on -

"The fact remains, however, that it was a terrible time and so far as the Reed Group was concerned it was particularly bad for those men who drove company vehicles through the heavy snow, the icy roads, the frozen drizzle, the slush and the fog. Their job was to keep open the lines of distribution, and

Above: Although the number is indiscernible, this is no.24 - XKN 846, the only Foden artic with fixed tandem axle trailer. The untreated road must have been a struggle for the driver.

Top: The driver of Aylesford's no.88 - 970 SKJ, an Atkinson FC 5LW/Scammell tractor - waits with his load as a roadman clears snow and ice from his, and the Hillman Minx's, path.

they had to get up early in the morning to do so. What was it like for the three hundred or so Reed drivers during this inordinately protracted spell of Arctic weather?"

The article later on covers night services as follows:

"Night services between Thatcham and London, Thatcham and Aylesford, Thatcham and Wigan, Aylesford and Wigan, Gravesend and London, and Gravesend and Wigan kept going throughout the period."

Without taking anything away from the difficulties experienced by the day drivers, the following is an account from one of the Aylesford night trunk drivers at that time, George Smith.

"I recall one night I was driving 226 to Dunchurch and noticed the engine was inclined to cut out. On arriving at Dunchurch I informed the Wigan driver of the problem. He informed me that several drivers on the way down had found the fuel was freezing - waxing - thereby starving the engine. We had never experienced this situation before. As it was very cold I decided to return home via the A5 rather than the M1 thinking the engine would have to work harder on hills, etc. (George's vehicle back was Foden FG6/24 no.241, 36 AKK which was paired with no.226).

When I approached Stow Hill just south of Weedon, I found Frank Spohr, one of the other Aylesford trunkers, had broken down. I stopped and went back to him and enquired what was wrong. He replied he had fuel problems and the engine would not start. I told him what the Wigan driver had told me about the fuel waxing. I suggested he could take out the first fuel filter element situated in front of the

out and wrapped rags, etc around the filter bowl to protect it from the freezing air. I bled the engine and got it started and proceeded home arriving at Aylesford two hours late. When I reported the next night for work, the Duty Foreman gave me a letter from Bert Bryant (the Fleet Engineer) which stated I could have damaged the engine and the letter would be placed on (my) file. I personally did not agree. The next night when I reported for work, the Foreman gave me another letter. The content was that on further enquiries taking that particular element out would not cause any damage. The first letter was deleted from file."

Returning to the 'Papyrus' magazine, the article finished - "Reed Transport's designation as a service company acquired a new significance during these difficult nights and days," commented W.C.Dale, Director and General Manager of Reed Transport. And he added "The staff put up a most credible performance."

And finally back to George Smith and his night trunking job. From 1961, the vehicles allocated for the Aylesford to Wigan trunk service were progressively replaced by the S21 tractors and the use of rigids had come to an end.

Right: Caught in blizzard conditions, probably at the bottom of Wrotham Hill on the A20 (pre M20 days) is the only tractor and fixed tandem axle trailer in the fleet, Foden FGTU6/25 24 - XKN 846. Attempting to overtake in this winter 1960 scene is one of the Aylesford A Licence fleet's Fodens. Note the Reed Transport headboard rather than the Reed Paper Group.

fuel tank. He replied we would not be allowed to remove the element and was going to ring for assistance. I said I would carry on.

About five miles south 241 petered out and I found the filter element waxed solid and had stopped the fuel flowing onto the next main filter. I left the filter

Overleaf: Foden no.240 - YKT 173, a FG6/15, had a flat fronted fibreglass cab, builder unknown. It is pictured here climbing up New Hythe Lane away from Aylesford Depot on a wintry day in 1963, radiator well muffled. It was almost certainly being driven by it's regular driver, Bill Featherstone.

Chapter Twenty

Vehicle Specifications, Livery and Identification

Many makes passed through Reed Transport's fleet between 1954 and 1991. For heavies, pre 30 tons gross, Foden predominated purchases in the early years with S18, S20 and S21 models, perhaps a policy inherited from Perkins & Glover after the demise of Maudslay into the AEC fold. Gardner superceded the Foden two-stroke engine fitted to the earlier purchases. Interestingly, Foden was already the favoured supplier of heavies to Cropper & Colthrop. Foden was the predominant supplier of eight-wheel rigids, the last one being no 747 for Thatcham in early 1962. However, there were two AEC Mammoth Majors nos 225 and 227 and one Leyland Octopus no. 226 purchased in 1960, the latter separately featured due to it's uniqueness.

From 1961, 23 S21 'Mickey Mouse' cabbed tractors entered the fleet, the last one being no.744 for Thatcham in December 1963. In 1967, an AEC Mercury no.49 entered service as a trial to be followed by 19 more from 1969 to 1971 with the AV505 engine. The last vehicles for carrying 15 ton payloads was a batch of Ford DA2418s purchased in 1975. The later DA2418s, in 1979/1980, were for the Corrugated Cases fleets and not for paper deliveries.

Then came the ERF LV cab 64CU period from 1965 to 1967 with the first 30 ton gvw tractors, 32 recorded in Appendix 17. Six 30 ton gvw Atkinsons were also purchased, three fitted with Gardner 6LX engines for Thatcham in 1965 and another three for Aylesford in 1966, this time with Cummins engines. There followed a short period from 1968 to 1970 with 24 AEC Mandator tractors, not proven to be the most reliable of heavies with the cooling system problems of the AV760 engine. One further Mandator entered the fleet in October 1971, a 2TG4R signifying

it's twin steer configuration. The fleet number is unknown and little is recalled of this one-off tractor. The registration archives quote the supplier as 'manufacturer' whereas the other AECs were supplied by Sparshatts. It was registered in the name of Reed Transport, but might have been an AEC long term demonstrator, perhaps supplied to counter in some way for the frustrations caused by the unreliable AV760 engine of the TG4Rs.

The year 1969 saw the first of many Scanias, both 110s and 80s/81s. The first 110s were the three 6x2s mentioned earlier for the Tilbury shuttle. The remainder were 4x2s for several depots. The 80s/81s continued for the south east depots in 1975, 1976 and 1979 with the last one in January 1980. By then, a total of 59 Scanias had been bought. All had day cabs.

In between, there was a Foden revival with purchases of two with S39 cabs and Gardner 6LX engines for Aylesford in 1970 and 26 with S40 cabs and 6LXB engines in 1972 for Aylesford, Darwen and Thatcham.

The next new make was MAN, first introduced to Thatcham in 1974 followed by more for Darwen in 1976, 1978 and 1979, and for Thatcham in 1978 and 1981, 19 in total. Eleven Cummins engined Seddon Atkinsons came in 1977 for Aylesford and Darwen.

The Volvo marque appeared for the first time in 1974 in the shape of 12 F88s for Aylesford and Wigan followed by four more in 1976, two each for Aylesford and Wigan. The early 12 had day cabs whilst the later four were full sleepers. Aylesford's nos 74 and 75 were the two used on continental deliveries, see Chapter Ten, whilst nos 987 and 988 were roamers from Wigan. In the words of Bill Parr "These Volvos really were the Ferraris of the haulage world." Then, 14 F10s followed for Aylesford and Wigan in 1978 and 1979.

An original from the Perkins & Glover fleet. Maudslay Meritor eight wheeler KLC 996 is seen with a full 15 ton load of reels. It went on the road in October 1949. This picture is the inspiration for the painting reproduced in the colour section of this book.

Left: FBL 48, was one of eleven magnificent Foden FG6/15 S18 eight wheel rigids in the Cropper & Colthrop fleet acquired by Reed. Dating from 1949 it first ran under the T.R.T.S flag along with seven similar examples (the other three being acquired during BRS ownership). No.744 and the Guy alongside - one of the 'Nellies' - are fully loaded with packing cases with the Foden's load being complimented with a well positioned - and roped - load of RSJs. The packing cases carry a 'Made in U.K.' logo and are reminiscent of those carried by the TRTS Albion pictured earlier in the book. Maybe the same customer who has stood by the haulier since those pre-nationalisation days?

Below: No.17, a Foden FE6/15 S18 eight-wheel rigid went on the road in July 1951 being one of seven of the type to enter the Aylesford Paper Mills' fleet in the year when the Festival of Britain was held.

Above: No.214, a Foden FG6/15 S18 eight-wheel rigid, seen being put through its paces at a LDoY event was bought in 1956 being a replacement vehicle for one of the time-expired vehicles that came with the ex BRS fleet purchase.

Left: Same number, different vehicle. No.17 - LYP 184, pictured above was transferred to the 'A' licence fleet in 1955 and renumbered 220 as a consequence of the previous no.220, a Mammoth Major, being stolen. The replacement for the 'C' licence fleet was this FG6/24 - XKL 320, again numbered 17, which joined the fleet in May 1956. Note that 'Radio Times' features in the destination box at the vehicle's rear.

Above: No.16 in a striking pose. Loaded with 20 reels of newsprint from Imperial Paper Mills, the 1958 registered Foden FG6/24 S20 eight-wheel rigid is pictured with driver Len Valsler at the wheel. There is a stronger link with the Imperial name as Len Valsler Senior was an ex Imperial driver, he transferring to Reed upon the acquisition of the company. No.16 was transfered from Aylesford during the period when the older Imperial AEC six wheelers were being phased out.

Right: Rear view of no.784 - OBL 501, a Foden KG6/24 S20 eight-wheel rigid, one of a batch of three that entered service with Cropper & Colthrop in October 1957. It is pictured at Thatcham, by now under Reed Transport ownership.

Left: A well sheeted no.734 at Thatcham in the early 1960s. By now the S18 had given way to the Foden KG6/24 6LK S20 eight-wheel rigid but the days of the eightwheeler in the Reed Transport fleet were already numbered. Articulation was the way to go and S21 tractors were already taking over some of the duties of 504 SKK. No.734 along with No.741 were later cut down to tractors.

Above: No.47 - LUV 240, Maudslay badged AEC Mammoth Major MkIII pictured in P&G/Reed livery when first built in October 1950. In late 1956/early 1957, the London based fleet was reduced, some vehicles were transferred to Aylesford and some drivers relocated, including no.47's regular pilot, Harry Stratford. The author well remembers, as a young traffic clerk, the Friday afternoon when Harry and no.47 roared into the depot to start their new lives. Harry later went on to become a black cab driver in London. No.47 was later rebuilt with a fibreglass cab. Note the destination blind right rear and the P&G type headboard.

Above: A rare view of Leyland Octopus No.226 - 953 MKE seen here at a Reed LDoY competition in the early 1960s.

Left: An Aylesford contestant is using AEC Mammoth Major MkV no.225 - 417 KKT, new in 1960, at a 1966 LDoY event.

No.226 - 953 MKE

Out of the 1400 vehicles identified within this history, operated by Reed Transport or one of it's predecessors, the award for the most unique or unusual must surely go to the one and only Leyland Octopus in the fleet. But that in itself is not the full reason for the award. It had two pedal control with a pneumocyclic gearbox and is believed to have been one of only two so built by Leyland making it an extremely rare vehicle.

Listed in Appendix 17, it's details are as follows:

* First registered on 29th September 1960
* Chassis number 601707
* 0680 engine, 150 bhp
* 24ft flat platform body
* Unladen weight $7\frac{1}{2}$ tons

This was the second vehicle in the fleet to carry the number 226. Perhaps it's predecessor warrants the consolation prize for uniqueness? It was the ex BRS AEC Mammoth Major 8 wheeler JXE 232 which eventually was modified to haul a drawbar trailer, listed in Appendix 5. But back to 953 MKE.

It's first regular driver was George Smith. His previous vehicle was Foden two-stroke eight wheeler no 220 - LYP 184 which had been transferred out of the former Perkins & Glover fleet into the A Licence fleet, see Appendix 6. George continues :

"I was very pleased to be allocated a revolutionary vehicle i.e. no clutch pedal. There was no gear stick as such, a short lever situated on top of a pedestal with the old fashioned gate change indicating the various gears. You could pre-select the gear you would need and to change gear you eased your foot on the throttle.

The actual gear change was operated by air - a very good system when in London traffic. It needed at least 500 revs or more to take up the drive. Anything less allowed the vehicle to 'free wheel'. The original type - pneumocyclic spinner clutch - was later replaced by a fluid flywheel".

No.226 was then transferred to London Depot to work on the Wigan trunk, as detailed in Chapter 19. After a short period, 226 was exchanged for a tractor and returned to Aylesford and George. A further 'George and 226' story is also in Chapter 19.

When George Smith came into the Traffic Office, 226 briefly passed to Percy Ottaway but very soon after, it was taken over by Ken Wratten who has described it's driving characteristics through three occasions.

"As the gear changes were so quick as opposed to the normal gearbox and clutch, a more constant and smoother speed was obtained. It was less tiring for the driver. All in all it was an HGV driver's dream. It was a pleasure to drive during the Sixties but it did have it's little differences. One day I was proceeding to Portslade with $16\frac{1}{2}$ tons of paper. On entering Lewes, I was confronted with a steep hill lined on each side with parked cars. As I got half way up the hill, a car came down. As there was hardly room to pass I had to stop. This was where trying to take off became a problem being heavily laden. As I had no clutch, I could not increase the engine revs and feather the clutch as was the normal way under such circumstances. When I engaged 1st gear, revved the engine and released the hand brake, the engine stalled. The way I eventually took off was to rev the engine to half power, engage 1st gear and release the hand brake at the same time. Fortunately it took off as smoothly as ever. That day I had learned of one of the vehicle's little quirks. With a little thought and some luck we overcame the problem.

On another day, I was delivering newsprint to the Radio Times at Park Royal, London NW10. We had to back onto a bank to offload. The trouble was that this bank sloped slightly upwards. With a normal loaded vehicle, this was no problem as all you did was to increase the revs and feather the clutch. But I had no clutch and when I got the revs right to reverse, I was going towards the bank rather quickly. I found out that the only way I could control the vehicle at a slow speed was to use the footbrake as you would a clutch.

Another characteristic of this vehicle when empty was that it could move off from standing nearly as fast as the cars of that era. I had one such experience on returning home one day. Coming down the Old Kent Road (London SE1), at the canal bridge there were four lanes, two each way. I pulled up at the lights on the nearside. Some distance ahead, the road narrowed to one lane each way. I was in the near side lane and on my offside were two London buses which at that time would have had Wilson pre-selector gearboxes. The ploy of these drivers was to come up on the offside knowing that having a quicker gear change they would soon overtake the normal lorry and across into the single lane. On this day they tried this manoeuvre but 226 was quicker off the mark! The last I saw of them was trying to get into the nearside some way back. I suppose they would get their own back when I was loaded.

In summary, I must repeat that it was a pleasure to drive such an HGV but in retrospect could see it's shortcomings in the commercial goods transport world".

Ken suggests that only two were ever built by Leyland with the pneumocyclic gearbox and that the other one was operated by Leyland Service, delivering parts and carrying their fleet number 36.

The next vehicle to carry the number 226 was a 1970 Scania LB110 - VKL 734H, not quite the same as it's predecessor.

12 EC14s and two EC10s. The EC14s were split between Aylesford and Thatcham. One Foden completed the scene, another ex demonstrator no 85, mentioned later in connection with it's striking livery.

These 38 tonners were all 6x2s and all had Cummins engines. However, there was one other 38 tonner to record, the only 4x2. Foden no.225 was purchased for operations out of Tilbury with PCL Rolaload trailers (automated unloading systems) to the east London newsprint houses. The extra weight of the trailers put a 6x2 at a disadvantage so no.225 gave a 1.5 tonnes benefit for the customer. Twenty-two reels could be carried instead of 21 with a 6x2 tractor.

No.989 - XKL 537S - new in 1978, with Bill Parr as driver, was entered in the Volvo national fuel consumption economy test held over a 20 consecutive working days period. Over 1000 drivers competed and Bill was to become the national winner in category 1A. An average fuel consumption of 9.44 mpg was achieved with 97.8 % loaded running. Bill wore carpet slippers for the test!

ERFs were to reappear in 1977 and 1978 with eleven B Series for Aylesford, London and Thatcham. Leyland was to make a comeback into the fleet with 15 Roadtrains between 1980 and 1982 for Aylesford, Darwen and Thatcham, four of which were ex demonstrators or manufacturer's 'seed' vehicles. A solitary Foden Fleetmaster no.62, an ex demonstrator, was trialed and purchased in 1980 for Aylesford. Another 'seed' Roadtrain no.65 was purchased for Aylesford in 1985 and the final 32 tonner came a year later for Gravesend, no 220, in 1986.

There was a return to the ERF marque in 1986 when the first 38 tonner entered service, a demonstrator C Series with Cummins engine, fleet no. 66. Thirteen Leyland Roadtrains followed for Aylesford, Darwen and Gravesend, the first one also being an ex demonstrator. Thereafter came 14 ERFs -

Above: GKN 446D all sheeted up and ready for it's driver to take it on the road. It was one of a batch of five ERF LV 64CU NHE180 tractors that joined the Thatcham fleet in the spring of 1966.

Left: A view of some of the Aylesford fleet from 1966. No.8 - DKO 732C, a Gardner powered ERF 5LW LV 54G leads the line-up. Behind is AEC Mammoth Major MkV no.225 - 417 KKT new in June 1960 and a Foden eight wheeler.

Left below: New in 1961, no.221 - 457 NKP was numerically the first of 23 S21 cabbed Fodens tractors. The square load cannot be identified and the hanging rope at the rear offside suggests that roping up had not been completed. This Roger Kenney shot dates from the mid 1960s.

Below: No.713 - EKT 182C, an Atkinson FC 6LX tractor was the second of three examples of the type that joined the Thatcham fleet in 1965. This Steve Wimbush picture dates from 1966.

Above: No.65 - LKK 937F was one of the last ERF LV64CUs to enter service in 1967. This unusual shot was taken at Imperial Paper Mills with Gravesend driver Bill Spunner about to sheet an unpalletised load of 'flat' paper destined for Spicers at Battersea. Typically, loading would have taken at least three hours and unloading nearly all day.

Left: Plated for a 20 ton payload was this Atkinson 'Silver Knight' artic no.17 - JKT 119E of 1967 vintage. It's regular driver was 'Dickie' Watts. It is seen here when still new and ready for the Saturday night trunk parked on the site now occupied by the current depot although at that time the original Thatcham depot was still in use.

Below: The Scania LB110 4x2 tractor first saw service with Reed Transport in 1970 and a fair number were purchased over the years. This example loaded with a mixed load of reels, Thatcham's no.755, dates from July 1974.

Left above: No.49 was the first of 20 AEC Mercurys to be purchased and was allocated to Aylesford in June 1967 although this was the only TGM4B in the fleet, the others being TGM4Rs. The vehicle was photographed by Steve Wimbush.

Left: The similarly cabbed AEC Mandator was not a successful vehicle as far as Reed were concerned, they buying some 25 examples over a three year period beginning in 1968. Cooling system problems beleaguered the type which was seen as a successor to the ERF LV 64CU then in service with the company. The next manufacturer of choice - Scania - was not to present such problems to the company's transport management.

Right: Scania 110 SKK 660M, numbered 221 in the Reed fleet, was purchased in the summer of 1974 and allocated to Gravesend. Later, along with two similar vehicles it was transferred to Tilbury although it was to retain its orginal number. It was to transfer again, this time to London, as the Tilbury fleet was reduced. It is pictured here in its London days on the M4, the driver undoubtedly being London depot's 'Lofty' Grist.

Below: No.712 - EKT 121L, a Foden 'S40' artic new in 1972, is pictured in May 1977 with driver Derek Appleby at the wheel. The Thatcham based unit was later sold to dealer in Bishops Waltham and by 1980 was providing the motive power for a showman's living van trailer, having by then been fitted with air horns and plenty of chrome adornments.

Above: A brace of Foden 'S40' artics from Aylesford depot unload reels at RCC Thatcham in February 1975. The AG18/30 6LXB S40 tractor units, nos. 91 & 92 - BKT 191K and BKT 192K respectively, were delivered new to the company in January 1972.

Left: No.784 - GKP 590V, a Ford D2418TR tractor was one of a batch of six similar examples to join Thatcham's RCC fleet in the spring/summer of 1980. The previous vehicle to carry this fleet number was a Bedford TK, again in RCC livery. The Ford D2418 was first purchased in August 1973 for the Reed Transport fleet but unfortunately no pictures exist of the type in RT livery.

Above and right: Two views of MAN power. No.759 (above), registered TKO 978N, was a Thatcham 16.232 tractor dating from 1974 being one of the Reed units that undertook continental work. No.765 (right), AKK 461T, was a 280FTN acquired for Thatcham in September 1978.

Left: Between October and December 1977 eight Seddon Atkinson T36C250 tractors were purchased for the Reed Transport fleet, four for Darwen and four for Aylesford. The latter depot's no.83 was captured on film running back to its home base. Note the heap of slings on the trailer.

Below: No.984 - TKM 856N was one of four Volvo F88s allocated to Wigan Depot in 1974. Vehicle Inspector Jim Sullivan has given it an inspection at Wigan Depot.

Left below: This brand new F88 was the first of 16 examples of the type to be purchased. As no.59 - SKK 881M, it was allocated to Aylesford depot.

Left: The next Volvo type to enter service with Reed was the F10. No.79 - AKK 457T, an Aylesford based unit, one of 14 similar units to be purchased. The load is imported kraft linerboard which did not need to be fully sheeted.

Left below: Thatcham's no.763 looks a little tired in this 1980s picture. Eleven ERF B Series tractors were purchased in the late 1970s, over a decade since last examples of the marque were acquired.

Below: How the unit would have looked when new complete with white banding beneath the windscreen as featured here on no.88 - VKP 140S.

Right: This actually is Thatcham's no.772 before it was acquired in October 1981. At the time the picture was taken the Leyland T45 Roadtrain was being run as dealer demonstration vehicle. Apart from this unit Seventeen 4x2 Roadtrain tractors - 16-28 and 17-28 models - were to be purchased in total. Later in the 1980s batches of the 20-32 6x2 tractor were to be put on the road.

Left: The driver of this Leyland Roadtrain 16-28 tractor looks quizzically on as the photographer takes this shot of the Aylesford unit parked up in a London Street waiting to load.

Below: No.67 - C705 MTW, a Leyland Roadtrain 38 tonner was, like HEU 860X, a former dealer demonstrator vehicle. Stuart Wise was on hand to take this picture during a visit it made to Thatcham sometime soon after its acquisition in July 1986.

Left bottom: The first ERF to be allocated to Thatcham for many years was no.778 - E343 TKE, a 38 tonner that arrived on 9th November 1987. Allocated to Tom Ralph, it is seen shortly after arrival in December a few days before Christmas.

Bottom: Foden S104 no.225 - H959 AKL was the only vehicle to be painted in SCA livery prior to Reed Transport being confirmed as a welcome part of SCA rather than being sold.

For the middle range there was a requirement for tractors with single axle trailers operating at 20 tons gvw, particularly for the London newsprint customers such as Daily Telegraph where vehicle length was restricted. Typically, many paper customers called off in 10 to 12 tons orders. Many had difficult premises to be negotiated. This need was filled in the early years with Bedford and Austin tractors. There then followed in 1959 a batch of eight Leyland Comets followed by a further two in 1960 with the LAD cab. Three Commer TS3s were purchased for Thatcham. All had Scammell type automatic couplings.

From 1961, a large number of Atkinson FC/Gardner 5LW tractors were introduced, not the most endearing of vehicles from the driver's point of view. The 'five pot'

might have been reliable but lacked power. Most had autocouplings but later entrants into the fleet had 5th wheel couplings. Many were subsequently converted to 5th wheel from auto couplings. The final one entered the fleet in January 1966 and in Appendix 17, a total of 101 such tractors have been identified. There may have been one or two more. In 1965 these were joined by 10 ERF LV cab 54Gs, also with 5LW engines and 5th wheel couplings. Four went to Aylesford and the other six were allocated to Gravesend and were particularly used on the shuttle into the Daily Telegraph in Shoe Lane, London EC4.

In 1966, 12 Seddons with Perkins P6.354 engines were purchased, six for Aylesford, two for Thatcham and four for Wigan. No 38 - HKK 145D was used by Seddon in a trade advertisement suggesting twenty-five examples had been purchased by Reed Paper Group. Whilst in addition to the 12, a few may have been purchased for other Group companies and there were the four acquired from the Darwen Mills in 1969 but purchased by Reed Transport on their behalf in 1967, the claim by Seddon of 25 may have been optimistic.

By now, customers' needs were changing and the need for 12 tonners for use on paper deliveries was rapidly disappearing. However, a few Ford DA2014s were bought for Darwen and Gravesend in 1973 to meet their local mills needs.

For the Corrugated Cases factories at Aylesford and Thatcham, the early tractors were Austin/Scammells. For the early years at Wigan, Austin/Scammells were transferred from the paper fleet in the South as Atkinson 5LWs came into the fleet. In 1968, there followed 20 Ford D600s (130 bhp) for Aylesford and 20 Bedford TKs for Thatcham, then 20 D600s for Wigan in 1969 and 1970. A further five D600s for Aylesford joined the fleet in 1970. These were 16ton gvw., powerwise just adequate for 24ft flat trailers, but nevertheless the high loads created considerable drag.

As trailers became longer (and heavier) and curtainsiders were being introduced, so there was a need for greater power. Ford DA1911s and DA2114s (150 bhp) were supplied for Aylesford, Thatcham and Wigan and, in 1979/1980, DA2418s for these depots. A Bedford TM2300 demonstrator was taken into the fleet as a trial in late 1976.

The next marque introduced, in 1980, was the Leyland Clydesdale for New Hythe and Thatcham. This model was superceded by the Cruiser, the first one taken in 1982. A total of 50 were purchased for the three Corrugated Cases factories' operations to 1989. The Clydesdales and early Cruisers had Albion six-speed + overdrive gearboxes and were considered extremely

Above: Two pictures of Austin/Scammells that served the Corrugated Cases factories. In the top picture a former Aylesford Austin 5K/FED3/TE no.162 is flanked by a pair of Thatcham based FFK/240 models both of which entered service in April 1964. In the lower picture one of those same two FFKs, no.727, is pictured when new coupled to an early build example of the company's 'Pallet Carrier'.

reliable. The later Cruisers had ZF 12 speed (six-speed + splitter) boxes which were less reliable.

In 1987 two Mercedes were added to the Wigan fleet for comparison whilst at New Hythe a Dodge demonstrator in 1981 and two Ford Cargos in 1982 were tried. In early 1990. a trial ERF E8-265 tractor, no.759, was purchased for Thatcham, followed by similar tractors for New Hythe and Wigan in late October 1990 - nos 146 and 981. Their suitability proved, and just as Reed Transport became SCA Transport, this model was being introduced to Wigan.

Above: Atkinson no.114, an FC 5LW tractor with a nice even two-high load pictured in Aylesford depot.

Left: An impressive line-up of sixteen Atkinson 12-ton units pictured at Aylesford Depot in 1964.

Left below: A rare make in the Thatcham fleet was the Seddon. Two arrived from Aylesford on 1st June 1966 and. no.795 - GKP 170D is seen in this Stuart Wise picture a year later. Along with sister vehicle no.794 it was tranferred to Wigan in 1969, then to Darwen in 1971.

Below: No.715 - FKE 608D, was nearly the last vehicle purchase that would bear the Austin name. The FJK360 Mastiff tractor dates from January 1966 as is pictured at Thatcham coupled to one of the 'pallet carriers'.

Above: RKE 308G and other Bedford TKs parked up at Thatcham during an open day.

Right: No.118 - JKJ 116N was one of many Ford DA2114s bought for the RCC Aylesford operation. This example was new in 1975.

Below: One of Thatcham's Leyland Clydescale units, no.787 - SKN 724, new in August 1981. No.784 alongside, a Ford D2418TR tractor dates from March 1980.

Above: One of the Leyland Cruisers allocated to Wigan depot. No.972 - C315 GKR was a 16-17 tractor, one of many examples of the type purchased for the RCC fleets in the 1980s.

Left: In 1990, three ERF E8 tractors were purchased as trials for Aylesford, Thatcham and Wigan RCC operations. This is Wigan's no.981 - H558 DKK but although in RCC livery, did not have a headboard.

Left: Inside the old TRTS garage at Thatcham in the early 1960s. Parked between the two Austin FFK tractors is Commer TS3 MMO 296 which was later to be converted into a gully emptier for Colthrop Board Mills. An ex Brentford FFK boxvan and two Foden FGTU6/24 6LX S21 artics complete the lineup.

Below: The Austin seven ton rigids for the A Licence fleet at Aylesford were not fitted with side panels. No.202 was new in 1956, registered XKR 107 and was a replacement vehicle for one of the ex BRS Vulcans.

Left below: RKK 793G was one of three Bedford KM rigids that commenced their working life at Thatcham on 14th March 1969. Numbered 804 the new vehicle is pictured at it's home base.

The need for four-wheel rigids was continually diminishing. Initially, Austin filled this requirement until 1965. Commer TS3s were purchased in 1960 and 1962 for Thatcham and from 1969 Bedford KM and Ford D800 provided most of the chassis for both flat platform and boxvan bodies.

A solitary Dodge was taken into the fleet in late 1972, initially trialled with a drawbar trailer with dolly for splitting into a semi trailer. Allocated to Darwen as no. 904, it was in a plain white livery with a black lettered Reed Transport headboard and Crown Paints logo on the cab doors. A photograph has been included of this 'one off' vehicle. It was introduced for the bulk delivery of paint to Uxbridge with backloading of multi drop loads of paper and paper sacks from Aylesford back to the North. In concept, it was before it's time but it was too long and was increasingly used as a rigid only, the

customers didn't like it and it was accident prone.

In a final attempt to make a success of the trial, the Darwen Foreman John Norris took it on for about a month with a better result. However, overall the trial was deemed a failure and the outfit was transferred to Aylesford, repainted green and renumbered 104. The vehicle was absorbed into the New Hythe Depot fleet and the trailer was thereafter only occasionally used as a semi trailer. Nevertheless, such trials and innovations are necessary in any haulage company to ensure that opportunities are not missed and whilst this one was a failure, it did not detract from the Company's desire to stay ahead of the game wherever practical and financially viable.

The first of many Leyland Clydedales joined the fleet in 1980 at Aylesford for the Reed Medway Sacks contract. There followed 18 more, all for the

Right: A one-off purchase was Dodge rigid and drawbar trailer no.904 - FKO 495L for Crown Paints whose logo can be seen on the cab. The unit was introduced for the bulk delivery of paint to Uxbridge. It was later transferred to Aylesford, painted green and renumbered no.104. This picture of the outfit parked at a transport café was taken by Roger Kenney.

Key/Caradon Terrain contract, up to 1985. For the Corrugated Cases factories, six Freighters were purchased, two for each factory and one more for the Reed Medway Sacks contract, all with curtainside bodies. In between, in 1979, a Boxer was taken also for the K/CT contract.

A brief mention should be made of the need for robust tractors for the Aylesford Paper Mills internal stock and raw materials operation. Having relied upon Bedford O and S tractors during the early 1950s, in 1957 five Douglas Tugmasters were purchased with Humber/Commer petrol engines and half cabs to be joined in 1958/1959 by a further five. Designed for 12 tons payloads, at times they were grossly overloaded within the mill. The operation passed back to the mill in the early 1960s. Between 1964 and 1966, five Atkinson half cab tractors with Gardner 5LW engines, six-speed David Brown gearboxes and Kirkstall special low ratio rear axles limiting the top speed to around 28 mph, were specified by Reed Transport and purchased on behalf of Aylesford Paper Mills, replaced the Tugmasters. Although never actually owned by Reed Transport, they have been included at Appendix 18 as a point of interest.

An attempt has been made to identify most vehicles which were operated by the Company within the Appendices at the back. There is a gap in records between about 1960 to 1974 so some of the detail has been derived from memory and photographs rather than hardcopy. In addition, many hours have been spent searching for and checking registration numbers and dates together with makes and models, at Kent County Council's Centre for Kentish Studies where records of vehicle registrations at Maidstone LTO since 1903 until the advent of the DVLA have been archived. The list of vehicles at Appendix 17 is probably 98% complete.

The list at Appendix 19 recorded as new from August 1974 is believed to be complete. Original cost, where known, has been included. Many vehicles were delivered in factory primer to be painted in the Company's own paintshop. Others were delivered factory finished, particularly Fords whilst others were painted by local contractors. The 'orig cost' may therefore not always reflect the final 'on road' cost.

Every attempt has been made for accuracy throughout but there are inevitably some errors and some vehicles missing from the lists. Some creative guess work has been applied. Where there is any doubt, a question mark has been used. In some Appendices, early vehicles have been included as operated by Group Companies because the records existed and it added to the interest within each list.

Apart from the few ex Demonstrators and Manufacturers' 'seed' vehicles, all new vehicles were Kent registered. The Company was also responsible for sourcing and supplying hundreds of commercial vehicles for other Reed owned companies. Where a significant number of vehicles were expected into the fleet, blocks of registration numbers were obtained, as Appendix 19 will clearly show. These were occasionally used up over a period of several months. Gaps in sequences may therefore have been used on other Group purchases.

The standard livery was Middle or Mid Brunswick Green with red chassis and wheels. The 'Reed' Green was a superbly durable coach enamel always supplied by International Paints. From about 1980 the red was replaced by black. A few outsiders considered the green with red livery somewhat reminiscent of fairground vehicles. Those within the Company thought that the move to black, however justified for practical and cost reasons, took something distinctive away from the fleet at that time.

Headboards and lettering need a special mention. The P&G fleet, certainly up to no.47 - LUV 240, originally carried a straight headboard simply lettered AYLESFORD in capitals in gold on green. All rigids and fixed artics possibly up to no.74 - WKE 472 and some early replacements, by then as Reed Transport, were built with side and rear panels to the flat platform bodies. Foden eight-wheeler no.16 - 76 BKR (see page 141) was the last to be so built. Appendices 3 and 17 cover these vehicles.

Forward of the rear wheels was the lettering AYLESFORD, this positioned above PAPER MILLS in smaller case as illustrated below on a P&G/RT Maudslay. To the rear of the rear wheels, nearside and offside on the eight-wheelers, was fitted a bus style destination blind (featured below) showing the publication to which the load was destined - RADIO TIMES, DAILY EXPRESS etc - white capitals on a black blind. This was a unique customer and public relations innovation for the period. It is believed that Foden eight-wheeler no.17 - XKL 320 was the last to be fitted with destination blinds. The later three eight-wheelers, the last for the Aylesford C Licence fleet, no.51 - 653 BKO, no.52 - 108 BKP and no.16 above, all carried the Reed Paper Group logo to the rear of the rear wheels in place of the blinds. Similarly, the last four-wheel rigids to carry panelled sides and rear were the Austins no.14 - XKO 267, no.13 - XKP 847, no. 75 - XKT 214 and no.117 - YKK 907. See Appendices 3 and 4.

The headboards had been changed to show the wording REED AYLESFORD, with 'Reed' surmounting Aylesford like a crown. The 'Reed' was always in Corporate style whilst Aylesford was in italicised capitals

- as detailed above and below on XKL 320. The Tovil & Bridge fleet carried similar livery, the headboards showing REED MAIDSTONE as per the layout of Aylesford vehicles and the side panels TOVIL & BRIDGE PAPER MILLS with 'Paper Mills' beneath the 'Tovil & Bridge' name but in a smaller case.

Similarly, London Paper Mills vehicles carried headboards thus REED DARTFORD and side panels LONDON and 'Paper Mills' as previously described.

The next change was to 'Reed' surmounting 'Paper Group' or 'Transport', whichever was appropriate. Again 'Reed' was in Corporate style above italicised capitals. Lettering continued to be in gold. Fleet numbers in gold were contained within a gold circle. Next came straight headboards depicting REED PAPER GROUP or REED TRANSPORT in raised green fibreglass moulded lettering on a white facia. Finally, with the introduction of cab caps, often illuminated, the two options were merely black capitals on a white or clear background.

The cab doors on the early P&G fleet carried AYLESFORD in a slightly semi circular format

with 'Paper Mills' beneath.

The next change, as 'Reed' appeared on the headboards, was to have Reed with PAPER GROUP or TRANSPORT in a semi circle underneath as detailed below. There were some 'Transport' headboarded vehicles, i.e. A Licence fleet, which carried Reed Paper Group cab logos! When the name Reed Paper Group ceased to exist, the new Reed logo of four diminishing white squares centred around a small REED on a white background became the new cab logo as seen right on Volvo F10 no.94. Fleet numbers were now white within a white square to balance with the logo.

In 1970 there was a variation made to the livery for the

first, and all subsequent, Scanias taken into the fleet - the radiator grilles were painted white. There had already been a move towards white cab caps on some makes and the Scanias were also included. In addition, a white band below the windscreen was added, extended to the cab doors and rear of the cab. This change occurred at a time when the anti juggernaut lobby was growing. The one thing that the large expanse of white to the front of the Scania did was to emphasise the sheer size and height of a 110's cab (see picture on page 62, Chapter Six) and public opinion was increasingly against 'large' lorries. There was an opinion within the Company that this was not such a good idea. The '80s also given the treatment didn't stand out so much. Perhaps all green cabs on the Scanias would have been more appropriate?

A photograph has been included here of no.755 - SKL 570M, one of Thatcham's Scania 110s. The panel below the windscreen carrying the S C A N I A name was finished in green rather than white together with the panel immediately above the bumper. The reduction to the expanse of white as on the earlier 110s provides an interesting comparison.

The scheme was to be repeated later when S40 cabbed Fodens and Seddon Atkinsons received the 'white' radiator treatment although the corner panels remained in green. The Volvos with the factory black radiators were exempt! Not that the white didn't work on all makes. The

application for example to the lower half of the fronts of Ford D Series and Bedford KMs looked smart but then those cabs were much lower overall. Those vehicles provided to the Corrugated Cases factories were in Ambassador Blue, the dark blue, with cab caps and wheels in a lighter blue, Naples Blue. Trailers were painted in Ambassador Blue. The vehicles carried full customer lettering.

In November 1989, a Foden 6x2 demonstrator was received, no.85 - F247 VVT. The colour was a striking Jade Green metallic. The Company was in limbo, owned now by SCA but still trading as Reed Transport. The future was uncertain and there was very little activity on the vehicle purchase side. Managing Director Ron Adkins, in an attempt perhaps to breathe a fresh image

into the Company during this period, considered the 'Reed' green livery had become outdated.

Not everyone was so enthusiastic about Jade Green. Fleet Engineer Graham Day was later to describe it as "that awful sickly metallic green". Readers can judge for themselves from the photographs included of no.85 - before and after. A curtainside trailer was also relettered in Jade Green. A second vehicle, ERF 6x2 no.86, was repainted in Jade Green but before any major decision could be made regarding future livery, SCA declared that the Company was to remain a part of the Group and therefore all vehicles were to be repainted in the SCA corporate livery. During this period of reflection, the Foden had been purchased by Reed Transport. Nos 85 and 86 became the first to be repainted in SCA livery, no. 86 having worn three different liveries in under two years.

Fleet numbering followed a general system related to original Depot allocation. Up to 1960, it was as follows :

1 to 100	C Licence fleet - Aylesford & London
101 upwards	Local fleet - Aylesford
201 upwards	A Licence fleet - Aylesford
700 upwards	A Licence fleet - Thatcham
800 upwards	C Licence (Corrugated Cases) fleet - Thatcham

Subsequently, the fleet acquired from Imperial Paper Mills at Gravesend were numbered ?175 to 199, additions and replacements taking numbers below 181. The first new vehicles for Wigan, the four 1966 Seddons, were numbered 141 to 144 but when the batch of Ford D600s

Below and right: Before and after. This is ex demonstrator Foden S106TS, no.85 - F247 VVT, which arrived in a striking Jade Green metallic livery. Lettered up together with a Southfields curtainside trailer, it was during the period of uncertainty for Reed Transport when SCA were not sure about the Company's future and a new 'more modern' livery was being considered. The company became SCA Transport on 15th August 1991 and no.85 was one of the first vehicles to be repainted in SCA livery. The vehicle is featured in the colour section in both the Jade Green and SCA liveries.

were delivered in 1969, the range of numbers allocated to Wigan began at 950.

The background to the numbering of the original RCC owned Commer tractors as 964 to 969, see Appendix 11, is unknown but clearly had influence on the adoption of the 950 series of numbers later. Darwen, the younger of the two northern depots, had already been allocated the range from 900 although the ex WPM vehicles had earlier been numbered between 850 and 891. Interestingly, two Ford DA2014s bought for Darwen in 1973 were numbered 884 and 885, tacked on the end of the sequence including the ex Hollins Seddons, see Appendix 15.

By the mid 1970s, the small London fleet had been allocated 151 upwards and Gravesend including Tilbury 201 upwards. By now, all Aylesford and New Hythe vehicles were numbered below 200. The need to distinguish between A Licence and C Licence vehicles

nearside of the cabs. 'A' for Aylesford, D,G,L,T and W etc. Tilbury based vehicles carried a 'G' for Gravesend, the depot responsible for the maintenance. All trailer numbers were in blocks segregated by type, length and payload and prefixed 'T' with the depot allocation as a suffix thus T1517D. Depot identification was introduced when a Chairman of the Company expressed a wish to be able to identify a vehicle's home base when seen on the road. The many photographs included in this book illustrate the variety of livery styles used and also the destination blinds on the early eight-wheelers.

Two interesting photographs of display boards, dated 9th September 1960, have been unearthed (next page) which show that the Company explored the practicalities of incorporating the depot name into the Reed Paper Group and Reed Transport logos. A few photographs exist confirming that this practice was introduced on some rigids and trailers. However, it was abandoned to be replaced much later with the letters on cabs as described above.

had gone. Also, by a natural process, the progressive contraction of the Thatcham fleet saw all that depot's vehicles being numbered below 800.

The general principal was to allocate vehicles with previously used numbers, often those of vehicles immediately replaced, with some gap filling and some tacking on the end of a series. The system may have appeared illogical to some but in the end a number was only a number. The TRTS and later the C&C fleet didn't carry fleet numbers. An arrangement with the local Taxation Office made it possible for a consecutive sequence of numbers to be allocated to new vehicles. A glance at Appendices 7 and 8 shows this clearly.

Another company which clearly had an influence with the Maidstone LTO was Imperial Paper Mills. A study of Appendix 12 will show that it's fleet of AECs from 1951 to 1957 had numbers ending 1 to 25. However, Imperial still saw the need to use fleet numbers 1 to 25.

Inter depot transfers or reallocations of vehicles usually resulted in a renumbering, but not on every occasion. Every depot looked forward to new vehicles, so when transfers occurred, this was usually unpopular and the retention of the 'old' fleet number attracted charges of 'Secondhand Rose' or 'depot X's castoffs'. The Notes to the various Appendices record many of the transfers and renumbering but inevitably some have gone unrecorded. Particularly through the period of cutbacks vehicles were being continually moved and there was also the continuing need to update and replace worn out shunt and internal vehicles.

Depot identification on vehicles was practiced for a period by applying white letters to the offside and

Specific types of trailer have been briefly mentioned already, where appropriate. But trailers and full articulation played a vital part throughout the Company's history. In some locations, it was necessary to provide over three trailers for each tractor to cover the 24 hours / 7 days loading demands as well as the forward loading for the many short distance loads delivered from every depot. Many customers demanded trailers for forward loading by several days to alleviate the need to provide warehousing capacity.

There was also the practice of mass loading at a month end for deliveries on the first days of the next month. Orders despatched but not necessarily delivered allowed invoicing and thus false sales figures to enhance monthly results. 'Spare' trailers were a cost which the Company often struggled to justify but nevertheless provided as part of the service.

Early full articulation in the 1950s was limited to 24ft flat platform single-axle auto-coupling trailers carrying up to 12 tons payloads. Manufacturers included Carrimore, Convoys, Mereworth and Scammell. The first such trailers in the C Licence fleet were lettered LA, LB etc - L for London - rather than numbered. LX was reached. From the late 1950s, trailers were numbered, as mentioned earlier. The early L lettered trailers were eventually relegated to Mill internal operations.

The first tandem-axle heavies built by Eagle have already been described in Chapters Three and Five, the 14 for Aylesford and four for Thatcham for use with the nine S20 Fodens of 1958/59. Throughout RT's history until it's final full year, 1990, all heavies were flat platforms. The paper industry required reels to be carried

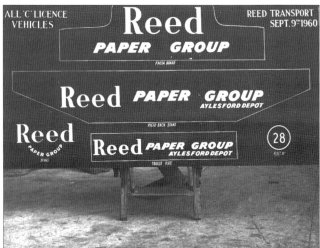

'on the roll'. Heavier reels were loaded and mainly unloaded by overhead crane. Mills did experiment using fork trucks with extended forks as the photograph of the new procedure at Tovil & Bridge Mills illustrates in Chapter Three, page 18. But this was the exception rather than the rule. Two and three high loads of 15tons and more produced high centres of gravity. Sideways sway with the related stresses demanded trailers with 18 inches deep I-beam chassis. Prefabricated chassis frames were not acceptable.

After the original Eagle trailers, 'own' build trailers met the Company needs at 33ft 6in, 35ft, 38ft 6in and 40ft lengths. There were even a few 30ft tandem axles exclusively for deliveries to the Daily Mirror at Stamford Street, SE1. Floorboards were of two layers of timber

with strictly no side raves. They needed to withstand a reel in excess of two tons dropping heavily during loading or unloading and with no slip for wedges and scotchboards. Headboards were required to prevent reels pushing forward during heavy braking. As RT ceased manufacturing trailers, so the developed designs were passed on to Fromant who became the sole supplier of heavy trailers.

Finally in 1990, the mills and customers had begun the transition towards large reels being loaded to and offloaded from the 'on end' position. Fork trucks with squeeze and rotating clamps were being introduced. To meet the new challenge, in February 1990 Southfields supplied two 40ft tandem-axle openspan curtainsiders to their Fleetloada design for general reel deliveries from Aylesford. They were numbered T1900/1A. The only other curtainside heavies introduced were the first three built with the PCL Rolaload system on Fromant chassis for operation out of Tilbury, as described in Chapter Fifteen. Thereafter, the Company became SCA Transport and curtainside heavies became the norm.

The lightweight fleet had a different demand. In the early 1960s, single-axle flat platforms were built to 24ft, 27ft, 30ft and 33ft for both paper and corrugated cases deliveries. A handful of four-in-line trailers were introduced but were not considered successful. By the late Sixties, the Corrugated Cases factories were succeeding in palletisation and so the early curtainsiders in full RCC livery began to be introduced, described in Chapter Seven. Apart from 'own' build, manufacturers included HWP and Fromant. By the time this fleet moved to 40ft, Fromant was the builder. There were curtainsiders also supplied for wallcoverings deliveries from Darwen and pockets of other customers. Of course, large fleets of single-axle auto coupling trailers were inherited from Cropper & Colthrop, Tovil & Bridge Mills and other acquisitions.

Specialist trailers were provided to customers. Chapter Thirteen mentions three tipper trailers introduced for loose wastepaper deliveries. In 1958, four tanker trailers were introduced for internal movements at Aylesford Paper Mills, two on Convoys chassis for size and two on Scammell chassis for liquid china clay. During the Seventies, a single axle tanker trailer was purchased secondhand to carry heavy oil for the mills' boiler houses during times of industrial disputes, for example by tanker drivers. There was also an 'own' build tandem-axle trailer specifically designed to carry machine rolls weighing in excess of 30 tons between machine houses within Aylesford Paper Mills. To operate in conjunction with the Douglas Tugmaster tractors mentioned earlier, also for Aylesford Paper Mills, a fleet of auto coupling tandem axle trailers was provided.

Left above: Boards displaying 'A' and 'C' fleet styling in 1960.

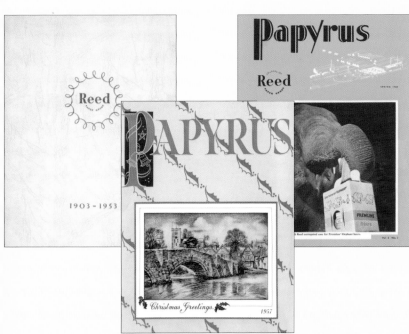

Above: This painting of a Maudslay Meritor hung in the office of the Fleet Engineer at Aylesford for many years, certainly it saw out many occupants of that post. The actual vehicle, no.39 was new in 1949 to Perkins & Glover and predates the company name change to Reed Transport by several years. It does epitomize the P&G fleet of heavies, just as Foden was to do in the 1950s for Reed Transport when its eight wheelers became the hallmark of that fleet.

Far left: In 1953 to mark the 50th anniversary of the incorporation of Albert E Reed and Company the Directors published this booklet which illustrated and described the activities of the Company and its subsidiaries of what by then was widely known as the Reed Paper Group.

Left: Reed, especially in the earlier days of Albert E Reed and the Reed Paper Group was quite paternalistic. Papyrus magazines reported not only the developments of the Group but also weddings, retirements, sport and achievements of employees from every part and at all levels.

Above: Mick Perry, a former fitter at Thatcham, joining Cropper & Colthrop in 1957, took a number of images of vehicles at the Berkshire depot during the 1960s. The line-up of six Austin tractors is of great interest, they are coupled to early Reed designed curtainside trailers - known then as 'pallet carriers' and were used mainly on the lightweight corrugated cases distribution.

Left: An Atkinson FC 5LW, no.44, 619 PKL, being refuelled at Aylesford. Drivers considered them underpowered for the task.

Left below: No.748 - 619 SKM, a Foden FGTU6/24 6LX S21 powered unit caught by the camera of Peter Davies at Thatcham.

Below: No.38 - HKK 145D was one of twelve Seddon 13:four P6.354 tractors purchased in 1966; a further four joining the fleet with the acquisition of WPM Paper Mills in July 1969.

Left: No.796 - RKE 308G heads a line-up of eighteen of the twenty Thatcham based Bedford TK nine-ton units that were purchased in 1968/69 for Reed Corrugated Cases work. The type was viewed as a successful acquisition.

Below: Another Mick Perry photograph taken at the same Thatcham location as that opposite, this time featuring three Atkinson 5LW tractors coupled to loaded trailers.

Above: The role of the rigid four wheeler had diminished significantly by the time that Bedford KM rigid no.804 - RKK 793G joined the Reed Thatcham fleet in 1969.

Left top: CRX 675, the ex TRTS ERF/AEC 7.7 C15 recovery tractor which carried fleet number 719 in its Reed days at Thatcham has survived into preservation.

Left: Aylesford's AEC Matador has just recovered to the depot this RCC Ford D series artic which has been involved in a collision.

Below: The 1970s replacement for Aylesford's Matador; again built in the company's workshop.

Left below: Thatcham's Matador replacement was this Foden S21 unit, its origins being in a eight wheel mixer chassis.

Left: This 1970s picture is significant as it collectively features the liveries carried at the time. The Key Terrain Ford D800 rigid numbered K2 features the original Key Terrain livery of red with white lettering whilst alongside is Ford D600 Series no.147 - RKL 327G in the Reed Corrugated Cases colours of Ambassador Blue (dark) and Naples Blue (light). No.213 - WKO 247J, a Foden 4AX6/30 6LX S39 tractor from Aylesford depot coupled to a well-sheeted tandem axle tractor, features the mid Brunswick Green livery and red wheels representative of the main Reed fleet.

Right: The mid 1970s saw a considerable number of Ford DA2114 tractor units being purchased for the RCC fleet. This example being Wigan's no.983 - JKJ 118N.

Below: No.758 - TKO 303N, a MAN 16.232 unit was one of five similar Thatcham tractors that undertook TIR haulage to the continent in the second half of the 1970s. Aylesford depot was also involved in the operation using Scania and Volvo units.

Right below: No.59 was the first of sixteen Volvo F88 tractors taken into the fleet from 1974 and was registered SKK 881M. This was one of twelve units fitted with day cabs.

Above: No.235 - SKN 894H, one of the three Scania LBS110 6x2 tractors photographed outside Head Office with a new 38ft 6in trailer.

Left: A standard Scania 110, no 229 - WKO 249J from 1970 with another in the background are pictured at Aylesford ready for the night trunk to Wigan.

Left below: Leyland Freighter, B998 XKN, new in 1985 was numbered K14 in the Key Terrain fleet and equipped with a Ray Smith demountable body. It is pictured here in the later Caradon Terrain livery after Reed Group sold the company but continued to supply it's vehicles on contract hire.

Below: Looking very purposeful with a well sheeted load is no.64 - SKN 726X, one of 17 Leyland Roadtrain 4x2 tractors purchased between 1980 and 1986.

Above: Entitled 'Paper-Making at Aylesford' the acclaimed artist Terence Cuneo was commissioned by the Company in the early 1950s to reproduce this dramatic scene of one of Aylesford's giant machines in production with it's staff in attendance. A trademark of Cuneo's work was the small mouse that normally appeared somewhere within his paintings but perusal of a larger version of this picture has yet to reveal the location of the small creature so closely associated with the late artist.

Right: Leyland Freighter no.50 - D850 KKN was bought in 1986 for New Hythe Depot for weekly hire to Medway Packaging. This photograph was taken in a very clean Aylesford Garage.

Left and below: In an attempt to revitalise the image of the company in the early days of SCA ownership when the future of Reed Transport was undecided this ex demonstrator Foden S106TS, no.85 - F247 VVT, arrived in this striking Jade Green metallic livery. Pictured at Aylesford with a similarly lined and lettered Southfields curtainside trailer, the vehicle's paint scheme was not to everyone's liking. However, the matter was to resolve itself in August 1991 when the company became SCA Transport and no.85 was one of the first vehicles to be repainted in that livery. The lower picture reveals no.85 under its new ownership alongside another reliveried vehicle, Leyland Cruiser no.140 - E146 AKN, now in SCA Packaging colours.

Postscript

Chapter 15 told of the last few weeks of Reed Transport in name. We had survived two years owned by Reedpack which was then purchased by Svenska Cellulosa Aktiebolaget, SCA, in July 1990. Having tested the market for a buyer, SCA Packaging Business Group decided to keep us and, after Due Diligence processes, the Company became SCA Transport Ltd on 15th August 1991. Managing Director, and my boss, Ron Adkins retired six weeks later on 30th September.

I was appointed MD as from 1st October. We had already been placed in the Packaging Business Group since the Reedpack acquisition. It was a natural home alongside many of our customers - three of the corrugated cases plants and the kraft (brown paper) mills. Now we had to prove ourselves to remain profitable and to produce an acceptable return on capital in line with SCA's benchmarks. It was to be a tough challenge for us all.

There were pressing issues to be attended to. A budget had to be produced and approved, effective from 1st January 1992. The whole fleet had to be reliveried and trailers recurtained. Every item of documentation was retitled, accounting periods and reporting procedures adjusted and Operators Licences changed. Non Group customers needed reassurance that service levels would

continue - that we were still in business for them. Very quickly, every physical identification of Reed Transport had been wiped away but in many ways the culture of RT still continued, at least for the immediate future.

Within three weeks of my appointment, I was attending a Logistics Meeting at Malmo where I met officially for the first time Colin Williams, President of the Packaging Business Group responsible for the corrugated cases plants and kraft paper mills throughout Europe. I was told to take over the transport operations at all the other UK corrugated cases plants. When asked about a time schedule, the short answer was "Tomorrow".

On completion, our involvement with the corrugated cases factories had doubled and we now had an excellent national network of depots, management and fleets on which we could build for the future. Life would never be quite the same again.

Left above: This picture was taken soon after the change of name to SCA Transport. The author is flanked by two close operations colleagues both at RT and SCAT. Chris Halliwell (left) was Northern Area Manager whilst Ken Lewis (right) was Southern Area Manager. Both feature in this book on a number of occasions.

Above: The author pictured in the autumn of 1995 in front of the then new Aylesford Newsprint Mill. Behind are examples of the modern fleet operated by SCA Transport.

Appendices

The layout of Appendices 3 to 19 - Vehicle Details - needs some explanation:

All - with the exception of Appendix 8 - list fleet number, registration number, make, model and type, and date or year first registered.

Original purchase cost, where known, has been shown in Appendices 3,4,6, part of 17 and 19.

Payload has been shown in all Appendices except 19, where gross vehicle weight or gross train weight in metric was considered more appropriate.

Appendices 5 and 7 show, where known, the original owner of each vehicle.

Appendices 17 and 19 show in the extreme right hand column the original Depot of allocation, by letter.

A = Aylesford, D = Darwen, G = Gravesend, L = London,
N = New Hythe, T = Thatcham, W = Wigan

Appendix 1 - Certificate of Incorporation
Perkins & Glover Limited, July 7th 1930

No. 249321

Certificate of Incorporation

I Hereby Certify, That

PERKINS & GLOVER LIMITED

is this day Incorporated under the Companies Act, 1929, and that the Company is Limited.

Given under my hand at London this ___seventh___ day of ___July___ One Thousand Nine Hundred and ___thirty___.

Registrar of Companies.

(88305) 4685/25152A 5,000 3/30 M. & S. Gp. 103

Appendix 2 - Change of Name Certificate
Perkins & Glover Limited
to Reed Transport Limited, October 14th 1954

No C.172.

No. 249321

Change of Name.

Certificate *pursuant to Section 18(3) of the Companies Act, 1948.*

I Hereby Certify that

PERKINS & GLOVER LIMITED

having, with the sanction of a Special Resolution of the said Company and with the approval of the BOARD OF TRADE, changed its name, is now called

REED TRANSPORT LIMITED

and I have entered such new name on the Register accordingly.

Given under my hand at London, this **fourteenth** day of **October** One thousand nine hundred and fifty **four.**

Registrar of Companies.

28804/4469 1M (1) 12/53 (P.4601) 42967/290 2500 (1) 4/54 AT&S. 811/1.

Appendix 3 - Perkins & Glover / Reed Transport 'C' Licence fleet 1945 - 1956

Vehicles Purchased before but sold or scrapped after 1945

Fleet No	Reg'n No	Make, Model and Type	Date Reg'd	Disposal Notes
?	AUM 452	Not known		Sold 15.12.45 for £200.
?	XJ 1103	Not known		Scrapped 31.12.47.
?	XK 8834	Not known		Scrapped 31.12.47.
?	EV 5831	Dennis van uw 4t.19c.3q.	29.4.32.	Scrapped 31.12.47.
?	APH 253	Ford van		Scrapped 31.12.47.
?	XN 1363	Not known		Scrapped 31.3.49.
?	XT 6420	Not known		Scrapped 31.3.49.
?	EJJ 29	Not known		Scrapped 30.9.49.
?	DUG 180	Austin		Sold 30.1.54 for £220.

NOTES:
1 Registration numbers and disposal details taken from old ledger.
2 Registers relating to Leeds registered vehicles AUM 452 and DUG 180 are missing but an index card with West Yorkshire Archive Service confirms DUG 180 as being an Austin. No other details.
3 A Vehicle Licence Register held by Essex County Council Heritage Services confirms EV 5831 as first registered to Sydney Phillips of Bull Garage, Dagenham, model unknown.
4 The Kithead Trust confirms APH 253 as a Ford van, no other details.

Vehicles Purchased from 1945

Fleet No	Reg'n No	Make, Model and Type	Date Reg'd	Original Cost	Payload
11	GYF 997	ERF tractor + fixed s/axle trailer	1.1.45.	£2270.0s.0d	? 12 tons
12	HGN 348	Dennis Max 4 wheel rigid	7.1.46.	£1715.8s.0d	? 8 tons
? 13					
? 14		Dennis Max 4 wheel rigid	7.1.46.	£1715.8s.0d	? 8 tons
? 15		Dennis Max 4 wheel rigid	4.4.46.	£1717.4s.0d	? 8 tons
? 16		Leyland ? Hippo 6 wheel rigid	21.5.46.	£1550.0s.0d	
? 17	LME 132	Not known	15.7.46.	£2000.0s.0d	
? 18		Austin	12.3.47.	£951.19s.0d	? 9 tons
? 19		Austin	25.7.47.	£994.4s.3d	? 9 tons
? 20		Not known - possibly an Austin	25.8.47.	£1032.4s.3d	
21	HGK 928	Maudslay Maharanee + fxd s/a trl	1.8.47.	£2749.17s.8d	13 tons
22	HYR 196	Maudslay Maharanee + fxd s/a trl	1.9.47.	£2749.17s.8d	13 tons
23	JXD 213	Maudslay Maharanee + fxd s/a trl	1.12.47.	£2749.17s.8d	13 tons
24	JXD 212	Maudslay Maharanee + fxd s/a trl	16.2.48.	£2749.17s.8d	13 tons
25	JXL 198	Maudslay Mogul 4 wheel rigid	21.5.48.	£2200.2s.6d	8 tons
26	JXL 199	Maudslay Maharanee + fxd s/a trl	20.7.48.	£2779.15s.2d	13 tons
27	JXP 549	Maudslay Mogul 4 wheel rigid	11.8.48.	£2198.17s.6d	8 tons
28	JXT 657	Austin tractor + fixed s/axle trl	11.11.48.	£1120.12s.6d	9 tons
29	JXU 804	Austin tractor + fixed s/axle trl	26.1.49.	£1128.17s.6d	9 tons
30	KGN 79	Austin tractor + fixed s/axle trl	25.2.49.	£1128.17s.6d	9 tons
31	KGN 80	Maudslay Meritor 8 wheel rigid	1.2.49.	£3170.5s.0d	15 tons
32	KGN 850	Maudslay Maharanee + fxd s/a trl	31.3.49.	£2975.2s.3d	13 tons
33	KGW 238	Austin tractor + fixed s/axle trl	28.4.49.	£1075.0s.0d	9 tons
34	KGW 240	Austin tractor + fixed s/axle trl	14.5.49.	£1075.0s.0d	9 tons
35	KGY 278	Maudslay Meritor 8 wheel rigid	16.6.49.	£3170.5s.0d	15 tons

Appendix 3 continued:

Fleet No	Reg'n No	Make, Model and Type	Date Reg'd	Original Cost	Payload
36	KJJ 263	Maudslay Meritor 8 wheel rigid	10.8.49.	£3172.7s.6d	15 tons
37	KJJ 264	Austin 4 wheel rigid	20.7.49.	£748.10s.0d	6 tons
38	KLB 181	Maudslay Meritor 8 wheel rigid	21.9.49.	£3287.8s.6d	15 tons
39	KLC 996	Maudslay Meritor 8 wheel rigid	13.10.49.	£3292.8s.6d	15 tons
40	KXY 875	Austin K4 4 wheel rigid			6 tons
41	KXY 966	Maudslay Meritor 8 wheel rigd	1.2.50.	£3177.7s.6d	15 tons
42	KXY 44	Scammell 'Mechanical Horse'			
43	KXY 974	Austin tractor + fixed s/axle trl	31.3.50.	£1181.16s.6d	9 tons
44	KXY 975	Austin tractor + fixed s/axle trl	31.3.50.	£1134.6s.5d	9 tons
45	KYH 521	Maudslay Meritor 8 wheel rigid	30.3.50.	£3339.5s.0d	15 tons
46	LLX 234	Austin tractor + fixed s/axle trl	31.7.50.		9 tons
47	LUV 240	Maudslay badged AEC 8 wheel rigid	1.10.50.	£3276.10s.6d	15 tons
48	LYF 571	AEC M Major + fixed s/axle trailer	1.10.50.	£3528.18s.8d	13 tons
49	LYF 575	AEC Mammoth Major 8 wheel rigid	28.2.51.	£4093.17s.9d	15 tons
15	LYP 177	Foden FE6/15 S18 8 wheel rigid	14.6.51.	£4216.0s.4d	15 tons
10	LYP 178	Foden FE6/15 S18 8 wheel rigid	14.6.51.	£4216.0s.4d	15 tons
? 50	NKR 183	Austin A40 van	23.6.51.	£511.14s.0d	A/Depot
17	LYP 184	Foden FE6/15 S18 8 wheel rigid	2.7.51.	£4105.13s.10d	15 tons
52	MLK 139	Foden FE6/15 S18 8 wheel rigid	2.10.51.	£4446.11s.0d	15 tons
16	MLD 725	Foden FE6/15 S18 8 wheel rigid	22.10.51.	£4446.11s.0d	15 tons
51	MLF 156	Foden FE6/15 S18 8 wheel rigid	30.10.51.	£4448.6s.7d	15 tons
53	MLL 255	Foden FE6/15 S18 8 wheel rigid	20.12.51.	£4471.11s.0d	15 tons
54	MUL 540	Austin Loadstar 4 wheel rigid	28.2.52.	£1073.17s.5d	6 tons
55	MXD 544	Foden FE6/15 S18 8 wheel rigid	2.1.52.	£4459.19s.1d	15 tons
56	MXL 220	Bedford S/Scammell tractor	31.5.52.	£1133.6s.10d	10 tons
57	MXL 982	Foden FE6/12 S18 6 wheel rigid	31.5.52.	£4836.4s.4d	12 tons
58	MXL 740	Bedford S/Scammell tractor (see notes 12/14)			10 tons
59	MXV 580	Bedford S/Scammell tractor	15.8.52.	£1186.7s.9d	10 tons
60	NGN 52	Foden FE6/15 S18 8 wheel rigid	31.10.52.	£4830.18s.6d	15 tons
61	NGO 52	Foden FETU6/20 S18 + s/axle trl	31.10.52.	£4473.11s.8d	13 tons
62	NLR 354	Foden FE6/12 S18 6 wheel rigid	31.1.53.	£4925.7s.7d	12 tons
100	OLC 444	Austin A70 pickup	30.11.53.	£735.9s.7d	L/Depot
63	OLL 534	Bedford S/Scammell tractor	7.5.54.	£1530.4s.1d	10 tons
64	JFN 193	Bedford S/Scammell tractor	7.5.54.		10 tons
59	JFN 194	Bedford S/Scammell tractor	7.5.54.	£1532.18s.4d	10 tons
65	TKR 100	Bedford S/Scammell tractor	10.11.54.	£1479.3s.7d	10 tons
66	TKR 98	Bedford S/Scammell tractor	10.11.54.	£1479.3s.7d	10 tons
67	UKE 515	Austin KR/WA Loadstar 4whl rigid	28.12.54.	£1511.11s.10d	6 tons
68	UKO 94	Foden FG6/12 S18 6 wheel rigid	28.3.55.	£4150.7s.6d	12 tons
69	UKP 155	Foden FG6/12 S18 6 wheel rigid	9.4.55.	£4150.7s.6d	12 tons
70	UKP 406	Foden FG6/12 S18 6 wheel rigid	22.4.55.	£4162.16s.11d	12 tons
72	VKE 741	Foden FG6/12 S18 6 wheel rigid	26.5.55.	£4282.10s.7d	12 tons
73	VKM 733	Foden FG6/12 S18 6 wheel rigid	20.7.55.	£4289.8s.1d	12 tons
71	VKM 955	Foden FG6/12 S18 6 wheel rigid	16.8.55.	£4286.13s.9d	12 tons
74	WKE 472	Foden FG6/12 S18 6 wheel rigid	31.10.55.	£4221.3s.9d	12 tons
17	XKL 320	Foden FG6/24 S18 8 wheel rigid	9.5.56.	£4802.0s.0d	15 tons
24	XKN 846	Foden FGTU6/25 S18 + t/axle trl	14.6.56.	£4537.11s.10d	15 tons
? 14	XKO 267	Austin 7K/FED3 4 wheel rigid	22.6.56.	£2062.13s.6d	8 tons
13	XKP 847	Austin 7K/FED3 4 wheel rigid	16.7.56.	£2065.7s.11d	8 tons
28	XKR 654	Austin 5K/FED3/Scammell tractor	30.7.56.	£1584.15s.6d	12 tons
20	XKR 655	Austin 5K/FED3/Scammell tractor	30.7.56.	£1601.10s.6d	12 tons
75	XKT 214	Austin 7K/FED3 4 wheel rigid	15.8.56.	£2062.11s.11d	8 tons
58	YKE 121	Austin 5K/FED3/TE/Scam tractor	6.9.56.	£1601.17s.6d	12 tons
56	YKE 122	Austin 5K/FED3/TE/Scam tractor	6.9.56.	£1601.11s.6d	12 tons

Appendix 3 continued:

NOTES:

1. Reference those vehicles set against fleet nos 11 to 20, a number of assumptions have been made, based on ledger entries from 1945 to 1947. A copy of ledger page 4 has been included at Appendix 21. No.11 was definitely an ERF tractor with fixed single axle trailer and a posed side view photograph is featured below. It may have been the new lorry supplied by Maskells on 1st January 1945 at a cost of £2250 + £20.
To fit the remaining unidentifiable ledger entries into the fleet list, it has been assumed that 13 was missed out. No.12 was definitely a Dennis Max, as were certainly 14 & 15. The ledger costs suggest they were all the same. The 2 Austins were probably tractors with fixed single axle trailers as the cost prices compare with those of identified Austin artics 28 etc. The unknown vehicle set against 20 was also probably the same judging by the cost. The Leyland and LME 132 remain mysteries.
2. Ledger page 5 is also included in Appendix 21, this covering identifiable vehicles down to 38 - KLB 181.
3. 21 - HGK 928 and 22 - HYR 196 were both accident write offs.
4. 24 - JXD 212 was an accident write off in November 1955.
5. 42 - KXY 44. A ledger entry shows this vehicle as being sold 29.1.55. Logic suggests the number was 42.
6. 43 and 44 - KXY 974/975 were on hire to Reed Corrugated Cases, Brentford.
7. 47 - LUV 240 was Maudslay badged.
8. 48 - LYF 571 was believed to have been Maudslay badged.
9. 47 - LUV 240, 49 - LYF 575, 15 - LYP 177, 10 - LYP 178 and 55 - MXD 544 were later fitted with RT built fibreglass cabs and wraparound windscreens, see photographs.
10. 50 - NKR 183 is believed to have been based at Aylesford.
11. Four of the 1951 Foden S18 rigids LYP 184, MLK 139, MLF 156 and MLD 725 were transferred to the A Licence fleet and renumbered 220, 216, 218 and 217. See Appendix 6.
12. A ledger entry dated 26.9.53. confirms MXL 740 as stolen with an original cost of £2737.8s.3d. This would have included the cost of two trailers purchased at the same time. A further entry shows the write-off reduced by depreciation of £905.8s.3d and another entry related to one trailer not stolen and reinstated at £600. It has been confirmed as being no 58 although 59 seems more likely.
13. The explanation for 60 and 61 as 1952 vehicles carrying 52 as part of their registration numbers can be explained by the fact that they were included on the Foden's Motor Show stand in that year. Both were fitted with distinctive cream steering wheels, Foden practice for Show exhibits.
14. Several Bedford S tractors appear in asset registers but it is uncertain which ones started life in the C Licence fleet and which in the Local fleet. It is also likely that some were transferred from road work to internal Mill work as the Austin tractors came into the fleet in 1956. If JFN 194 was the replacement for stolen MXL 740 then it seems logical that MXL 740 was 59 and MXV 580 was 58. Unfortunately the registration date of MXL 740 is unknown which would have helped confirm this view.
15. The Foden build sheet for 24 - XKN 846 shows the original customer entered as Maskells/Reeds Transport Ltd. This was then crossed through and another operator - West Transport Ltd, Johnson Brook Garage, Ashton Road, Newton, Hyde, Ches. added. One might speculate that RT tried to cancel the order after build had commenced, Foden found another customer but RT then had a change of mind and reinstated the order?
16. The number of XKO 267 is uncertain. However, a photograph exists of an unregistered 14, almost certainly XKO 267.

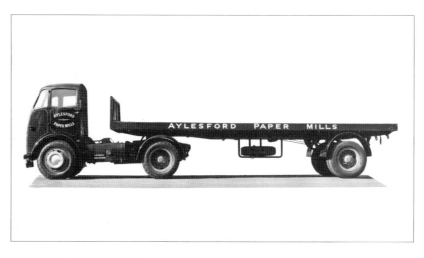

Appendix 4 - Aylesford 'Local' vehicles of Albert E. Reed absorbed into Reed Transport fleet with subsequent additions 1954 - 1956

Fleet No	Reg'n No	Make, Model and Type	Date Reg'd	Original Cost	Payload
?	DKP 814	Dennis	7.5.37.		?
?	DKP 815	Dennis	7.5.37.		?
?	GKO 18	Dennis - model unknown,uw 4t.10c.	31.8.39.		?
?	GKR 601	Austin	27.11.41.		?
106		Austin tractor + fixed s/axle trl			9 tons
107					
108		Dennis Max 4 wheel rigid			7/8 tons
109		Dennis Max 4 wheel rigid			7/8 tons
110	HKM 153	Commer 14A 4 wheel rigid	9.2.46.		? 6 tons
111	See note 6				
112	See note 6				
113	See note 2				
114	KKK 785	Vulcan 4 wheel rigid	16.2.48.		7 tons
115	KKK 278	Austin K45V tractor +fixed s/a trl	1.7.48.	£987.10s.6d	9 tons
116	KGH 324	Bedford O/Scammell tractor	10.1.49.	£674.0s.0d	10 tons
117	LKK 956	Vulcan 4 wheel rigid	8.3.49.		7 tons
118	HMU 801	Morris Commercial van			?
119	MKE 439	Vulcan 6VF 4 wheel rigid	21.11.49.		7 tons
120	MKM 194	Austin Loadstar K4WA 4 whl rigid	6.4.50.	£687.0s.0d	6 tons
121	NKM 406	Commer Superpoise 27A 4 whl rigid	16.2.51.	£968.0s.0d	6 tons
122	LYL 72	Bedford O/Scammell tractor			10 tons
123	MLA 776	Bedford O/Scammell tractor	18.7.51.	£1035.19s.6d	10 tons
124	OKE 220	Morris Comm. FV12/5 4 whl rigid	23.7.51.	£1004.5s.7d	6/7 ton
125	MLF 42	Bedford O/Scammell tractor	16.11.51.	£895.8s.1d	10 tons
126	OKR 548	Scammell Scarab tractor	5.5.52.		6 tons
127	MUL 437	Bedford	5.2.52.	£1668.11s.11d	Garage
?	MXL 219	Bedford S/Scammell tractor	16.4.52.	£1127.16s.10d	10 tons
?	NGF 613	Bedford O/Scammell tractor	4.11.52.	£971.15s.8d	10 tons
130	RKN 454	Austin Loadstar K4WA 4 whl rigid	1.8.53.	£999.14s.10d	6 tons
131	SKE 39	Bedford A5STO 4 wheel tipper	1.12.53.		?
132	SKE 590	Bedford A5SCO 4 wheel tipper	12.12.53.	£1434.7s.4d	?
133	SKJ 406	Bedford A5SCO 4 wheel tipper	1.1.54.	£1434.7s.4d	?
?	SKK 297	Commer D4 van	29.1.54.	£542.12s.1d	Garage
? 137	NGX 582	Bedford S/Scammell tractor	26.11.52.	£1187.17s.6d	10 tons
? 145	NUW 845	Bedford S/Scammell tractor	31.10.53.	£1105.9s.1d	10 tons
?	OLD 270	Bedford S/Scammell tractor	20.2.54.	£1067.12s.7d	10 tons
138	CEW 504	AEC 6 wheel rigid	30.9.41.	Ex BRS	10 tons
139	KKR 492	Vulcan 6PF 4 wheel rigid	1.9.48.	Ex BRS	7 tons
140	WKJ 241	Karrier 71A refuse collector	31.10.55.	£818.10s.0d	?
?	OKT 468	Morris Commercial JR van	13.6.52.		?
?	UKR 608	Commer pickup	2.6.55.	£520.5s.4d	Garage
118	XKM 545	Austin LDO2A van	1.7.56.	£1011.15s.0d	1 1/2 ton
117	YKK 907	Austin 7K/FED3 4 wheel rigid	2.11.56.	£2078.12s.1d	8 tons

NOTES :

1   DKP 814 is ledger recorded as being scrapped in November 1955. No information exists on DKP 815, GKO 18 and GKR 601 except within the Local Taxation Office archives. Fleet numbers of all four are unknown although the Dennises may have been numbered 7, 8 and 9 pre Reed Transport, see Chapter 3

2   Original fleet number 13 (113) probably didn't exist.

3   106,108,109,117 and 139 were used on general deliveries mainly for the Paper Mill.

Appendix 4 continued:

4   Attempts have been made to identify the registration numbers of 108 and 109. They had the post War "rounded" cab and were probably the C7 model. Both were in service in 1956. Searches of LTO archives failed to find any more Kent registered Dennisses. Which leaves the possibility that they were transferred from the Perkins & Glover fleet, see Appendix 3, speculatively identified as 12, 14 or 15 dating from 1946 and were London registered.

5   110 - HKM 153 had a side access enclosed body and used for the collection and delivery of reel centres for the Paper Mill.

6   JXA 923 was a Bedford O/Scammell tractor probably numbered 111 or 112

7   114 and 115 were used for internal reelstock movements for the Corrugated Cases factory.

8   118 - HMU 801 was the so called Town Van. See Chapter 3.

9   The role of 119 - LKK 956 is unknown.

10   120 and 130 were used on multi drop Home Counties deliveries for Brookgate Industries.

11   121 - NKM 406 was the Home Counties delivery vehicle for Brookgate Industries Towelling Division.

12   124 and 126 were used for internal reelstock movements for Medway Paper Sacks. No 126 worked with three small Scammell trailers.

13   127 - MUL 437 was a mobile workshops used on-site for the maintenance of cranes and miscellaneous plant.

14   The 3 tippers Nos 131, 132 and 133 worked for the Paper Mill clearing boiler house waste etc to various disposal sites.

15   Bedford O and S tractors appear in an asset register as "Local Fleet", fleet numbers not shown. An unofficial note sets no 137 against NGX 582 and no 145 against NUW 845.These cannot be verified and throw the numbering sequence in relation to registration dates out of sequence. 126,127,130,131,132,133,138,139 and 140 are definitely correct.

16   Refer to Appendix 5 for more details on 138 and 139.

17   138 - CEW 504 mainly operated on-site for the Paper Mill Civil Engineers.

18   140 - WKJ 241 cleared general rubbish throughout the Aylesford site.

19   All the Bedford/Scammell tractors were used within the Paper Mill moving raw materials and finished stock on a 24 hour day shift operation.

20   118 - XKM 545 was a straight replacement for the older van HMU 801

21   117 - YKK 907 was a straight replacement for the Vulcan LKK 956.

22   OKT 468 was registered new to Hygiene Products (Great Britain) Ltd and was presumably a secondhand purchase. It carried the fleet no 820 by unknown date - a post 1960 Thatcham number. Everything about this van remains a mystery.

Appendix 5 - Vehicles acquired from BRS 1955

BRS 61F no.	RT flt no	Reg'n No	Make, Model and Type	Date Reg'd	Payload	Orig or pre - BRS Owner
75	201	JKO 369	Vulcan 9VFA tractor+fixed s/a trlr	2.7.47.	10 tons	Kent Carriers
102	202	KYF 310	Vulcan 6PF 4 wheel rigid	25.3.50.	7 tons	BRS
103	203	KYF 309	Vulcan 6PF 4 wheel rigid	25.3.50.	7 tons	BRS
104	204	KYF 308	Vulcan 6PF 4 wheel rigid	25.3.50.	7 tons	BRS
107	205	KYF 313	Vulcan 6PF 4 wheel rigid	25.3.50.	7 tons	BRS
122	206	KKR 492	Vulcan 6PF 4 wheel rigid	1.9.48.	7 tons	R&W Tolhurst
123	207	KKR 500	Vulcan 6PF 4 wheel rigid	1.10.48.	7 tons	R&W Tolhurst
187	208	JKO 209	Bedford OXC/Scammell tractor	1.6.47.	10 tons	W.Arnold
188	209	GKP 616	Bedford OWSC/Scammell tractor	24.4.44.	10 tons	W.Arnold
189	210	KKT 711	Bedford OSS/Scammell tractor	15.9.48.	10 tons	W.Arnold
224	211	KKK 604	Bedford OSS/Scammell tractor	1.2.48.	10 tons	Harper
251	212	HME 185	AEC 4 wheel Matador 0346 rigid	30.9.38.	7 tons	Medway Trans
			originally taxed as a wagon and trailer with Carrimore drawbar T61F321			
254	213	BEW 473	AEC Mammoth Major 6 wheel 0366L rigid	9.3.39.	12 tons	Medway Trans
256	214	BEW 458	AEC Mammoth Major 8 wheel 0386 rigid	1.3.39.	15 tons	Medway Trans
257	215	HKK 445	Atkinson M1266 FC 6 wheel rigid	30.11.45.	12 tons	Medway Trans
258	216	HG 6801	AEC Mammoth Major 8 wheel 0386 rigid	17.10.38.	15 tons	Medway Trans
259	217	BEW 486	AEC Mammoth Major 8 wheel 0386 rigid	11.3.39.	15 tons	Medway Trans
261	218	BEW 535	AEC Mammoth Major 8 wheel 0386 rigid	25.3.39.	15 tons	Medway Trans
262	219	CEW 504	AEC Mammoth Minor 6 wheel 0366L rigid	30.9.41.	12 tons	Medway Trans
266	220	HKT 142	AEC Mammoth Major 8 wheel 0386 rigid	1.9.46.	15 tons	Medway Trans

Appendix 5 continued:

BRS 61F no.	RT flt no	Reg'n No	Make, Model and Type	Date Reg'd	Payload	Orig or pre - BRS Owner
269	221	KKP 875	AEC Mammoth Major 8 wheel 0386 rigid	21.7.48.	15 tons	Medway Trans
275	222	KXY 430	Vulcan 6PF 4 wheel rigid	18.1.50.	7 tons	BRS
276	223	KXY 429	Vulcan 6PF 4 wheel rigid	17.1.50.	7 tons	BRS
278	224	DYY 182	AEC Mammoth Major 8 wheel 0386 rigid	1.8.37.	15 tons	Thomas Tilling
280	225	JXE 231	AEC Mammoth Major 8 wheel 0386 rigid	23.1.48.	15 tons	Thomas Tilling
281	226	JXE 232	AEC Mammoth Major 8 wheel 0386 rigid	10.2.48.	15 tons	Thomas Tilling
296	227	KKT 749	Vulcan 6PF 4 wheel rigid	12.10.48.	7 tons	See note 9
301	228	LLU 302	AEC Mammoth Major 8 wheel 3871 rigid	20.6.50.	15 tons	BRS
303	229	LLU 321	AEC Mammoth Major 8 wheel 3871 rigid	1.7.50.	15 tons	BRS
305	230	LLX 523	Vulcan 6PF 4 wheel rigid	15.9.50.	7 tons	BRS
310	231	LLX 536	Vulcan 6PF 4 wheel rigid	22.9.50.	7 tons	BRS
319	232	LLX 534	Bedford O/Scammell tractor	22.9.50.	10 tons	BRS
327	233	LUC 840	Vulcan 6PF 4 wheel rigid	10.11.50.	7 tons	BRS
371	234	LKR 140	Vulcan 6PF 4 wheel rigid	1.10.49.	7 tons	HJ.Manwaring
374	235	LKT 752	AEC Matador 3472 + fixed Dyson single axle trailer (ex BRS T61F345)	13.9.49.	12 tons	HJ.Manwaring
376	236	MKT 795	AEC Matador 3472 + fixed 'homemade' s/axle trailer (ex BRS T61F377)	16.8.50.	12 tons	HJ.Manwaring
380	237	MLC 101	Vulcan 6PF 4 wheel rigid	11.7.51.	7 tons	BRS
404	238	MLC 184	Vulcan 6PF 4 wheel rigid	1.9.51.	7 tons	BRS
414	239	HKE 378	Vulcan 6PF 4 wheel rigid	1.12.44.	7 tons	C.Hitch

NOTES:

1   It is clear that the fleet number range 201 to 239 was allocated in the same sequence as the BRS 61F numbering. Therefore a logical assumption has been made regarding some of the vehicles for which records no longer exist.

2   201 - JKO 369 was scrapped about 9/55 and was a fixed artic with trailer SA1 attached. SA1 was retained and converted to full auto coupling.

3   Six 24ft Scammell type auto coupling flat platform trailers were included in acquisition. They were allocated numbers SA2 to SA7 (Special A)

4   206 - KKR 492 was transferred to the Local Fleet, renumbered 139. See Appendix 4.

5   213 - BEW 473 and 217 - BEW 486 were first registered to Greenwoods of Ramsey. Other Huntingdon registered vehicles may have been similarly registered originally.

6   219 - CEW 504 is recorded as being first registered to 'Greenwoods for Medway' It was a 6 wheel rigid with single wheels trailing axle, probably originally a 4 wheel rigid extended by Greenwoods or Medway Transport. It was transferred to the Local Fleet and renumbered 138. See Appendix 4

7   220 - HKT 142 according to LTO records was described as ex WD and registered to Medway Transport Ltd on 1.9.46. Actually manufactured in February 1942, chassis no 0386 654, supplied to Bouts-Tillotson Transport Ltd from whom it was presumably requisitioned by the WD. It was stolen in 1955, recovered as a complete wreck.

8   224 - DYY 182, 225 - JXE 231 and 226 - JXE 232 were originally transferred from Newington Butts Group, of which Thomas Tilling was also a part, to Mid Kent Group in 1950.

9   227 - KKT 749 according to the LTO Records was first registered to Bristow, no address given. BRS records show it was acquired from Rede Court Transport Ltd, 'Brooklyn', Chatham Road, Sandling, Maidstone on 27.6.50 as Unit A383.

10   236 - MKT 795 was fitted with a 11.3 litre engine.

11   Trading addresses of original or pre BRS owners are as follows:
         The main base of the Thomas Tilling Ltd operation was Searles Road, London SE1.
             Their London Road, Larkfield Depot was to become Unit 66/6554 for tendering.
         W.Arnold & Sons Ltd., Branbridges, Paddock Wood.
         Harper's Transport, 130 London Road, Southborough, Tonbridge.
         C. Hitch & Sons, Padsole Lane, Maidstone.
         Kent Carriers Ltd, Sutton Road, Maidstone. Also Balls Pond Road, London N1.
         H.J.Manwaring, 'The Nortons', Maidstone Road, Collier Street, Marden.
         Medway Transport Ltd, Pump Lane, Rainham, Gillingham.
         R & W. Tolhurst, Ashford Road, Bearsted, Maidstone.

12   This appendix was compiled with additional information kindly provided by Mike Houle and John Mollett.

Appendix 6 - Vehicle Replacements for ex BRS Fleet 1955 - 1958

Transfers from Perkins & Glover London Fleet
- renumbered with numbers reused

Fleet No	Reg'n No	Make, Model and Type	Date Reg'd	Original Cost	Payload
220	LYP 184	Foden FE6/15 S18 8 wheel rigid	2.7.51.	£4105.13s.10d	15 tons
216	MLK 139	Foden FE6/15 S18 8 wheel rigid	2.10.51.	£4446.11s.0d	15 tons
218	MLF 156	Foden FE6/15 S18 8 wheel rigid	30.10.51.	£4448.6s.7d	15 tons
217	MLD 725	Foden FE6/15 S18 8 wheel rigid	22.10.51.	£4446.11s.0d	15 tons

New Purchases - most numbers reused

Fleet No	Reg'n No	Make, Model and Type	Date Reg'd	Original Cost	Payload
206	WKN 130	Austin 7K/FED3 4 wheel rigid	1.1.56.	£1710.6s.8d	7 tons
214	WKN 311	Foden FG6/15 S18 8 wheel rigid	1.1.56.	£4666.18s.4d	15 tons
238	WKR 81	Austin 7K/FED3 4 wheel rigid	17.2.56.	£1746.7s.5d	7 tons
224	XKE 422	Foden FG6/24 S18 8 wheel rigid	25.3.56.	£4693.3s.9d	15 tons
231	XKK 694	Austin 7K/FED3 4 wheel rigid	11.5.56.	£1696.15s.10d	7 tons
213	XKK 698	Foden DFG5/17 S18 6 wheel rigid	1.5.56.	£4018.0s.5d	11 tons
219	XKK 699	Foden DFG5/17 S18 6 wheel rigid	1.5.56.	£4018.0s.5d	11 tons
204	XKO 972	Austin 7K/DKD3 4 wheel rigid	3.7.56.	£1853.10s.6d	7 tons
207	XKP 846	Austin 7K/FED3 4 wheel rigid	16.7.56.	£1872.18s.0d	7 tons
202	XKR 107	Austin 7K/FED3 4 wheel rigid	19.7.56.	£1870.16s.9d	7 tons
201	XKR 653	Austin 5K/FED3 Scammell tractor	30.7.56.	£1601.17s.9d	10 tons
205	XKT 24	Austin 7K/FED3 4 wheel rigid	8.8.56.	£1878.3s.4d	7 tons
215	YKP 105	Foden FG6/24 S20 8 wheel rigid	6.2.57.	£4704.9s.8d	15 tons
240	YKT 173	Foden FG6/24 8 whl rigid (note 3)	11.3.57.	£4875.1s.2d	15 tons
209	401 AKJ	Austin 5K/FED3T Scammell tractor	10.4.57.	£1549.18s.6d	10 tons
241	36 AKK	Foden FG6/24 S20 8 wheel rigid	16.4.57.	£4713.4s.10d	15 tons
208	564 AKK	Austin 5K/FED3T Scammell tractor	25.4.57.	£1602.9s.8d	10 tons
211	565 AKK	Austin 5K/FED3T Scammell tractor	25.4.57.	£1602.5s.0d	10 tons
232	566 AKK	Austin 5K/FED3T Scammell tractor	25.4.57.	£1576.8s.4d	10 tons
242	164 AKM	Foden FG6/24 S20 8 wheel rigid	14.5.57.	£4713.11s.6d	15 tons
210	170 AKM	Austin 5K/FED3T Scammell tractor	18.5.57.	£1556.19s.2d	10 tons
231	109 CKR	Austin MKC/FED3 4 wheel rigid	22.5.58.	£2295.16s.8d	7 tons

NOTES:
1   Replacement vehicles took the fleet numbers of those specific ex BRS vehicles they replaced.
    The three Fodens 240, 241 and 242 probably on paper replaced several 4 wheel rigids to keep within the SA
    Licence rules of unladen weights hence the extension to the numbering beyond 239. See Appendix 5.
2   231 - XKK 694 was written off and scrapped by 1.4.58.
3   240 - YKT 173 had a fibreglass cab, not an S20. See photograph. A copy of the original build sheet was
    obtained from Foden archives held by Chester Record Office but cab details were not indicated.
4   231 - 109 CKR had a fibreglass cab. A replacement for the earlier 231 - XKK 694. See photograph.

Appendix 7 - Vehicles acquired in 1960 from Cropper & Colthrop

Fleet No	Reg'n No	Make, Model and Type	Date Reg'd	Payload	Orig Owner
710	ARX 611	Albion CX27 twin steer 6 whl rigid	10.11.37.	10 tons	TRTS
711	RMO 630	Foden KG6/24 S20 8 wheel rigid	1959	15 tons	C&C
712	BMO 858	Albion CX27 twin steer 6 whl rigid	28.2.39.	10 tons	TRTS
714	SMO 640	Commer TS3 4 wheel rigid	11.5.59.	7 tons	C&C
715	CJB 61	Albion CX5 5 cyl 6 whl rigid	30.4.40.	10 tons	TRTS
716	RMO 639	Austin BMC/Scammell tractor	1959	10 tons	C&C
717	CRX 50	Foden DG6/12 6 wheel rigid	14.2.44.	11 tons	TRTS
718	CRX 674	ERF/AEC 7.7 C15 tractor	26.9.45.	10 tons	TRTS
719	CRX 675	ERF/AEC 7.7 C15 recovery tractor	27.7.46.	-	TRTS
720	CDP 738	Morris Commercial van	1946	2 tons	Talbot Serpell
721	PBL 817	Austin BMC/Scammell tractor	1958	10 tons	C&C
722	RMO 631	Foden KG6/24 S20 8 wheel rigid	1959	15 tons	C&C
723	EBL 933	Foden DG5/10 6 wheel rigid	28.11.47.	11 tons	TRTS
724	EBL 843	Foden DG5/10 6 wheel rigid	31.10.47.	11 tons	TRTS
725	EBL 342	Foden DG6/15 8 wheel rigid	22.8.47.	15 tons	TRTS
726	ERX 249	Albion CX7 8 wheel rigid	1.11.48.	15 tons	TRTS
727	EJB 525	Foden DG5/10 6 wheel rigid	21.2.48.	11 tons	TRTS
728	EJB 435	Foden DG5/10 6 wheel rigid	21.2.48.	11 tons	TRTS
729	EJB 637	Foden DG5/10 6 wheel rigid	11.3.48.	11 tons	TRTS
730	EJB 445	Foden DG5/10 6 wheel rigid	21.2.48.	11 tons	TRTS
731	GOR 582	Vulcan 4 wheel canvas tilt rigid	1948	6 tons	Hutton
732	CRD 477	AEC Mammoth Major 8 wheel rigid	1948	15 tons	Talbot Serpell
733	EJB 562	Bedford OSS/Scammell tractor	28.2.48.	10 tons	TRTS
734	EMO 164	Bedford OSS/Scammell tractor	30.6.48.	10 tons	TRTS
735	EMO 966	Bedford OLB 4 wheel rigid	1.10.48.	6 tons	TRTS
736	EJB 470	Bedford OSB 4 wheel tipper	1.4.48.	4 tons	TRTS
737	EMO 683	Thornycroft/Coles mobile crane	1942	-	Ex RAF 1948
738	FBL 234	Albion Chieftain 4 wheel rigid	1949	7 tons	TRTS
739	ERX 627	Foden FG6/15 S18 8 wheel rigid	1.1.49.	15 tons	TRTS
740	FBL 932	Foden FG6/15 S18 8 wheel rigid	1949	15 tons	TRTS
741	FJB 36	Foden FG6/15 S18 8 wheel rigid	1949	15 tons	TRTS
742	ERX 641	Foden FG6/15 S18 8 wheel rigid	1.1.49.	15 tons	TRTS
743	ERX 646	Foden FG6/15 S18 8 wheel rigid	1.1.49.	15 tons	TRTS
744	FBL 48	Foden FG6/15 S18 8 wheel rigid	1949	15 tons	TRTS
745	FJB 952	Foden FG6/15 S18 8 wheel rigid	1949	15 tons	TRTS
746	FJB 971	Foden FG6/15 S18 8 wheel rigid	1949	15 tons	TRTS
747	EDP 438	AEC Mammoth Major 8 wheel rigid	1949	15 tons	Talbot Serpell
748	FMO 308	Foden FG6/15 S18 8 wheel rigid	1950	15 tons	BRS
749	FMO 609	Foden FG6/15 S18 8 wheel rigid	1950	15 tons	BRS
750	FMO 728	Foden FG6/15 S18 8 wheel rigid	1950	15 tons	BRS
751	ERD 610	AEC Mammoth Major 8 wheel rigid	1950	15 tons	Talbot Serpell
752	FRX 867	Albion Chieftain 4 wheel rigid	1950	7 tons	BRS
753	GBL 68	Albion Chieftain 4 wheel rigid	1950	7 tons	BRS
754	FRX 272	Albion Chieftain 4 wheel rigid	1950	7 tons	BRS
755	GBL 573	Albion Chieftain 4 wheel rigid	1950	7 tons	BRS
756	NEL 553	Guy Otter Perkins P6 4 whl rigid	1953	7 tons	BRS
757	NEL 554	Guy Otter Perkins P6 4 whl rigid	1953	7 tons	BRS
758	NEL 555	Guy Otter Perkins P6 4 whl rigid	1953	7 tons	BRS
759	NEL 556	Guy Otter Perkins P6 4 whl rigid	1953	7 tons	BRS
760	NEL 557	Guy Otter Perkins P6 4 whl rigid	1953	7 tons	BRS
761	NEL 558	Guy Otter Perkins P6 4 whl rigid	1953	7 tons	BRS
762	NEL 560	Guy Otter Perkins P6 4 whl rigid	1953	7 tons	BRS

sponsored by# Reed *TRANSPORT*

Appendix 7 continued:

Fleet No	Reg'n No	Make, Model and Type	Date Reg'd	Payload	Orig. Owner
763	NEL 561	Guy Otter Perkins P6 4 whl rigid	1953	7 tons	BRS
764	NEL 562	Guy Otter Perkins P6 4 whl rigid	1953	7 tons	BRS
765	NEL 563	Guy Otter Perkins P6 4 whl rigid	1953	7 tons	BRS
766	NEL 585	Guy Otter Perkins P6 4 whl rigid	1953	7 tons	BRS
767	NEL 586	Guy Otter Perkins P6 4 whl rigid	1953	7 tons	BRS
768	NEL 588	Guy Otter Perkins P6 4 whl rigid	1953	7 tons	BRS
769	NEL 793	Guy Otter Perkins P6 4 whl rigid	1953	7 tons	BRS
770	NEL 794	Guy Otter Perkins P6 4 whl rigid	1953	7 tons	BRS
771	NEL 795	Guy Otter Perkins P6 4 whl rigid	1953	7 tons	BRS
772	LRX 401	Albion Chieftain/Scammell tractor	1955	10 tons	C&C
773	LRX 402	Albion Chieftain/Scammell tractor	1955	10 tons	C&C
774	LRX 403	Albion Chieftain/Scammell tractor	1955	10 tons	C&C
775	LRX 404	Albion Chieftain 4 wheel rigid	1955	7 tons	C&C
776	LRX 405	Albion Chieftain 4 wheel rigid	1955	7 tons	C&C
777	LRX 406	Albion Chieftain 4 wheel rigid	1955	7 tons	C&C
778	LRX 407	Albion Chieftain 4 wheel rigid	1955	7 tons	C&C
779	MMO 208	Albion Chieftain /Scammell tractor	1956	10 tons	C&C
780	MMO 209	Albion Chieftain /Scammell tractor	1956	10 tons	C&C
781	MMO 210	Albion Chieftain /Scammell tractor	1956	10 tons	C&C
782	MMO 211	Albion Chieftain /Scammell tractor	1956	10 tons	C&C
783	MMO 296	Commer TS3 4 wheel rigid	1956	7 tons	C&C
784	OBL 501	Foden KG6/24 S20 8 wheel rigid	2.10.57.	15 tons	C&C
785	OBL 502	Foden KG6/24 S20 8 wheel rigid	2.10.57.	15 tons	C&C
786	OBL 503	Foden KG6/24 S20 8 wheel rigid	2.10.57.	15 tons	C&C
787	OJB 712	Austin BMC/Scammell tractor	1957	10 tons	C&C
788	OJB 714	Austin BMC/Scammell tractor	1957	10 tons	C&C
789	OJB 715	Austin BMC/Scammell tractor	1957	10 tons	C&C
790	ORX 116	Austin BMC 4 wheel rigid	1957	7 tons	C&C
791	PBL 818	Austin BMC/Scammell tractor	1958	10 tons	C&C
792	PBL 819	Austin BMC/Scammell tractor	1958	10 tons	C&C
793	PBL 820	Austin BMC/Scammell tractor	1958	10 tons	C&C
794	PRX 921	Austin BMC/Scammell tractor	1958	10 tons	C&C
795	PRX 922	Austin BMC/Scammell tractor	1958	10 tons	C&C
796	PRX 923	Austin BMC/Scammell tractor	1958	10 tons	C&C
797	PRX 924	Austin BMC/Scammell tractor	1958	10 tons	C&C
798	RJB 326	Foden FGTU6/20 S20 tractor	1.11.58.	15 tons	C&C
799	RJB 329	Foden FGTU6/20 S20 tractor	1.11.58.	15 tons	C&C
	Trlrs 43-46	Eagle t/axle air suspension trlrs	1958		C&C

NOTES:
1. 710 - ARX 611 served at Dunkirk in the Second World War.
2. 719 - CRX 675 is now restored in preservation.
3. All Austin BMC and Albion tractors and Guy Otter rigids had Eaton 2 speed axles.
4. 723, 724, 727, 728, 729, 730 Fodens had single wheel rear axles.
5. 726 - ERX 249 cost £3024 new and was ex 1948 Commercial Motor Show.
6. 735 - EMO 966 cost £627 new and was the half millionth Bedford off the line.
7. 737 - EMO 683 was an Amazon 6 wheel petrol rigid dating from 1942 but first registered in 1948.
8. Talbot - Serpell of Cardiff Road, Reading became BRS Reading.
9. 748, 749, 750 Fodens and 752 to 755 Albions were ordered by TRTS but delivered new to BRS.
10. 783 - MMO 296 was sold to Colthrop Board Mills, converted to a gully emptier.
11. This appendix was compiled from information kindly supplied by Stuart Wise.

Appendix 8 - Vehicles operated by TRTS and Cropper & Colthrop between 1934 and 1959, none acquired by Reed Transport

Reg'n No	Make, Model and Type	Year Reg'd	Payload
JB 4001	Albion 6 wheel rigid	1934	12 tons
JB 4002	Albion 6 wheel rigid	1934	12 tons
JB 4003	Albion 6 wheel rigid	1934	12 tons
JB 4004	Albion 6 wheel rigid	1934	12 tons
JB 4005	Albion 6 wheel rigid	1934	12 tons
JB 4006	Albion 6 wheel rigid	1934	12 tons
JB 5240	Albion 6 wheel rigid	1934	12 tons
JB 5241	Albion 6 wheel rigid	1934	12 tons
JB 5242	Albion 6 wheel rigid	1934	12 tons
JB 5243	Albion 6 wheel rigid	1934	12 tons
JB 6145	Albion 6 wheel rigid	1935	12 tons
JB 6146	Albion 6 wheel rigid	1935	12 tons
JB 6147	Albion 6 wheel rigid	1935	12 tons
JB 6148	Albion 6 wheel rigid	1935	12 tons
JB 6149	Albion 6 wheel rigid	1935	12 tons
JB 6150	Albion 6 wheel rigid	1935	12 tons
JB 7144	Albion 6 wheel rigid	1935	12 tons
JB 9924	Albion 4 wheel rigid	1936	7 $\frac{1}{2}$ tons
JB 9925	Albion 4 wheel rigid	1936	7 $\frac{1}{2}$ tons
JB 9926	Albion 4 wheel rigid	1936	7 $\frac{1}{2}$ tons
JB 9927	Albion 4 wheel rigid	1936	7 $\frac{1}{2}$ tons
JB 9928	Albion 4 wheel rigid	1936	7 $\frac{1}{2}$ tons
JB 9929	Albion 4 wheel rigid	1936	7 $\frac{1}{2}$ tons
JB 9930	Albion 4 wheel rigid	1936	7 $\frac{1}{2}$ tons
JB 9931	Albion 4 wheel rigid	1936	7 $\frac{1}{2}$ tons
JB 9932	Albion 4 wheel rigid	1936	7 $\frac{1}{2}$ tons
JB 9933	Albion 4 wheel rigid	1936	7 $\frac{1}{2}$ tons
JB 9934	Albion 4 wheel rigid	1936	7 $\frac{1}{2}$ tons
JB 9935	Albion 4 wheel rigid	1936	7 $\frac{1}{2}$ tons
JB 9936	Albion 4 wheel rigid	1936	7 $\frac{1}{2}$ tons
JB 9937	Albion 4 wheel rigid	1936	7 $\frac{1}{2}$ tons
JB 9938	Albion 4 wheel rigid	1936	7 $\frac{1}{2}$ tons
JB 9939	Albion 4 wheel rigid	1936	7 $\frac{1}{2}$ tons
AJB 707	Albion 4 wheel rigid	1937	6 tons
BBL 551	Albion 4 wheel rigid	1938	6 tons
BBL 552	Albion 4 wheel rigid	1938	6 tons
BBL 553	Albion 4 wheel rigid	1938	6 tons
BBL 554	Albion 4 wheel rigid	1938	6 tons
BMO 155	Albion 4 wheel rigid	1938	6 tons
BMO 156	Albion 4 wheel rigid	1938	6 tons
BMO 857	Albion 4 wheel rigid	1938	6 tons
BMO 908	Albion 4 wheel rigid	1938	6 tons
BMO 909	Albion 4 wheel rigid	1938	6 tons
BMO 910	Albion 4 wheel rigid	1938	6 tons
BMO 912	Albion 4 wheel rigid	1938	6 tons
BMO 914	Albion 4 wheel rigid	1938	6 tons
BMO 915	Albion 4 wheel rigid	1938	6 tons
BMO 916	Albion 4 wheel rigid	1938	6 tons
BMO 917	Albion 4 wheel rigid	1938	6 tons
BMO 918	Albion 4 wheel rigid	1938	6 tons

Appendix 8 Continued:

Reg'n No	Make, Model and Type	Year Reg'd	Payload
BMO 919	Albion 4 wheel rigid	1938	6 tons
BMO 920	Albion 4 wheel rigid	1938	6 tons
BMO 921	Albion 4 wheel rigid	1938	6 tons
BMO 922	Albion 4 wheel rigid	1938	6 tons
BMO 923	Albion 4 wheel rigid	1938	6 tons
CJB 60	Albion 6 wheel rigid	1940	10 tons
EBL 751	Albion 4 wheel rigid	1947	6 tons
EJB 463	Bedford 4 wheel rigid	1948	6 tons

NOTE:
This appendix was compiled from information kindly supplied by Stuart Wise.

Appendix 9 - Tovil & Bridge Mills fleet 1945 - 1976

Vehicles operated by Tovil & Bridge Mills, Disposal by 1959

Fleet No	Reg'n No	Make, Model and Type	Date Reg'd	Payload
-	?	Tilling Stevens petrol electric		
-	DKN 690	Dennis 4 cyl petrol 4 wheel rigid	30.12.36.	
-	DKN 991	Dennis 4 cyl petrol 4 wheel rigid	30.12.36.	
-	DKT 4	Dennis 4 wheel rigid	20.3.37.	
-	GKT 364	Austin 4 wheel tipper	29.5.42.	
-	FVU 319	Ford		1 ton
-	JXB 120	Albion 6 wheel rigid		12 tons
-	JXF 314	Albion 6 wheel rigid		12 tons
-	JXF 616	Albion 6 wheel rigid		12 tons
-	JXV 919	Albion 6 wheel rigid		12 tons
-	JXU 408	Bedford O/Scammell tractor		10 tons
-	KGU 678	Bedford O/Scammell tractor		10 tons
-	LUC 989	Bedford O/Scammell tractor		10 tons
-	OKE 295	Karrier Bantam 69A	27.8.51.	2 tons

NOTES:
1   The reg'n nos of the Ford, Albions and Bedfords are from memory and cannot be verified except for JXB 120, see photograph.
2   The 4 Albions were ex War Dept. See ch 4.
3   The Bedfords were supplied by Penfolds, hence the London reg'n nos.
4   OKE 295 replaced FVU 319 as the Mill 'runabout'. It was eventually owned by Alan Firmin, reregistered AF 158 on 9.2.61.

Vehicles ex Tovil & Bridge Mills at 28.9.59, Including Others Retained

Fleet No	Reg'n No	Make, Model and Type	Date Reg'd	Payload
1	OKM 35	Albion HD57 doubledrive 6 wheel rigid	1.12.51.	12 tons
2	PKM 726	Albion HD57 doubledrive 6 wheel rigid	1.11.52.	12 tons
3	SKE 411	Albion HD57 doubledrive 6 wheel rigid	1.2.53.	12 tons
4	SKM 412	Albion HD57 doubledrive 6 wheel rigid	27.2.54.	12 tons
5	SKR 71	Albion HD57 doubledrive 6 wheel rigid	1.5.54.	12 tons
6	TKJ 157	Albion HD57 doubledrive 6 wheel rigid	28.6.54.	12 tons
?	UKP 161	Albion Chieftain/Scammell tractor	14.4.55.	12 tons
?	VKM 728	Albion Chieftain/Scammell tractor	20.7.55.	12 tons
32	WKR 378	Albion Chieftain/Scammell tractor	1.3.56.	12 tons
?	YKL 544	Albion Chieftain/Scammell tractor	19.11.56.	12 tons
7	HJG 897	Bedford S/Scammell tractor	25.3.54.	12 tons
?	HJG 898	Bedford S/Scammell tractor	31.3.54.	12 tons
?	JJG 112	Bedford S/Scammell tractor	6.10.54.	12 tons
?	PGK 817	Bedford S/Scammell tractor		12 tons
29	WKL 614	Albion Claymore 4 wheel rigid	11.12.55.	
-	YKK 906	Albion Chieftain MR7L 4 wheel tipper	1.11.56.	
26	YKL 951	Albion Chieftain MRL 4 wheel rigid	13.10.56.	7 tons
?	YKP 483	Albion Claymore 74L85F 4 wheel rigid	14.2.57.	
-	102 AKT	Albion Claymore 4 wheel rigid	22.7.57.	

NOTES:
1   1 and 2 had Albion engines, 3 to 6 Leyland 600 9.8 litre engines
2   29 - WKL 614 was registered to Southern Paper Stock Ltd, a small wastepaper trading subsidiary but considered a part of the Tovil & Bridge Mills fleet.
3   YKK 906,102 AKT and two or three of the Albion Chieftain or Bedford S tractors did not transfer, retained for internal Mill or Tovil to Aylesford shuttle operations. See chapter 4.

Appendix 9 Continued:

Vehicles operated by Tovil & Bridge Mills between 1959 and 1976

Fleet No	Reg'n No	Make, Model and Type	Date Reg'd	Payload
-	318 SKN	Albion Chieftain/Scammell tractor	24.1.62.	12 tons
-	319 SKN	Albion Chieftain/Scammell tractor	24.1.62.	12 tons
-	657 YKL	Albion Chieftain/Scammell tractor	29.7.63.	12 tons
-	660 YKL	Albion Chieftain/Scammell tractor	1.8.63.	12 tons
-	HKL 448D	Leyland Comet 12C.4 tractor	4.8.66.	12 tons
-	HKL 837D	Leyland Comet 12C.4 tractor	15.8.66.	12 tons
-	TKJ 622H	Seddon	23.10.69.	
-	UKL 419H	Leyland tractor	19.3.70.	12 tons

NOTE:
TKJ 622H may have been a tipper.

Vehicles Ex Tovil & Bridge Mills 1976

Fleet No	Reg'n No	Make, Model and Type	Date Reg'd	Payload
105	GKE 972L	Seddon tractor	19.10.72.	12 tons
127	OKM912M	Leyland Chieftain 12 spd splitter tractor	19.10.73.	12 tons
128	GKP 646N	Leyland Chieftain 6 speed tractor	1.12.74	12 tons

Appendix 10 - Medway Corrugated Paper Company fleet 1936 - 1953 and those vehicles acquired in 1958 from Reed Corrugated Cases

Vehicles operated by Medway Corrugated Paper Company 1936 - 1953

Fleet No	Reg'n. No	Make, Model and Type	Year Reg'd	Date Reg'd.	Payload
?	DKE 829	Dennis		23.6.36.	n/a
?	DKK 607	Dennis		21.10.36.	n/a.
?	EKJ 339	Dennis		13.5.37.	n/a.
?	FKN 745	Commer		29.12.38.	n/a.
?	GKE 633	Commer - model unknown, uw 2t.8c.1q.		16.5.39.	n/a.
?	HKE 379	Commer 4 wheel pantechnicon		29.12.44.	n/a.
?	HKJ 614	Commer Q4 4 wheel pantechnicon		28.9.45.	n/a.
?	KKE 850	Karrier 64A		20.11.47.	n/a.
?	KKM 379	Karrier 64A		4.5.48.	n/a.
?	MKE 895	Commer A 4 wheel pantechnicon		3.11.49.	n/a.
(30)	NKE 164	Austin Loadstar K4WA 4 wheel pantechnicon		11.10.50.	n/a.
?	NKL 646	Commer 25A		16.2.51.	n/a.
?	OKL 278	Ford van		13.11.51.	n/a.
?	OKL 964	Austin K2WA		18.1.52.	n/a.
?	PKE 597	Commer 32A		16.7.52.	n/a.
?	PKR 413	Austin K2WA		25.3.53.	n/a.

NOTES:
1 These vehicles were disposed of long before the acquisition but are included out of interest. All were registered in the name of Medway Corrugated Paper Co.
2 A photograph exists of two Fordson Thames pantechnicons in MCPC livery. OKL 278 had chassis no 7260693 but this doesn't help identify the model.
3 The fleet number 30 was that of RCC.

Vehicles Operated by Reed Corrugated Cases and acquired in 1958

Fleet No	Reg'n. No	Make, Model and Type	Year Reg'd	Date Reg'd.	Payload
(6)	?	Austin 5K/FED3/Scammell tractor		?	n/a.
?	?	Austin 5K/FED3/Scammell tractor		?	n/a.
?	XKR 542	Commer 91A 4 wheel van		31.8.56.	n/a.
?	YKJ 717	Commer D91A 4 wheel van		1.11.56.	n/a.
?	YKJ 720	Commer D91A 4 wheel van		1.11.56.	n/a.
?	YKT 481	Austin 4K/FED3 4 wheel pantechnicon		15.3.57.	n/a.
?	YKT 944	Austin 4K/FED3 4 wheel pantechnicon		21.3.57.	n/a.
?	451 BKR	Commer D98A 4 wheel pantechnicon		9.1.58.	n/a.
?	453 BKR	Commer D98A 4 wheel pantechnicon		6.2.58.	n/a.
?	118 DKO	Austin DER/15 4 wheel pantechnicon		22.9.58.	n/a.
?	159 DKR	Austin 5K/FED3/Scammell tractor		15.10.58.	n/a.
171	296 GKM	Commer D98A 4 wheel pantechnicon		31.7.59.	n/a.
121	7292 MM	Commer ? 4 wheel pantechnicon		1961	n/a.

NOTES:
1 At the time of the acquisition, 3 Austin/Scammell tractors were included. A photograph of unregistered no 6 (RCCs number) is included. It's registration number and that of the second tractor are unknown.
2 121 - 7292 MM may have been ordered by RCC, Brentford but never transferred to Thatcham, hence the Middlesex registration. Records for xxxx MM registrations no longer exist so the date of registration and original registered owner cannot be verified.

Appendix 11 - Reed Corrugated Cases, Wigan fleet 1959/1960 and that part of the fleet merged into Wigan Depot operation February 1960

Fleet No	Reg'n No	Make, Model and type	Date Reg'd	Payload
?	?	Austin 4 wheel flat platform rigid		
?	?	Bedford 4 wheel pantechnicon		
?	?	Albion 4 wheel flat platform rigid with drawbar trailer		
?	?	Van		Samples
964	41 GKK	Commer HD 5th wheel tractor	30.6.59.	12 tons
965	42 GKK	Commer HD 5th wheel tractor	30.6.59.	12 tons
966	750 JKM	Commer HD 5th wheel tractor	8.2.60.	12 tons
967	164 JKN	Commer HD 5th wheel tractor	15.2.60.	12 tons
968	659 JKN	Commer HD 5th wheel tractor	16.2.60.	12 tons
969	901 JKO	Commer HD 5th wheel tractor	24.2.60.	12 tons

NOTE:
This appendix was compiled with the kind help of Bill Parr.

Appendix 12 - Vehicles operated by and acquired from Imperial Paper Mills in 1961

Fleet No	Reg'n No	Make, Model and type	Date Reg'd	Payload
? 175	NKL 211	AEC Mammoth Major 3671 6 wheel rigid	1.1.51.	12 tons
? 176	NKL 212	AEC Mammoth Major 3671 6 wheel rigid	1.1.51.	12 tons
? 177	NKL 213	AEC Mammoth Major 3671 6 wheel rigid	1.1.51.	12 tons
? 178	NKL 214	AEC Mammoth Major 3671 6 wheel rigid	1.1.51.	12 tons
? 179	NKL 215	AEC Mammoth Major 3671 6 wheel rigid	1.1.51.	12 tons
? 180	NKL 216	AEC Mammoth Major 3671 6 wheel rigid	1.1.51.	12 tons
-	OKR 692	Dodge 103/T 4 wheel tipper	13.5.52.	?
181	PKM 7	AEC Mammoth Major 3671 6 wheel rigid	11.11.52.	12 tons
182	PKM 8	AEC Mammoth Major 3671 6 wheel rigid	11.11.52.	12 tons
183	PKM 9	AEC Mammoth Major 3671 6 wheel rigid	29.11.52.	12 tons
184	PKM 10	AEC Mammoth Major 3671 6 wheel rigid	29.11.52.	12 tons
185	PKM 11	AEC Mammoth Major 3671 6 wheel rigid	29.11.52.	12 tons
186	PKM 12	AEC Mammoth Major 3671 6 wheel rigid	17.10.52.	12 tons
187	RKR 913	AEC Mammoth Major 3671 6 wheel rigid	15.12.53.	12 tons
188	RKR 914	AEC Mammoth Major 3671 6 wheel rigid	2.1.54.	12 tons
189	RKR 915	AEC Mammoth Major 3871 8 wheel rigid	17.12.53.	15 tons
190	RKR 916	AEC Mammoth Major 3671 6 wheel rigid	2.1.54.	12 tons
191	RKR 917	AEC Mammoth Major 3871 8 wheel rigid	5.1.54.	15 tons
192	RKR 918	AEC Mammoth Major 3671 6 wheel rigid	2.1.54.	12 tons
193	VKP 919	AEC Mammoth Major 3671 6 wheel rigid	9.11.55.	12 tons
194	VKP 920	AEC Mammoth Major 3671 6 wheel rigid	9.3.56.	12 tons
195	VKP 921	AEC Mammoth Major 3671 6 wheel rigid	28.4.56.	12 tons
196	VKP 922	AEC Mammoth Major 3671 6 wheel rigid	1.7.56.	12 tons
197	VKP 923	AEC Mammoth Major 3671 6 wheel rigid	9.8.56.	12 tons
198	VKP 924	AEC Mammoth Major 3671 6 wheel rigid	?	12 tons
199	VKP 925	AEC Mammoth Major 3871 8 wheel rigid	17.1.57.	15 tons

NOTES:
See opposite for notes on Appendix 12 - Imperial Paper Mills fleet listing.

Appendix 13 - Vehicles Operated by and acquired from London Paper Mills in 1961

Fleet No	Reg'n No	Make, Model and type	Date reg'd	Payload
?	EKK 726	Dennis	7.10.37.	
?	KKK 784	Vulcan 4 wheel rigid	13.2.48.	7 tons
?	KKM 555	Vulcan 6VF 4 wheel rigid	30.4.48.	7 tons
?	NKL 573	Morris LC3	4.1.51.	
(6)	RYO 578	Austin K/FED3 4 wheel rigid	?	? 6 tons
(1)	RYO 579	Austin ?K/FED3 4 wheel rigid	?	? 6 tons
(10)	SKO 747	Bedford SAO/Scammell tractor	7.4.54.	10 tons
(2)	WKN 165	Bedford S/Scammell tractor	1.1.56.	10 tons
27	XKT 479	Austin 5K/FED3 4 wheel rigid	28.9.56.	7 tons
?	XKT 480	Austin 5K/FED3 4 wheel rigid	28.9.56.	7 tons

NOTES to the above:
1. EKK 726, KKK 784 and KKM 555 would have been disposed of long before the acquisition but are included out of interest.
2. The bracketed fleet numbers were those of LPM.
3. Apart from 27 - XKT 479, there is no evidence that any others transferred into the RT fleet in 1961.

NOTES - Appendix 12 - Acquired Imperial Paper Mills vehicles
1. The 25 AECs carried the fleet numbers 1 to 25 under Imperial ownership.
2. Tipper OKR 692 was operating within the Mill after takeover. It is not known whether it remained as Mill owned or RT owned. It was later replaced by a Bedford.
3. It is believed that the six 1951 AECs were sold very soon after the acquisition and replaced by Albion and Foden rigids transferred from Aylesford.
4. Photographs confirm that RKR 914 and RKR 915 were numbered 188 and 189. It seems likely and logical that the remainder were numbered in sequence from 181 although no evidence can be found to confirm.
5. PKM 11 was eventually sold to haulier C.Bates of Snodland who continued to use it on it's A Contract Licence for the Company at Aylesford.
6. RKR 915 and RKR 917 were built as 3671 6 wheelers, later returned to AEC for conversion to 3871 8 wheelers. LTO archives record them as 3671s.
7. The first registration date of VKP 924 is unreadable in the LTO records.
8. This appendix compiled with additional information kindly provided by Len Valsler.

Appendix 14 - Vehicles acquired from Reed Corrugated Cases as part of factory move from Brentford to Thatcham in 1961 and 1962

Fleet No	Reg'n No	Make, Model and Type	Date Reg'd	Payload
820	GZ 4373	Bedford OX/Scammell tractor	1.6.46.	10 tons
819	WMY 723	Bedford O/Scammell tractor		10 tons
814	965 JHX	Albion Claymore 4 wheel rigid boxvan		
800	611 MMU	BMC Series 3/Scammell tractor	1956	10 tons
817	193 SML	BMC Series 3 4 wheel rigid		7 tons
801	85 UMP	Austin FFK/Scammell tractor	2.3.59.	10 tons
802	86 UMP	Austin FFK/Scammell tractor	2.3.59.	10 tons
803	2157 MK	Austin FFK/Scammell tractor	21.4.60.	10 tons
804	6422 HX	Austin FFK/Scammell tractor	23.5.60.	10 tons
805	4186 MV	Austin FFK/Scammell tractor	15.7.60.	10 tons
806	6212 MV	Austin FFK/Scammell tractor	1.11.60.	10 tons
807	8215 MP	Austin FFK/Scammell tractor	1.12.60.	10 tons
815	3567 MM	Austin FFK 4 wheel rigid boxvan	1.6.61.	
816	4192 MM	Austin FFK 4 wheel rigid boxvan	1.6.61.	
812	632 TKK	Austin FFK140 4 whl rigid 1250 cu ft boxvan	9.4.62.	7 tons
811	828 TKK	Austin FFK140 4 whl rigid 1250 cu ft boxvan	11 4.62.	7 tons
813	104 TKN	Austin FFK140 4 whl rigid 1250 cu ft boxvan	1.5.62.	7 tons
818	153 TKP	Austin FFK/Scammell tractor	17.5.62.	10 tons
810	154 TKP	Austin FFK/Scammell tractor	17.5.62.	10 tons
809	155 TKP	Austin FFK/Scammell tractor	17.5.62.	10 tons
821	684 UKK	Austin FFK ? See note 3.	10.7.62.	
808	685 UKK	Austin FFK/Scammell tractor	10.7.62.	10 tons
822	431 UKT	Austin FFK140 4 whl rigid 1250 cu ft boxvan	25.9.62.	7 tons

NOTES :

1   820 - GZ 4373 was ex Reed Corrugated Cases, Warrenpoint, N.Ireland and was a shunt unit. It was last road taxed to 31.12.64.

2   819 - WMY 723 was a shunt unit.

3   821 - 684 UKK. It is not known whether this was a rigid or a tractor.

4   The nine 1962 vehicles were originally sourced by Reed Transport as part of it's Group vehicle purchasing role, hence the Kent registrations.

5   This appendix was compiled from information kindly supplied by Stuart Wise

Appendix 15 - Vehicles acquired from WPM Paper Mills 28th July 1969

Fleet No	Reg'n No	Make, Model and Type	Date Reg'd	Payload	Orig Mill
850	TUA 954G	Bedford 4 wheel rigid van	24.7.69.	2/3 tons	See note 3
851	CXJ 396C	Commer 4 wheel rigid	26.8.65.	8 tons	Darwen PM
852	AVU 833B	Seddon 4 wheel rigid	25.9.64.	9 tons	Darwen PM
860	956 UTJ	Leyland/Scammell tractor	7.6.61.	10 tons	Hollins PM
861	8117 TD	Leyland/Scammell tractor	1.9.62.	10 tons	Hollins PM
862	8697 TD	Leyland/Scammell tractor	10.9.62.	10 tons	Hollins PM
863	144 FKT	Leyland Comet ECOS2/Scam tractor	20.5.59.	10 tons	Hollins PM
864	MTD 995C	Leyland/Scammell tractor	18.2.65.	10 tons	Darwen PM
865	MTD 996C	Leyland/Scammell tractor	18.2.65.	10 tons	Darwen PM
866	TTB 279D	Leyland/Scammell tractor	21.12.65.	10 tons	Darwen PM
867	NTB 679C	Leyland/Scammell tractor	1.5.65.	10 tons	Darwen PM
868	FTC 879B	Leyland/Scammell tractor	1.6.64.	10 tons	L.Darwen PM
869	116 GKE	Leyland Comet ECOS2/Scam tractor	29.5.59.	10 tons	Darwen PM
870	4106 NF	Commer/Scammell tractor	1.9.62.	10 tons	L.Darwen PM
871	WXJ 672	Commer/Scammell tractor	2.2.59.	10 tons	Hollins PM
880	MKE 107F	Seddon 13:four P6.354 tractor	9.11.67.	12 tons	Hollins PM
881	MKE 108F	Seddon 13:four P6.354 tractor	9.11.67.	12 tons	Hollins PM
882	MKE 109F	Seddon 13:four P6.354 tractor	9.11.67.	12 tons	Hollins PM
883	MKJ 535F	Seddon 13:four P6.354 tractor	24.11.67.	12 tons	Hollins PM
890	XTC 115D	ERF LV 64CU NHE180 tractor	1.7.66.	20 tons	Hollins PM
891	XTC 123D	ERF LV 64CU NHE180 tractor	12.7.66.	20 tons	Hollins PM

NOTES:
1   863 - 144 FKT & 869 - 116 GKE were previously transferred to the two Mills from Reed Transport probably written down at £1 each as shunt units. 144 FKT had a dual auto/5th wheel conversion. See Appendix 17 note 4.
2   The acquisition included the following trailers:
            16 Scammell 23ft to 25ft trailers from Darwen Paper Mill,
            9 Scammell 23ft and 25ft trailers from Lower Darwen Paper Mill.
            9 Scammell 20ft and 24ft 6in trailers, 8 Fromant 28ft trailers used with Seddons and
            6 Dyson 33ft trailers used with ERFs - all from Hollins Paper Mill
3   In accordance with Reed Paper Group rules, the above assets transferred at a book value of £13501.2s.6d.
    This excluded 850 - TUA 954G which, based on the registration date, was ordered prior to the acquisition by one of the Mills and delivered immediately after the transfer. It ended it's life as New Hythe depot's Equipment Store.
4   890 - XTC 115D sustained major accident damage in an M6 pile up. It was recovered to Aylesford and rebuilt by Aylesford Garage using replacement undrilled chassis frames, this work being done by hand.

Appendix 16 - Vehicles acquired from Reed Corrugated Cases, Tube Factory, Aylesford in 1976

Fleet No	Reg'n No	Make, Model and Type	Date Reg'd	Payload
108	?	Ford D800 4 wheel rigid		8 tons
110	XKJ 508J	Ford D800 tractor	1.2.71.	12 tons
112	DKJ 209K	Ford D600 tractor	1.4.72.	9 tons
?	NKN 232M	Ford D600 tractor	1.8.73.	9 tons
?	HKP 182N	Ford DA2114 tractor	24.2.75.	12 tons
?	JKR 223N	Ford DA2114 tractor	9.6.75.	12 tons

NOTES :
Views differ whether four or five tractors were involved. If only four then NKN 232M is probably the 'rogue' vehicle.

Appendix 17 - New Vehicle Purchases 1957 - 1974 (July) with Original Costs included for Early Vehicles

Fleet No	Reg'n No	Make, Model and Type	Date Reg'd	Orig Cost	Payload	Depot
KC1	YKJ 725	Austin 5K/FED3 4 wheel boxvan	10.10.56.	£2244.2s.2d	1650 cu.ft	-
KC2	YKL 681	Austin 5K/FED3 4 wheel boxvan	20.11.56.	£2241.6s.8d	1650 cu.ft	-
KC3	YKO 348	Austin 5K/FED3/T tractor	25.1.57.	£1491.15s.1d	-	-
KC4	YKR 101	Austin 3K/FED3 4 wheel boxvan	22.2.57.	£1732.1s.7d	?	-
-	-	Pantechnicon trailer for YKO 348	25.1.57.	£1505.8s.11d	2000 cu.ft	-
19	YKN 419	Austin 5K/FED3/T Scam tractor	3.1.57.	£1601.1s.6d	10 tons	A
18	YKN 420	Austin 5K/FED3/T Scam tractor	3.1.57.	£1601.1s.6d	10 tons	A
77	YKN 532	Austin 5K/FED3/TE Scam tractor	5.1.57.	£1607.2s.7d	10 tons	A
? 76	YKN 537	Austin 5K/FED3/TE Scam tractor	8.1.57.	£1604.5s.7d	10 tons	A
152	454 AKP	Douglas Tugmaster/Scam tractor	1.7.57.	£2952.18s.4d	12 tons	A
151	92 AKR	Douglas Tugmaster/Scam tractor	11.7.57.	£2954.4s.0d	12 tons	A
153	454 AKT	Douglas Tugmaster/Scam tractor	25.7.57.	£2984.6s.9d	12 tons	A
? 154	457 AKT	Douglas Tugmaster/Scam tractor	30.7.57.	£2966.8s.5d	12 tons	A
? 155	923 AKT	Douglas Tugmaster/Scam tractor	2.8.57.	£2952.8s.4d	12 tons	A
131	566 BKJ	Austin 7K/FEDS 4 wheel tipper	3.9.57.	£2184.3s.4d		A
42	715 BKK	Austin 5K/FED3/T Scam tractor	20.9.57.	£1608.9s.7d	10 tons	A
82	859 BKL	Austin 5K/FED3/TE Scam tractor	7.10.57.	£1628.3s.0d	10 tons	A
83	860 BKL	Austin 5K/FED3/TE Scam tractor	7.10.57.	£1626.13s.6d	10 tons	A
161	106 BKM	Austin 5K/FED3/TE Scam tractor	14.10.57.	£1625.11s.9d	10 tons	A
162	107 BKM	Austin 5K/FED3/TE Scam tractor	14.10.57.	£1625.11s.10d	10 tons	A
78	273 BKM	Austin 5K/FED3/TE Scam tractor	17.10.57.	£1619.11s.2d	10 tons	A
64	274 BKM	Austin 5K/FED3/TE Scam tractor	17.10.57.	£1619.11s.1d	10 tons	A
79	24 BKN	Austin 5K/FED3/TE Scam tractor	1.11.57.	£1648.15s.5d	10 tons	A
?	81 BKN	Austin LCFOA	13.11.57.	£1302.11s.1d	2 tons	A
110	89 BKN	Austin 5K/FED3 4 wheel rigid	12.11.57.	£1417.8s.5d	5 tons	A
50	421 BKN	Austin van	4.11.57.	£1133.0s.3d	Garage	A
80	127 BKO	Austin 5K/FED/T3 Scam tractor	18.11.57.	£1652.11s.10d	10 tons	A
51	653 BKO	Foden FG6/24 S20 8 wheel rigid	29.11.57.	£4674.5s.6d	15 tons	A
81	104 BKP	Austin 5K/FED/TE3 Scam tractor	6.12.57.	£1604.19s.2d	10 tons	A
52	108 BKP	Foden FG6/24 S20 8 wheel rigid	10.12.57.	£4676.11s.6d	15 tons	A
16	76 BKR	Foden FG6/24 S20 8 wheel rigid	1.1.58.	£4583.5s.0d	15 tons	A
?	921 CKL	Austin 3K/FED3 4 wheel rigid	15.4.58.	£1641.7s.1d	7 tons	A
109	732 CKR	Austin 5K/FED/TE3 Scam tractor	28.5.58.	£1645.16s.3d	10 tons	A
139	570 DKO	Austin 5K/FED/T3 Scam tractor	12.9.58.	£1502.5s.2d	10 tons	A
203	33 DKP	Austin 755/94 4 wheel rigid	22.9.58.	£1847.11s.3d	7 tons	A
124	743 DKR	Austin 755/94 4 wheel rigid	9.10.58.	£1723.6s.2d	7 tons	A
116	259 EKL	Douglas Tugmaster/Scam tractor	8.12.58.	£2964.10s.0d	12 tons	A
122	36 EKO	Douglas Tugmaster/Scam tractor	12.1.59.	£2964.10s.0d	12 tons	A
129	37 EKO	Douglas Tugmaster/Scam tractor	12.1.59.	£2964.10s.0d	12 tons	A
?	270 EKO	Douglas Tugmaster/Scam tractor	Jan 1959	£2964.10s.0d	12 tons	A
?	650 EKO	Douglas Tugmaster/Scam tractor	21.1.59.	£2964.10s.0d	12 tons	A
91	58 DKO	Foden FGTU6/20 S20 tractor	5.9.58.	£3490.16s.6d	15 tons	A
92	304 EKJ	Foden FGTU6/20 S20 tractor	7.11.58.	£3502.19s.1d	15 tons	A
93	305 EKJ	Foden FGTU6/20 S20 tractor	7.11.58.	£3506.18s.3d	15 tons	A
94	615 EKK	Foden FGTU6/20 S20 tractor	26.11.58.	£3507.9s.3d	15 tons	A
95	313 EKM	Foden FGTU6/20 S20 tractor	18.12.58.	£3505.12s.8d	15 tons	A
96	475 EKN	Foden FGTU6/20 S20 tractor	5.1.59.	£3486.13s.6d	15 tons	A
97	389 EKP	Foden FGTU6/20 S20 tractor	2.2.59.	£3486.13s.6d	15 tons	A
Trls 351-364		Eagle t/axle air suspension trlrs	1958/1959	£1312.16s 0d each		

Appendix 17 continued:

Fleet No	Reg'n No	Make, Model and Type	Date Reg'd	Payload	Depot
36	144 FKT	Leyland Comet ECOS2/Scammell tractor	20.5.59.	12 tons	A
23	145 FKT	Leyland Comet ECOS2/Scammell tractor	20.5.59.	12 tons	A
41	116 GKE	Leyland Comet ECOS2/Scammell tractor	29.5.59.	12 tons	A
39	117 GKE	Leyland Comet ECOS2/Scammell tractor	29.5.59.	12 tons	A
31	118 GKE	Leyland Comet ECOS2/Scammell tractor	29.5.59.	12 tons	A
21	119 GKE	Leyland Comet ECOS2/Scammell tractor	29.5.59.	12 tons	A
22	120 GKE	Leyland Comet ECOS2/Scammell tractor	29.5.59.	12 tons	A
33	431 GKE	Leyland Comet ECOS2/Scammell tractor	29.5.59.	12 tons	A
720	YCG 175	BMC FGK boxvan	1.5.60.	30 cwt	T
500	t/plates	AEC Matador 4x4 recovery	1960	Garage	A
84	70 KKM	Austin 583A/Scammell tractor	20.4.60.	10 tons	A
225	417 KKT	AEC Mammoth Major 8 wheel rigid	1.6.60.	15 tons	A
34	34 LKJ	Leyland Comet CS3.4R/Scammell tract.	16.6.60.	12 tons	A
35	35 LKJ	Leyland Comet CS3.4R/Scammell tract.	16.6.60.	12 tons	A
227	36 LKJ	AEC Mammoth Major 8 wheel rigid	16.6.60.	15 tons	A
85	126 LKL	Austin 583A/Scammell tractor	4.7.60.	10 tons	A
718	127 LKL	Commer QX T99Y 4 wheel rigid	4.7.60.	7 tons	T
735	128 LKL	Commer QX T99Y 4 wheel rigid	4.7.60.	7 tons	T
715	621 LKN	Commer HDY/Scammell tractor	28.7.60.	10 tons	T
712	622 LKN	Commer HDY/Scammell tractor	28.7.60.	10 tons	T
710	623 LKN	Commer HDY/Scammell tractor	28.7.60.	10 tons	T
226	953 MKE	Leyland Octopus 24.O/4 8 wheel rigid	29.9.60.	15 tons	A
-	562 MKJ	Austin Mini AV7 van	21.10.60.	-	KC
783	813 MKM	Commer VHD 25 cwt pickup	16.11.60.	Garage	T
123	244 NKL	Commer HDY/Scammell tractor	23.2.61.	10 tons	A
136	959 NKN	Commer HDY/Scammell tractor	20.3.61.	10 tons	A
222	456 NKP	Foden FGTU6/24 6LX S21 tractor	1.4.61.	15 tons	A
221	457 NKP	Foden FGTU6/24 6LX S21 tractor	1.4.61.	15 tons	A
-	271 NKT	Morris OEH1 van + 2 wheel van trailer	20.4.61.	5 cwt	KC
-	272 NKT	Morris OEH1 van + 2 wheel van trailer	20.4.61.	5 cwt	KC
-	273 NKT	Morris OEH1 van + 2 wheel van trailer	20.4.61.	5 cwt	KC
-	274 NKT	Morris OEH1 van + 2 wheel van trailer	20.4.61.	5 cwt	KC
-	275 NKT	Morris OEH1 van + 2 wheel van trailer	20.4.61.	5 cwt	KC
-	276 NKT	Morris OEH1 van + 2 wheel van trailer	5.5.61.	5 cwt	KC
-	277 NKT	Morris OEH1 van + 2 wheel van trailer	5.5.61.	5 cwt	KC
724	877 PKJ	Foden FGTU6/24 6LX S21 tractor	5.5.61.	15 tons	T
43	27 PKL	Atkinson FC 5LW/Scammell tractor	15.5.61.	12 tons	A
44	619 PKL	Atkinson FC 5LW/Scammell tractor	23.5.61.	12 tons	A
732	444 PKN	Foden FGTU6/24 6LX S21 tractor	4.6.61.	15 tons	T
723	445 PKN	Atkinson FC 5LW/Scammell tractor	7.6.61.	12 tons	T
717	446 PKN	Atkinson FC 5LW/Scammell tractor	7.6.61.	12 tons	T
731	650 RKJ	Austin 566A 4wheel rigid boxvan	26.7.61.	7 tons	T
103	871 RKJ	Foden FGTU6/24 6LX S21 tractor	26.7.61.	15 tons	A
104	872 RKJ	Foden FGTU6/24 6LX S21 tractor	26.7.61.	15 tons	A
728	478 RKN	Atkinson FC 5LW/Scammell tractor	13.9.61.	12 tons	T
736	479 RKN	Atkinson FC 5LW/Scammell tractor	13.9.61.	12 tons	T
45	146 RKP	Atkinson FC 5LW/Scammell tractor	2.10.61.	12 tons	A
755	432 RKP	Atkinson FC 5LW/Scammell tractor	6.10.61.	12 tons	T
729	433 RKP	Atkinson FC 5LW/Scammell tractor	6.10.61.	12 tons	T
46	802 RKP	Atkinson FC 5LW/Scammell tractor	10.10.61.	12 tons	A
746	829 RKT	Foden FGTU6/24 6LX S21 tractor	9.11.61.	15 tons	T
730	830 RKT	Atkinson FC 5LW/Scammell tractor	9.11.61.	12 tons	T
726	71 SKE	Atkinson FC 5LW/Scammell tractor	9.11.61.	12 tons	T
751	72 SKE	Atkinson FC 5LW/Scammell tractor	9.11.61.	12 tons	T
738	73 SKE	Atkinson FC 5LW/Scammell tractor	9.11.61.	12 tons	T
753	255 SKE	Atkinson FC 5LW/Scammell tractor	14.11.61.	12 tons	T

Appendix 17 continued:

Fleet No	Reg'n No	Make, Model and Type	Date Reg'd	Payload	Depot
223	256 SKE	Foden FGTU6/24 6LX S21 tractor	14.11.61.	15 tons	A
87	969 SKJ	Atkinson FC 5LW/Scammell tractor	8.12.61.	12 tons	A
88	970 SKJ	Atkinson FC 5LW/Scammell tractor	8.12.61.	12 tons	A
230	306 SKK	Foden FGTU6/24 6LX S21 tractor	15.12.61.	15 tons	A
733	307 SKK	Foden KG6/24 6LK S20 8 wheel rigid	15.12.61.	15 tons	T
754	308 SKK	Foden FGTU6/24 6LX S21 tractor	1.1.62.	15 tons	T
752	309 SKK	Atkinson FC 5LW/Scammell tractor	1.1.62.	12 tons	T
743	310 SKK	Foden FGTU6/24 6LX S21 tractor	1.1.62.	15 tons	T
734	504 SKK	Foden KG6/24 6LK S20 8 wheel rigid	18.12.61.	15 tons	T
86	745 SKK	Atkinson FC 5LW/Scammell tractor	19.12.61.	12 tons	A
89	746 SKK	Atkinson FC 5LW/Scammell tractor	19.12.61.	12 tons	A
90	913 SKK	Atkinson FC 5LW/Scammell tractor	1.1.62.	12 tons	A
98	655 SKL	Atkinson FC 5LW/Scammell tractor	2.1.62.	12 tons	A
750	618 SKM	Foden FGTU6/24 6LX S21 tractor	15.1.62.	15 tons	T
748	619 SKM	Foden FGTU6/24 6LX S21 tractor	15.1.62.	15 tons	T
742	620 SKM	Foden KG6/24 6LK S20 8 wheel rigid	15.1.62.	15 tons	T
233	631 SKM	Foden FGTU6/24 6LX S21 tractor	15.1.62.	15 tons	A
212	632 SKM	Foden FGTU6/24 6LX S21 tractor	15.1.62.	15 tons	A
15/747	629 SKN	Foden FGTU6/24 6LX S21 tractor	31.1.62.	15 tons	T
99	643 SKR	Foden FGTU6/24 6LX S21 tractor	2.3.62.	15 tons	A
101	139 TKE	Atkinson FC 5LW/Scammell tractor	20.3.62.	12 tons	A
102	140 TKE	Atkinson FC 5LW/Scammell tractor	20.3.62.	12 tons	A
? 232	561 TKE	Foden FGTU6/24 6LX S21 tractor	20.3.62.	15 tons	A
740	562 TKE	Foden KG6/24 6LK S20 8 wheel rigid	20.3.62.	15 tons	T
745	563 TKE	Foden FGTU6/24 6LX S21 tractor	20.3.62.	15 tons	T
48	573 TKJ	Foden FGTU6/24 6LX S21 tractor	18.3.62.	15 tons	A
749	815 TKJ	Foden KG6/24 6LK S20 8 wheel rigid	30.3.62.	15 tons	T
739	816 TKJ	Foden FGTU6/24 6LX S21 tractor	30.3.62.	15 tons	T
741	827 TKK	Foden KG6/24 6LK S20 8 wheel rigid	11.4.62.	15 tons	T
53	946 TKL	Foden FGTU6/24 6LX S21 tractor	18.4.62.	15 tons	A
747	121 TKO	Foden KG6/24 6LK S20 8 wheel rigid	8.5.62.	15 tons	T
119	611 UKO	Atkinson FC 5LW/Scammell tractor	24.8.62.	12 tons	A
120	612 UKO	Atkinson FC 5LW/Scammell tractor	24.8.62.	12 tons	A
126	156 UKP	Atkinson FC 5LW/Scammell tractor	1.9.62.	12 tons	A
128	157 UKP	Atkinson FC 5LW/Scammell tractor	1.9.62.	12 tons	A
757	769 UKP	Commer CADY887 4 wheel rigid	10.9.62.	7 tons	T
131	535 UKR	Atkinson FC 5LW/Scammell tractor	14.9.62.	12 tons	A
129	536 UKR	Atkinson FC 5LW/Scammell tractor	14.9.62.	12 tons	A
125	435 UKT	Atkinson FC 5LW/Scammell tractor	28.9.62.	12 tons	A
140	139 VKK	Atkinson FC 5LW/Scammell tractor	25.10.62.	12 tons	A
132	140 VKK	Atkinson FC 5LW/Scammell tractor	25.10.62.	12 tons	A
47	281 VKK	Atkinson FC 5LW/Scammell tractor	25.10.62.	12 tons	A
137	282 VKK	Atkinson FC 5LW/Scammell tractor	25.10.62.	12 tons	A
758	512 VKK	Commer CADY887 4 wheel rigid	29.10.62.	7 tons	T
759	513 VKK	Commer CADY887 4 wheel rigid	29.10.62.	7 tons	T
760	514 VKK	Commer CADY887 4 wheel rigid	29.10.62.	7 tons	T
756	515 VKK	Commer CADY887 4 wheel rigid	29.10.62.	7 tons	T
761	516 VKK	Commer CADY887 4 wheel rigid	29.10.62.	7 tons	T
138	611 VKK	Atkinson FC 5LW/Scammell tractor	30.10.62.	12 tons	A
700	t/plates	AEC Matador recovery	Nov 1962	Garage	T
762	626 VKN	Atkinson FC 5LW/Scammell tractor	5.12.62.	12 tons	T
763	627 VKN	Atkinson FC 5LW/Scammell tractor	5.12.62.	12 tons	T
765	628 VKN	Atkinson FC 5LW/Scammell tractor	5.12.62.	12 tons	T
768	629 VKN	Atkinson FC 5LW/Scammell tractor	5.12.62.	12 tons	T
-	412 WKT	Austin Mini Traveller	4.1.63.	Depot	T
711	74 YKL	Austin J4 van	23.7.63.	Garage	T

Appendix 17 continued:

Fleet No	Reg'n No	Make, Model and Type	Date Reg'd	Payload	Depot
?	301 YKM	Austin J4/PA	30.7.63		
?	803 YKM	Morris M/AV5	7.8.63.		
?	804 YKM	Austin J4/VA/M10	7.8.63.		
?	853 YKM	Ford D24C	14.8.63.		
59	148 YKP	Atkinson FC 5LW tractor	3.9.63.	12 tons	A
60	612 YKT	Atkinson FC 5LW tractor	19.9.63.	12 tons	A
57	7115 KM	Atkinson FC 5LW tractor	26.11.63.	12 tons	A
40	7720 KM	Atkinson FC 5LW/Scammell tractor	1.12.63.	12 tons	A
744	7721 KM	Foden FGTU6/24 6LX S21 tractor	1.12.63.	15 tons	T
37	7722 KM	Atkinson FC 5LW tractor	1.12.63.	12 tons	A
29	8354 KM	Atkinson FC 5LW tractor	6.12.63.	12 tons	A
61	8507 KM	Atkinson FC 5LW tractor	10.12.63.	12 tons	A
55	8508 KM	Atkinson FC 5LW tractor	10.12.63.	12 tons	A
62	9080 KO	Atkinson FC 5LW tractor	17.12.63.	12 tons	A
135	153 KO	Atkinson FC 5LW tractor	24.12.63.	12 tons	A
?	9408 KM	Atkinson FC 5LW tractor	1.1.64.	12 tons	
114	157 KO	Atkinson FC 5LW tractor	1.1.64.	12 tons	A
134	1178 KO	Atkinson FC 5LW tractor	7.1.64.	12 tons	A
12	1179 KO	Atkinson FC 5LW tractor	7.1.64.	12 tons	A
213	1425 KO	Atkinson FC 5LW tractor	8.1.64.	12 tons	A
201	1430 KO	Atkinson JC 5LW tractor	9.1.64.	12 tons	A
67	1980 KO	Atkinson FC 5LW/Scammell tractor	13.1.64.	12 tons	A
819	2204 KO	Atkinson FC 5LW/Scammell tractor	15.1.64.	12 tons	T
820	2208 KO	Atkinson FC 5LW/Scammell tractor	17.1.64.	12 tons	T
725	3471 KO	Atkinson FC 5LW/Scammell tractor	24.1.64.	12 tons	T
206	4585 KO	Atkinson FC 5LW/Scammell tractor	3.2.64.	12 tons	A
219	4586 KO	Atkinson FC 5LW tractor	3.2.64.	12 tons	A
13	6011 KO	Austin FHK160 4 wheel rigid	11.2.64.	8 tons	A
7	8710 KO	Atkinson FC 5LW tractor	28.2.64.	12 tons	A
727	5746 KP	Austin FFK240/Scammell tractor	14.4.64.	12 tons	T
737	5911 KP	Austin FFK240/Scammell tractor	15.4.64.	12 tons	T
766	7751 KP	Austin FFK240/Scammell tractor	24.4.64.	12 tons	T
764	8818 KP	Austin FFK240/Scammell tractor	1.5.64.	12 tons	T
100	935 KR	Austin van or pickup ?	14.5.64.		
767	939 KR	Austin FFK240/Scammell tractor	15.5.64.	12 tons	T
118	3966 KR	Austin JO2 PA16 van	3.6.64.		A
712	9670 KR	Atkinson FC 5LW/Scammell tractor	13.7.64.	12 tons	T
75	202 D	Austin FHK160 4 wheel rigid	13.7.64.	8 tons	A
202	1622 D	Austin FHK160 4 wheel rigid	23.7.64.	8 tons	A
4	1623 D	Atkinson FC 5LW tractor	23.7.64.	12 tons	
2	3418 D	Atkinson FC 5LW tractor	10.8.64.	12 tons	G
72	AKJ 244B	Austin FFK240/Scammell tractor	4.9.64.	12 tons	A
814	AKK 654B	Austin FFK240/Scammell tractor	15.9.64.	12 tons	T
69	AKL 296B	Austin FFK240/Scammell tractor	21.9.64.	12 tons	A
198	AKN 869B	Atkinson FC 5LW tractor	12.10.64.	12 tons	G
24	AKN 870B	Austin FFK240/Scammell tractor	12.10.64.	12 tons	A
5	AKO 219B	Atkinson FC 5LW tractor	13.10.64.	12 tons	
6	AKO 572B	Atkinson FC 5LW/Scammell tractor C	15.10.64.	12 tons	A
716	AKP 437B	Atkinson FC 5LW/Scammell tractor C	26.10.64.	12 tons	T
779	AKT 265B	Atkinson FC 5LW/Scammell tractor C	5.11.64.	12 tons	T
778	AKT 452B	Atkinson FC 5LW/Scammell tractor C	6.11.64.	12 tons	T
777	AKT 458B	Atkinson FC 5LW/Scammell tractor C	9.11.64.	12 tons	T
780	BKJ 509B	Atkinson FC 5LW/Scammell tractor C	24.11.64.	12 tons	T
774	BKK 312B	Atkinson FC 5LW/Scammell tractor C	4.12.64.	12 tons	T
? 205	BKL 233B	Atkinson FC 5LW/Scammell tractor	8.1.65.	12 tons	A
782	BKN 54C	Atkinson FC 5LW/Scammell tractor C	4.1.65.	12 tons	T

Appendix 17 continued:

Fleet No	Reg'n No	Make, Model and Type	Date Reg'd	Payload	Depot
192	BKN 56C	Atkinson FC 5LW/Scammell tractor C	4.1.65.	12 tons	G
199	BKN 57C	Atkinson FC 5LW/Scammell tractor	4.1.65.	12 tons	G
772	BKN 976C	Atkinson FC 5LW/Scammell tractor C	1.1.65.	12 tons	T
191	CKE 167C	Atkinson FC 5LW/Scammell tractor	5.2.65.	12 tons	G
?	CKE 634C	Atkinson FC 5LW/Scammell tractor	11.2.65.	12 tons	G
200	CKE 635C	Atkinson FC 5LW/Scammell tractor	10.2.65.	12 tons	G
773	CKK 675C	Atkinson FC 5LW/Scammell tractor C	1.3.65.	12 tons	T
188	CKN 531C	Atkinson FC 5LW tractor	8.3.65.	12 tons	G
19	CKO 461C	Atkinson FC 5LW tractor	12.3.65.	12 tons	A
189	CKO 793C	Atkinson FC 5LW tractor	19.3.65.	12 tons	G
11	CKP 515C	Atkinson FC 5LW tractor	22.3.65.	12 tons	A
179	CKP 519C	Atkinson FC 5LW tractor	25.3.65.	12 tons	G
187	DKE 852C	Atkinson FC 5LW tractor	13.4.65.	12 tons	G
194	DKE 853C	Atkinson FC 5LW tractor	13.4.65.	12 tons	G
787	DKJ 174C	Atkinson FC 5LW/Scammell tractor C	20.4.65.	12 tons	T
789	DKJ 175C	Atkinson FC 5LW/Scammell tractor C	20.4.65.	12 tons	T
776	DKJ 176C	Atkinson FC 5LW/Scammell tractor C	20.4.65.	12 tons	T
788	DKJ 177C	Atkinson FC 5LW/Scammell tractor C	20.4.65.	12 tons	T
781	DKJ 178C	Atkinson FC 5LW/Scammell tractor C	20.4.65.	12 tons	T
3	DKN 181C	ERF LV 54G 5LW tractor	28.5.65.	12 tons	A
8	DKO 732C	ERF LV 54G 5LW tractor	17.6.65.	12 tons	A
171	DKP 186C	Atkinson FC 5LW tractor	25.6.65.	12 tons	G
?	DKR 513C	Atkinson FC 5LW tractor	7.7.65.	12 tons	G
172	EKE 197C	ERF LV 54G 5LW tractor	1.8.65.	12 tons	G
703	EKE 462C	Atkinson FC 5LW tractor	1.8.65.	12 tons	T
9	EKL 146C	Austin FJK160 4 wheel rigid	6.8.65.	8 tons	A
173	EKJ 395C	Austin FJK160 4 wheel rigid	11.8.65.	8 tons	G
50	EYN 523C	Austin FGK van - mobile wokshops	24.8.65.	Garage	G
109	EKK 481C	Austin FJK160 4 wheel rigid	25.8.65.	8 tons	
15	EKK 482C	ERF LV 64CU NHE180 tractor	26.8.65.	20 tons	A
704	EKK 632C	Atkinson FC 5LW tractor	27.8.65.	12 tons	T
?	EKL 311C	Austin FJK160 4 wheel rigid	8.9.65.	8 tons	
174	EKL 312C	Austin FJK160 4 wheel rigid	8.9.65.	8 tons	G
177	EKM 832C	Austin FJK160 4 wheel rigid	1.10.65.	8 tons	G
180	EKN 448C	ERF LV 64CU NHE180 tractor	7.10.65.	20 tons	A
211	EKN 449C	ERF LV 64CU NHE180 tractor	7.10.65.	20 tons	A
181	EKN 450C	ERF LV 64CU NHE180 tractor	7.10.65.	20 tons	A
705	EKN 571C	Atkinson FC 6LX tractor	7.10.65.	20 tons	T
175	EKO 680C	ERF LV 54G 5LW tractor	1.11.65.	12 tons	G
178	EKR 371C	ERF LV 54G 5LW tractor	12.11.65.	12 tons	G
706	EKR 377C	Atkinson FC 6LX tractor	17.11.65.	20 tons	T
713	EKT 182C	Atkinson FC 6LX tractor	23.11.65.	20 tons	T
?	EKT 183C	Austin FJK360 tractor	1.12.65.	See note 15	
176	FKE 606D	ERF LV 54G 5LW tractor	1.1.66.	12 tons	G
154	FKE 607D	ERF LV 64CU NHE180 tractor	1.1.66.	20 tons	A
715	FKE 608D	Austin FJK360 Mastiff tractor	1.1.66.	12 tons	T
153	FKJ 670D	ERF LV 64CU NHE180 tractor	1.12.65.	20 tons	A
?	FKJ 696D	Austin FFK340 tractor	1.1.66.	See note 15	
?	FKL 468D	Atkinson FC 5LW tractor	11.1.66.	12 tons	G
190	FKL 642D	ERF LV 54G 5LW tractor	17.1.66.	12 tons	G
193	FKM 427D	ERF LV 54G 5LW tractor	1.2.66.	12 tons	G
155	FKP 220D	ERF LV 64CU NHE180 tractor	1.3.66.	20 tons	A
182	GKE 746D	ERF LV 64CU NHE180 tractor	23.3.66.	20 tons	A
157	GKK 550D	ERF LV 64CU NHE180 tractor	14.4.66.	20 tons	A
707	GKM 893D	ERF LV 64CU NHE180 tractor	28.4.66.	20 tons	T
164	GKM 894D	ERF LV 54G 5LW tractor	28.4.66.	12 tons	A

Appendix 17 continued:

Fleet No	Reg'n No	Make, Model and Type	Date Reg'd	Payload	Depot
708	GKN 446D	ERF LV 64CU NHE180 tractor	2.5.66.	20 tons	T
709	GKO 236D	ERF LV 64CU NHE180 tractor	12.5.66.	20 tons	T
719	GKO 238D	ERF LV 64CU NHE180 tractor	16.5.66.	20 tons	T
722	GKO 239D	ERF LV 64CU NHE180 tractor	16.5.66.	20 tons	T
794	GKP 169D	Seddon 13:four P6.354 tractor	27.5.66.	12 tons	T
795	GKP 170D	Seddon 13:four P6.354 tractor	27.5.66.	12 tons	T
165	GKR 129D	ERF LV 54G 5LW tractor	7.6.66.	12 tons	A
141	GKR 772D	Seddon 13:four P6.354 tractor	9.6.66.	12 tons	W
142	GKR 775D	Seddon 13:four P6.354 tractor	10.6.66.	12 tons	W
143	HKE 132D	Seddon 13:four P6.354 tractor	24.6.66.	12 tons	W
144	HKE 133D	Seddon 13:four P6.354 tractor	24.6.66.	12 tons	W
158	HKE 922D	ERF LV 64CU NHE180 tractor	1.7.66.	20 tons	A
26	HKE 923D	Seddon 13:four P6.354 tractor	1.7.66.	12 tons	A
20	HKE 924D	Seddon 13:four P6.354 tractor	1.7.66.	12 tons	A
14	HKE 925D	Seddon 13:four P6.354 tractor	1.7.66.	12 tons	A
183	HKJ 230D	Atkinson FC NHE180 tractor	11.7.66.	20 tons	A
27	HKJ 516D	Seddon 13:four P6.354 tractor	11.7.66.	12 tons	A
28	HKJ 935D	Seddon 13:four P6.354 tractor	1.8.66.	12 tons	A
38	HKK 145D	Seddon 13:four P6 354 tractor	20.7.66.	12 tons	A
159	HKL 450D	ERF LV 64CU NHE180 tractor	5.8.66.	20 tons	A
196	HKM 753D	ERF LV 64CU NHE180 tractor	6.9.66.	20 tons	G
195	HKM 754D	ERF LV 64CU NHE180 tractor	6.9.66.	20 tons	G
184	HKO 826D	Atkinson FC NHE180 tractor	10.10.66.	20 tons	A
160	HKP 373D	ERF LV 64CU NHE180 tractor	1.11.66.	20 tons	A
163	HKP 752D	ERF LV 64CU NHE180 tractor	1.11.66.	20 tons	A
-	JJJ 479D	Ford Escort Estate	1966	Depot	T
17	JKT 119E	Atkinson FC NHE180 tractor	1.4.67.	20 tons	A
10	KKJ 863E	ERF LV 64CU NHE180 tractor	1.5.67.	20 tons	A
22	KKJ 864E	ERF LV 64CU NHE180 tractor	1.5.67.	20 tons	A
30	KKK 340E	ERF LV 64CU NHE180 tractor	3.5.67.	20 tons	A
705	KKK 751E	ERF LV 64CU NHE180 tractor	8.5.67.	20 tons	T
710	KKL 151E	ERF LV 64CU NHE180 tractor	11.5.67.	20 tons	T
18	KKL 734E	ERF LV 64CU NHE180 tractor	1.6.67.	20 tons	A
42	KKL 735E	ERF LV 64CU NHE180 tractor	1.6.67.	20 tons	A
49	KKN 269E	AEC TGM4B Mercury tractor	7.6.67.	15 tons	A
56	KKN 371E	ERF LV 64CU NHE180 tractor	7.6.67.	20 tons	A
64	LKE 416F	ERF LV 64CU NHE180 tractor	21.7.67.	20 tons	A
63	LKE 417F	ERF LV 64CU NHE180 tractor	21.7.67.	20 tons	A
65	LKK 937F	ERF LV 64CU NHE180 tractor	1.9.67.	20 tons	A
66	LKK 938F	ERF LV 64CU NHE180 tractor	1.9.67.	20 tons	A
-	ENK 514F	Ford Escort van		Insp.	T
720	VLL 721G	Austin JU van	24.9.68.	Garage	T
?	OKN 662G	AEC TG4R Mandator tractor	5.8.68.	20 tons	A
70	OKN 664G	AEC TG4R Mandator tractor	8.8.68.	20 tons	A
?	OKN 665G	AEC TG4R Mandator tractor	8.8.68.	20 tons	A
74	OKR 773G	AEC TG4R Mandator tractor	19.9.68.	20 tons	A
73	OKR 774G	AEC TG4R Mandator tractor	19.9.68.	20 tons	A
?	OKR 775G	Ford Transit van	19.9.68.		
76	OKT 950G	AEC TGM4R Mercury tractor	7.10.68.	15 tons	A
77	PKE 675G	AEC TGM4R Mercury tractor	15.10.68.	15 tons	A
78	PKJ 118G	AEC TGM4R Mercury tractor	17.10.68.	15 tons	A
79	PKJ 664G	AEC TG4R Mandator tractor	1.11.68.	15 tons	A
80	PKJ 665G	AEC TG4R Mandator tractor	1.11.68.	15 tons	A
?	PKK 510G	AEC TG4R Mandator tractor	1.11.68.	20 tons	
?	PKK 626G	AEC TG4R Mandator tractor	1.11.68.	20 tons	
711	PKL 321G	Bedford TK tractor	11.11.68.	9 tons	T

Appendix 17 continued:

Fleet No	Reg'n No	Make, Model and Type	Date Reg'd	Payload	Depot
234	PKL 322G	Ford D1000 4 wheel rigid	11.11.68.	8 tons	L
?	PKL 323G	AEC TG4R Mandator tractor	11.11.68.	15 tons	
714	PKL 324G	Bedford TK tractor	11.11.68.	9 tons	T
?	PKL 448G	AEC TG4R Mandator tractor	14.11.68.	20 tons	
?	PKL 449G	AEC TG4R Mandator tractor	14.11.68.	20 tons	
721	PKM 192G	Bedford TK tractor	21.11.68.	9 tons	T
731	PKM 193G	Bedford TK tractor	1.12.68.	9 tons	T
106	PKM 702G	AEC TG4R Mandator tractor	1.12.68.	20 tons	A
108	PKM 703G	AEC TGM4R Mercury tractor	1.12.68.	15 tons	A
783	PKM 763G	Ford Transit van	1.12.68.	Garage	T
178	PKM 764G	Ford Transit van	1.12.68.	Garage	G
23	PKN 314G	Ford D600 tractor	5.12.68.	9 tons	A
21	PKN 315G	Ford D600 tractor	5.12.68.	9 tons	A
110	PKN 316G	AEC TGM4R Mercury tractor	6.12.68.	15 tons	A
735	PKN 317G	Bedford TK tractor	6.12.68.	9 tons	T
769	PKN 583G	Bedford TK tractor	11.12.68.	9 tons	T
750	PKN 584G	Bedford TK tractor	11.12.68.	9 tons	T
32	PKO 116G	Ford D600 tractor	17.12.68.	9 tons	A
31	PKO 117G	Ford D600 tractor	17.12.68.	9 tons	A
111	PKO 120G	AEC TGM4R Mercury tractor	19.12.68.	15 tons	A
784	PKO 793G	Bedford TK tractor	1.1.69.	9 tons	T
34	PKO 794G	Ford D600 tractor	1.1.69.	9 tons	A
33	PKO 795G	Ford D600 tractor	1.1.69.	9 tons	A
115	PKO 796G	AEC TGM4R Mercury tractor	1.1.69.	15 tons	A
?	PKO 797G	AEC TGM4R Mercury tractor	1.1.69.	15 tons	
117	PKO 799G	AEC TGM4R Mercury tractor	1.1.69.	15 tons	A
35	PKO 984G	Ford D600 tractor	2.1.69.	9 tons	A
?	PKO 985G	Ford Transit van	2.1.69.		
825	PKP 156G	Ford Escort van	2.1.69.	Depot	T
?	PKP 346G	Ford Escort van	7.1.69.		
36	PKP 347G	Ford D600 tractor	7.1.69.	9 tons	A
?	PKP 348G	AEC TG4R Mandator tractor	7.1.69.	20 tons	
785	PKP 349G	Bedford TK tractor	7.1.69.	9 tons	T
162	PKP 434G	AEC TGM4R Mercury tractor	10.1.69.	15 tons	G
?	PKP 435G	AEC TG4R Mandator tractor	10.1.69.	20 tons	
39	PKP 601G	Ford D600 tractor	10.1.69.	9 tons	A
148	PKP 604G	Ford D800 4 wheel boxvan	14.1.69.	8 tons	A
41	PKP 605G	Ford D600 tractor	14.1.69.	9 tons	A
?	PKP 904G	AEC TGM4R Mercury tractor	17.1.69.	15 tons	
52	PKP 905G	Ford D600 tractor	17.1.69.	9 tons	A
168	PKR 216G	AEC TGM4R Mercury tractor	17.1.69.	15 tons	G
51	PKR 217G	Ford D600 tractor	17.1.69.	9 tons	A
54	PKR 218G	Ford D600 tractor	17.1.69.	9 tons	A
?	PKR 220G	Ford D800 4 wheel boxvan	21.1.69.	8 tons	A
786	PKR 338G	Bedford TK tractor	22.1.69.	9 tons	T
?	PKR 339G	AEC TG4R Mandator tractor	22.1.69.	20 tons	
823	PKR 746G	Ford D800 4 wheel boxvan	1.2.69.	8 tons	T
824	PKR 747G	Ford D800 4 wheel boxvan	1.2.69.	8 tons	T
58	PKR 748G	Ford D600 tractor	1.2.69.	9 tons	A
156	PKT 293G	Ford D800 4 wheel boxvan	4.2.69.	8 tons	A
127	PKT 294G	Ford D600 tractor	4.2.69.	9 tons	A
790	PKT 591G	Bedford TK tractor	5.2.69.	9 tons	T
791	PKT 595G	Bedford TK tractor	7.2.69.	9 tons	T
203	PKT 795G	Bedford KM 4 wheel rigid	1.2.69.	9 tons	A
792	RKE 106G	Bedford TK tractor	11.2.69.	9 tons	T
793	RKE 109G	Bedford TK tractor	14.2.69.	9 tons	T

Appendix 17 continued:

Fleet No	Reg'n No	Make, Model and Type	Date Reg'd	Payload	Depot
796	RKE 308G	Bedford TK tractor	17.2.69.	9 tons	T
136	RKE 309G	Ford D600 tractor	17.2.69.	9 tons	A
139	RKE 492G	Ford D600 tractor	18.2.69.	9 tons	A
135	RKE 493G	Ford D800 4 wheel boxvan	18.2.69.	8 tons	A
797	RKE 495G	Bedford TK tractor	20.2.69.	9 tons	T
799	RKE 772G	Bedford TK tractor	21.2.69.	9 tons	T
145	RKE 773G	Ford D600 tractor	21.2.69.	9 tons	A
800	RKJ 482G	Bedford TK tractor	1.3.69.	9 tons	T
146	RKJ 483G	Ford D600 tractor	1.3.69.	9 tons	A
801	RKJ 793G	Bedford TK tractor	1.3.69.	9 tons	T
204	RKJ 794G	Bedford KM 4 wheel rigid	1.3.69.	9 tons	A
207	RKJ 795G	AEC TG4R Mandator tractor	1.3.69.	20 tons	A
802	RKK 167G	Bedford TK tractor	5.3.69.	9 tons	T
206	RKK 170G	Bedford KM 4 wheel rigid	6.3.69.	9 tons	A
208	RKK 448G	AEC TG4R Mandator tractor	12.3.69.	20 tons	A
806	RKK 792G	Bedford KM 4 wheel rigid	14.3.69.	9 tons	T
804	RKK 793G	Bedford KM 4 wheel rigid	14.3.69.	9 tons	T
803	RKK 794G	Bedford KM 4 wheel rigid	14.3.69.	9 tons	T
147	RKL 327G	Ford D600 tractor	20.3.69.	9 tons	A
102	SKJ 723G	Ford Transit van	27.6.69.	Garage	A
K1	SKJ 981G	Ford D800 4 wheel rigid	3.7.69.	8 tons	A
K2	SKK 314G	Ford D800 4 wheel rigid	17.7.69.	8 tons	A
K3	SKN 616H	Ford D800 4 wheel rigid	30.7.69.	8 tons	A
235	SKN 894H	Scania LBS110 6x2 tractor	5.8.69.	19 tons	A
900	SKO 511H	AEC TGM4R Mercury tractor	12.8.69.	15 tons	D
902	SKO 512H	AEC TGM4R Mercury tractor	12.8.69.	15 tons	D
901	SKO 513H	AEC TGM4R Mercury tractor	12.8.69.	15 tons	D
?	SKO 514H	AEC TG4R Mandator tractor	12.8.69.	20 tons	
K4	SKO 557H	Ford D800 4 wheel rigid	12.8.69.	8 tons	A
236	SKR 491H	Scania LBS110 6x2 tractor	9.9.69.	19 tons	A
K5	SKR 492H	Ford D800 4 wheel rigid	9.9.69.	8 tons	A
237	SKR 493H	Scania LBS110 6x2 tractor	9.9.69.	19 tons	A
K6	SKR 494H	Ford D800 4 wheel rigid	9.9.69.	8 tons	A
210	SKR 556H	AEC TG4R Mandator tractor	10.9.69.	20 tons	G
950	SKT 197H	Ford D600 tractor	18.9.69.	9 tons	W
952	SKT 416H	Ford D600 tractor	23.9.69.	9 tons	W
951	SKT 417H	Ford D600 tractor	23.9.69.	9 tons	W
953	SKT 418H	Ford D600 tractor	23.9.69.	9 tons	W
29	SKT 901H	AEC TGM4R Mercury tractor	1.10.69.	15 tons	A
K7	SKT 902H	Ford D800 4 wheel rigid	1.10.69.	8 tons	A
212	SKT 903H	AEC TG4R Mandator tractor	1.10.69.	20 tons	G
214	SKT 904H	AEC TG4R Mandator tractor	1.10.69.	20 tons	G
954	SKT 908H	Ford D600 tractor	1.10.69.	9 tons	W
955	SKT 909H	Ford D600 tractor	1.10.69.	9 tons	W
958	TKE 641H	Ford D600 tractor	7.10.69.	9 tons	W
957	TKE 642H	Ford D600 tractor	7.10.69.	9 tons	W
956	TKE 643H	Ford D600 tractor	7.10.69.	9 tons	W
959	TKE 649H	Ford D600 tractor	9.10.69.	9 tons	W
98	TKE 877H	Ford Escort van	13.10.69.	Garage	A
37	TKK 757H	AEC TGM4R Mercury tractor	14.11.69.	15 tons	A
-	TKL 175H	Ford Escort van	19.11.69.	Depot	A
202	TKL 371H	Ford Transit van	19.11.69.	Garage	A
43	TKL 376H	AEC TGM4R Mercury tractor	20.11.69.	15 tons	A
960	TKL 528H	Ford D600 tractor	25.11.69.	9 tons	W
44	TKM 368H	AEC TGM4R Mercury tractor	8.12.69.	15 tons	A
961	TKM 793H	Ford D600 tractor	15.12.69.	9 tons	W

Reed *TRANSPORT*

Appendix 17 continued:

Fleet No	Reg'n No	Make, Model and Type	Date Reg'd	Payload	Depot
962	TKM 794H	Ford D600 tractor	15.12.69.	9 tons	W
963	TKM 863H	Ford D600 tractor	16.12.69.	9 tons	W
964	TKN 162H	Ford D600 tractor	17.12.69.	9 tons	W
965	TKN 165H	Ford D600 tractor	18.12.69.	9 tons	W
966	TKN 168H	Ford D600 tractor	19.12.69.	9 tons	W
968	TKN 169H	Ford D600 tractor	1.1.70.	9 tons	W
967	TKN 170H	Ford D600 tractor	1.1.70.	9 tons	W
215	TKN 985H	AEC TG4R Mandator tractor	5.1.70.	20 tons	G
969	TKR 271H	Ford D600 tractor	1.2.70.	9 tons	W
216	TKR 272H	AEC TG4R Mandator tractor	1.2.70.	20 tons	G
47	TKR 275H	Ford D600 tractor	2.2.70.	9 tons	A
46	TKR 276H	Ford D600 tractor	2.2.70.	9 tons	A
45	TKR 277H	Ford D600 tractor	2.2.70.	9 tons	A
55	TKR 601H	Ford D600 tractor	4.2.70.	9 tons	A
57	TKR 826H	Ford D600 tractor	9.2.70.	9 tons	A
186	UKN 526H	Ford D800 4 wheel rigid	13.4.70.	8 tons	?
197	UKP 318H	Ford D ? 4 wheel rigid. See note 21.	1.5.70.	?	G
217	UKP 536H	Scania LB80 tractor	7.5.70.	20 tons	A
860	UKR 292H	Ford Escort van	11.5.70.	Depot	D
218	VKE 321H	Scania LB80 tractor	1.6.70.	20 tons	A
220	VKE 327H	Scania LB80 tractor	1.6.70.	20 tons	A
224	VKE 328H	Scania LB110 tractor	1.6.70.	20 tons	A
225	VKE 922H	Scania LB110 tractor	3.6.70.	20 tons	A
226	VKL 734H	Scania LB110 tractor	3.7.70.	20 tons	A
208	WKE 534J	Foden 4AX6/30 6LX S39 tractor	11.9.70.	20 tons	A
717	WKJ 739J	Ford D600 tractor	1.10.70.	9 tons	T
219	WKM 494J	Scania LB110 tractor	1.11.70.	20 tons	A
227	WKM 495J	Scania LB110 tractor	1.11.70.	20 tons	A
228	WKN 393J	Scania LB110 tractor	13.11.70.	20 tons	A
213	WKO 247J	Foden 4AX6/30 6LX S39 tractor	1.12.70.	20 tons	A
229	WKO 249J	Scania LB110 tractor	1.12.70.	20 tons	A
232	WKO 250J	Scania LB110 tractor	1.12.70.	20 tons	A
231	WKO 481J	Scania LB110 tractor	1.12.70.	20 tons	A
238	XKE 757J	Scania LB110 tractor	1.2.71.	20 tons	A
700	t/plates	Foden S21 6 wheel recovery	25.2.71.	Garage	T
239	XKO 321J	Scania LB110 tractor	11.3.71.	20 tons	A
771	YKM 543J	Ford Transit van	4.6.71.		
713	AKJ 618K	Ford Escort van	1.8.71.	Depot	T
?	BKJ 285K	AEC 2TG4R Mandator tractor	12.10.71.	20 tons	
94	BKT 181K	Foden AG18/30 6LXB S40 tractor	13.1.72.	20 tons	A
95	BKT 182K	Foden AG18/30 6LXB S40 tractor	10.1.72.	20 tons	A
912	BKT 183K	Foden AG18/30 6LXB S40 12 sp tractor	4.1.72.	20 tons	D
913	BKT 184K	Foden AG18/30 6LXB S40 12 sp tractor	14.1.72.	20 tons	D
910	BKT 185K	Foden AG18/30 6LXB S40 12 sp tractor	1.1.72.	20 tons	D
914	BKT 186K	Foden AG18/30 6LXB S40 12 sp tractor	4.1.72.	20 tons	D
87	BKT 187K	Foden AG18/30 6LXB S40 tractor	6.1.72.	20 tons	A
88	BKT 188K	Foden AG18/30 6LXB S40 tractor	10.1.72.	20 tons	A
89	BKT 189K	Foden AG18/30 6LXB S40 tractor	13.1.72.	20 tons	A
90	BKT 190K	Foden AG18/30 6LXB S40 tractor	10.1.72.	20 tons	A
91	BKT 191K	Foden AG18/30 6LXB S40 tractor	6.1.72.	20 tons	A
92	BKT 192K	Foden AG18/30 6LXB S40 tractor	14.1.72.	20 tons	A
93	BKT 193K	Foden AG18/30 6LXB S40 tractor	14.1.72.	20 tons	A
911	BKT 194K	Foden AG18/30 6LXB S40 12 sp tractor	1.1.72.	20 tons	D
100	CKJ 321K	Ford Transit pickup	10.1.72.	Stores	A
241	CKN 826K	Scania LB110 tractor	1.3.72.	20 tons	A
240	CKN 827K	Scania LB110 tractor	1.3.72.	20 tons	A

Appendix 17 continued:

Fleet No	Reg'n No	Make, Model and Type	Date Reg'd	Payload	Depot
96	CKO 978K	Foden AG18/30 6LXB S40 tractor	14.4.72.	20 tons	A
702	CKO 979K	Foden AG18/30 6LXB S40 12 sp tractor	13.4.72.	20 tons	T
915	EKJ 977K	Foden AG18/30 6LXB S40 9 spd tractor	1.7.72.	20 tons	D
916	EKJ 978K	Foden AG18/30 6LXB S40 9 spd tractor	1.7.72.	20 tons	D
917	EKJ 979K	Foden AG18/30 6LXB S40 9 spd tractor	1.7.72.	20 tons	D
918	EKJ 980K	Foden AG18/30 6LXB S40 9 spd tractor	1.7.72.	20 tons	D
704	EKM 376K	Foden AG18/30 6LXB S40 9 spd tractor	21.7.72.	20 tons	T
97	EKM 377K	Foden AG18/30 6LXB S40 tractor	11.7.72.	20 tons	A
712	EKT 121L	Foden AG18/30 6LXB S40 9 spd tractor	1.8.72.	20 tons	T
919	EKT 366L	Foden AG18/30 6LXB S40 9 spd tractor	1.8.72.	20 tons	D
920	EKT 368L	Foden AG18/30 6LXB S40 9 spd tractor	1.8.72.	20 tons	D
715	EKT 369L	Foden AG18/30 6LXB S40 9 spd tractor	7.8.72.	20 tons	T
748	FKK 430L	Ford D1000 tractor	11.8.72.	15 tons	T
904	FKO 495L	Dodge LDV 3V1029 rigid + drawbar trlr	1.11.72.	15 tons	D
155	t/plates	ERF LV 64CU NHE180 6 wheel recovery	?	Garage	A
703	HKL 305L	Ford D800 tractor	1.2.73.	12 tons	T
-	HKM 943L	Austin J4	1.2.73.	See note 30	
200	HKO 711L	Scania LB110 tractor	2.3.73.	20 tons	A
201	HKO 712L	Scania LB110 tractor	2.3.73.	20 tons	A
205	HKO 720L	Scania LB110 tractor	14.6.73.	20 tons	G
729	HKO 721L	Scania LB110 tractor	22.6.73.	20 tons	T
73	HKO 722L	Scania LB110 tractor	22.6.73.	20 tons	A
124	JKE 342L	Austin 1300 van	1.4.73.	Garage	A
716	JKE 846L	Ford D800 tractor	15.3.73.	12 tons	T
723	JKK 108L	Scania LB110 tractor	22.3.73.	20 tons	T
974	JKL 342L	Austin 1300 van	1.4.73.	Depot	W
718	JKM 161L	Ford D800 tractor	2.4.73.	12 tons	T
725	JKP 462L	Scania LB110 tractor	1.5.73.	20 tons	T
212	JKR 265L	Scania LB110 tractor	4.5.73.	20 tons	G
72	JKR 266L	Scania LB110 tractor	4.5.73.	20 tons	A
214	KKL 371L	Scania LB110 tractor	28.6.73.	20 tons	G
726	KKN 705L	Scania LB110 tractor	28.6.73.	20 tons	T
727	KKO 377L	Scania LB110 tractor	4.7.73.	20 tons	T
169	NKJ 674M	Ford DA2418 tractor	1.8.73.	15 tons	G
215	NKK 501M	Scania LB110 tractor	24.7.73.	20 tons	G
216	NKK 502M	Scania LB110 tractor	30.7.73.	20 tons	G
209	NKK 503M	Scania LB110 tractor	1.10.73.	20 tons	G
223	NKK 504M	Scania LB110 tractor	1.10.73.	20 tons	A
728	NKK 505M	Scania LB110 tractor	5.10.73.	20 tons	T
925	NKT 741M	Scania LB110 tractor	5.9.73.	20 tons	D
173	OKK 350M	Ford DA2014 tractor	1.10.73.	12 tons	G
K9	OKL 611M	Ford DA2014 tractor	5.10.73.	12 tons	N
970	OKL 612M	Ford DA2014 tractor	5.10.73.	12 tons	W
174	OKL 617M	Ford DA2014 tractor	8.10.73.	12 tons	G
884	OKL 851M	Ford DA2014 tractor	9.10.73.	12 tons	D
971	OKO 244M	Ford DA2014 tractor	1.11.73.	12 tons	W
177	OKO 245M	Ford DA2014 tractor	1.11.73.	12 tons	G
179	OKO 246M	Ford DA2014 tractor	1.11.73.	12 tons	G
885	OKO 973M	Ford DA2014 tractor	5.11.73.	12 tons	D
709	OKP 244M	Ford DA2014 tractor	6.11.73.	12 tons	T
972	OKP 957M	Ford DA2014 tractor	15.11.73.	12 tons	W
K10	OKR 413M	Ford DA2014 tractor	19.11.73.	12 tons	N
?	OKR 836M	Ford Transit van	27.11.73.		
973	OKR 837M	Ford Transit van	27.11.73.	Garage	W
706	PKJ 727M	Ford DA2014 tractor	1.1.74.	12 tons	T
701	PKK 126M	Ford Transit van	17.12.73.	Garage	T

Appendix 17 continued:

Fleet No	Reg'n No	Make, Model and Type	Date Reg'd	Payload	Depot
-	PKT 618M	Ford Escort van	4.3.74.	Insp.	T
198	RKE 639M	Ford Transit 175 van	18.3.74.	Garage	G
724	RKT 830M	Ford DA2014 tractor	1.6.74.	12 tons	T
16	SKE 211M	Bedford tractor. See note 45	1.6.74.	15 tons	A
714	SKE 212M	Ford DA2014 tractor	1.6.74.	12 tons	T
-	SKE 658M	Ford Escort van	5.6.74.	See note 46	
730	SKK 249M	Ford DA2014 tractor	1.7.74.	12 tons	T
221	SKK 660M	Scania LB110 tractor	1.7.74.	20 tons	G
59	SKK 881M	Volvo F88 tractor	1.7.74.	20 tons	A
242	SKL 286M	Scania LB110 tractor	2.7.74.	20 tons	A
755	SKL 570M	Scania LB110 tractor	8.7.74.	20 tons	T
756	SKL 671M	Scania LB110 tractor	8.7.74.	20 tons	T
69	SKL 839M	Volvo F88 tractor	16.7.74.	20 tons	A

NOTES:

1 The two batches of Douglas Tugmasters had half cabs and were fitted with Humber/Commer petrol engines, 4 speed gearboxes and Eaton 2-speed axles. They replaced Bedford O and S tractors on Aylesford Paper Mills internal operations.

2 50 - 421 BKN had a half canopy/half pickup body with an extendable canopy to slide back to cover the open area if necessary.

3 Leyland Comets 144/145 FKT, 116-120/431 GKE are recorded in LTO archives as Scammells. The later two, 34/35 LKJ, recorded as Leyland Scammells

4 Leyland Comets 36-144 FKT and 41-116 GKE were transferred to Hollins PM and Darwen PM respectively as shunt units before RT acquired the ex WPM fleet, see Appendix 14.

5 226 - 953 MKE Leyland Octopus had 2 pedal control, fitted with a pneumocyclic gearbox. It has been covered as a separate feature as RT's most unique vehicle.

6 500 - AEC Matador recovery was later renumbered 105.

7 731 - 650 RKJ was in Reed Cartons livery.

8 734 - 504 SKK and 741 - 827 TKK Foden 8 wheelers were eventually cut down to 4x2 tractors for road use and later site shunting. They had a rather strange appearance with their 12" deep chassis members. See note 25.

9 233 - 631 SKM was eventually rebuilt with a basic half cab by Wigan Garage for site shunting and named The Beast .

10 15/747 - 629 SKP was originally part of the C Licence fleet at Aylesford. A photo confirms that it was badly damaged in an accident. It was rebuilt, renumbered 747 and transferred to Thatcham in about 1965. It is remembered as arriving at Thatcham minus the Foden badge. It must have replaced Foden 8 wheeler 747 - 121 TKO, less than four months younger, which almost certainly had been written-off in an accident. It was itself replaced at Aylesford by ERF LV 64CU EKK 432C which then took the number 15

11 Foden 561 TKE fleet number was probably 232. A photograph shows it wrecked - probably a write off.

12 700 AEC Matador recovery had a c.1944 chassis ex West Yorkshire Road Car, rebuilt by Thatcham Garage.

13 Atkinson FC 5LW/Scammell tractors with a 'C' added were later converted to 5th wheel.

14 6 - AKO 572B Atkinson FC was exhibited at the 1964 Earls Court Commercial Motor Show.

15 Seddons 794/795 - GKP 169/170D were transferred to Wigan in Feb 1969, then Darwen in August 1971.

16 Austin FJKs EKT 183C and FKJ 696D are somewhat of a mystery. EKT 183C was registered in the name of Reed Paper Group - common practice for the C Licence fleet but also for other Group Companies' vehicles. FKJ 696D was registered in the name of Reed Transport. No records could be found of where they operated and there was no memory of them either! As FJK360 and FJK340 models, they were certainly tractors.

17 49 - KKN 269E was transferred to Gravesend, not renumbered.

18 102 - SKJ 723G was later transferred to Darwen, not renumbered.

19 Boxvans PKR 220G and 156 - RKE 493G later were transferred to the Key/Caradon Terrain contract, repainted and renumbered K8 and K11. See Ch 12

20 197 - UKP 318H was transferred to Wigan in later life, renumbered 957. It's original Depot and fleet number is unknown, neither is it's body type.

21 54 - PKR 218G, 55 - TKR 601H and 57 - TKR 826H were transferred to Thatcham, not renumbered. 57 later went on to Wigan.

Appendix 17 Notes continued:

22 47 - TKR 275H, 46 - TKR 276H and 45 - TKR 277H were transferred to Wigan.

23 235 - SKN 894H, 236 - SKR 491H and 237 - SKR 493H at the end of their road life were cut down to 4x2 tractors for site shunting. 235 and 237 were transferred to Tilbury, later to Gravesend for their quayside operation. For 236 see note 25.

24 217 - UKP 536H and 218 - VKE 321H were transferred to London, renumbered 154 and 158.

25 One priority was the continual updating of the Aylesford Depot internal fleet using vehicles relegated from the road . In 1981 those involved were renumbered in the low series, as follows :

      225 - VKE 922H renumbered 11, 226 - VKL 734L to 12, 72 - JKR 266L to 14,
      723 - JKK 108L to 15, 726 - KKN 705L to 16 and 236 - SKR 491H to 18.

Previously an earlier batch of internal replacements were:

      734 - 504 SKK not renumbered, 754 - 308 SKK renumbered 10, 741 - 827 TKK to 11
      and 222 - 456 NKP to 12.

26 700 Foden S21 recovery replaced the Matador and was built on a concrete mixer chassis ex Morsham of Ashton in Makerfield. It was registered as Q999 JKO on 1.1.88.

27 904 - FKO 495L Dodge 4 wheel rigid was first registered in the owner's name - Rolands Trailer Hire Ltd and operated experimentally with a drawbar trailer plus dolly. It was originally in all white livery, Reed Transport black lettered headboard and Crown Paints logo on the cab doors. The trial operation for Crown was unsuccessful , the outfit was transferred to New Hythe Depot, painted green and renumbered 104. The drawbar trailer was occasionally used as a semi trailer independently. At an unknown date it is assumed that it was purchased from Rolands.

28 155 ERF recovery replaced the Matador 500/105. It was based on a 6 wheel tipper chassis with running gear from 64CU tractor 155 - FKP 220D

29 Darwen Depot also received a continual flow of replacement vehicles for it's shunting and local needs. Vehicles included were :
748 - FKK 430L renumbered 903 later replaced by FKM 427D, fleet no unknown also to 903,
182 - GKE 746D to 900 for Hollins/Crown Paints shunting, 208 - WKE 534J to 904 for shunting
on road, 163 - HKP 752D not renumbered for Sun Paper Mills shunting, and 239 - XKO 321J for Garage use for trailer maintenance and testing.

30 The origin of YKM 543J is uncertain. Originally registered in the name of Reed International, it's fleet number suggests that it started life at Thatcham. transferred to Wigan as Sample Van for RCC, retaining it's 771 number. Later it went to Darwen, renumbered 902.

31 Van HKM 943L was hired to Lower Darwen Paper Mill.

The early 1970s saw a contraction in business as described in Chapter 10. As a consequence there were considerable inter Depot transfers of vehicles, some of which are recorded below. Some vehicles were renumbered, others were not. Not all transfers will have been included, details lost in the passing of time.

32 87 - BKT 187K was transferred to Thatcham for site shunting, not renumbered.

33 729 - HKO 721L was transferred to Gravesend, renumbered 207

34 124 - JKE 342L was transferred to Darwen, renumbered 901.

35 73 - HKO 722L and 72 - JKR 266L were transferred to Wigan, renumbered 981 and 980

36 212 - JKR 265L, 214 - KKL 371L, 215 - NKK 501M and 216 - NKK 502M were transferred to Darwen, renumbered 921, 922, 923 and 924

37 Initially, Tilbury was a Sub Depot to Gravesend, see Ch 10. When it became autonomous for p & l purposes, three Scanias were transferred from Gravesend, 212 - JKR 265L, 214 - KKL 371L
and 221 - SKK 660M, none renumbered. In addition, 981 - HKO 722L transferred again from Wigan to Tilbury, renumbered 206.

38 723 - JKK 108L was transferred to Aylesford, renumbered 71.

39 173 - OKK 350M was transferred to New Hythe, renumbered 108 or 115.

40 179 - OKO 246M was transferred to New Hythe but not renumbered.

41 973 - OKR 837M was transferred to Thatcham, renumbered 703.

42 884 - OKL 851M and 885 - OKO 973M were transferred to Wigan, but not renumbered.

43 69 - SKL 839M was transferred to Wigan, renumbered 982

44 16 - SKE 211M was a demonstrator, model not known. LTO records confirm the registered owner as Cummins Eng Co Ltd with Vauxhall Motors Ltd as agent.

45 Van SKE 658M was hired to Data Processing Dept, a Corporate Department at Aylesford.

Appendix 18 - New Vehicle Purchases 1964 - 1966

The following were owned by Aylesford Paper Mills but sourced by Reed Transport to replace Douglas Tugmasters on internal mill operations

Fleet No	Reg'n No	Make, Model and Type	Date Reg'd	Payload
-	BKE 516B	Atkinson half-cab SLW/Scammell tractor	18.11.64.	12 tons
-	BKK 372B	Atkinson half-cab SLW/Scammell tractor	Dec. 1964.	12 tons
-	BKL 961B	Atkinson half-cab SLW/Scammell tractor	1.1.65.	12 tons
-	FKL 466D	Atkinson half-cab SLW/Scammell tractor	14.1.66.	12 tons
-	FKO 412D	Atkinson half-cab SLW/Scammell tractor	11.2.66.	12 tons

NOTE:
These tractors had David Brown six-speed gearboxes and Kirkstall rear axles - a special low ratio version limiting top speed to about 28 mph. Although built to 20 tons gvw design weight, 18 ton payloads were not unknown internally. They were operated on exempted licences

Appendix 19 - New Vehicle Purchases from 1974 (August)

Fleet No	Reg'n No	Make, Model and Type	Date Reg'd	Orig Cost	GVW/GTW	D
70	TKL 867N	Volvo F88 tractor	1.8.74.		32520	A
60	TKL 868N	Volvo F88 tractor	1.8.74.		32520	A
905	TKL 869N	Ford DA2418 tractor	1.8.74.		24390	D
926	TKM 214N	Scania 110 tractor	1.8.74.		32520	D
927	TKM 215N	Scania 110 tractor	1.8.74.		32520	D
984	TKM 856N	Volvo F88 tractor	9.8.74.		32520	W
731	TKM 857N	Ford DA2114 tractor	9.8.74.	£3542.00	21340	T
61	TKM 858N	Volvo F88 tractor	9.8.74.		32520	A
62	TKN 336N	Volvo F88 tractor	14.8.74.		32520	A
105	TKN 591N	Ford DA2114 tractor	1.9.74.	£4465.50	21340	N
64	TKN 592N	Volvo F88 tractor	1.9.74.		32520	A
67	TKO 301N	Volvo F88 tractor	1.9.74.		32520	A
985	TKO 302N	Volvo F88 tractor	1.9.74.		32520	W
758	TKO 303N	MAN 16.232 tractor	1.9.74.		32520	T
757	TKO 304N	MAN 16.232 tractor	1.9.74.		32520	T
762	TKO 976N	MAN 16.232 tractor	2.9.74.		32520	T
760	TKO 977N	MAN 16.232 tractor	2.9.74.		32520	T
759	TKO 978N	MAN 16.232 tractor	2.9.74.		32520	T
761	TKO 979N	MAN 16.232 tractor	2.9.74.		32520	T
68	TKP 699N	Volvo F88 tractor	10.9.74.		32520	A
106	GKJ 442N	Ford DA2114 tractor	1.10.74.	£3805.16	21340	N
986	GKL 860N	Volvo F88 tractor	15.10.74.		32520	W
975	GKN 570N	Ford DA2114 tractor	1.11.74.	£4038.00	21340	W
906	GKO 215N	Ford DA2418 tractor	8.11.74.		24390	D
161	GKP 647N	Ford DA2418 tractor	1.12.74.	£5865.91	24390	G
107	GKP 648N	Ford DA2114 tractor	1.12.74.	£4460.81	21340	N
150	GKP 942N	Ford Transit van	2.12.74.		Smalls	L
109	GKP 943N	Ford DA2114 tractor	2.12.74.	£4261.09	21340	N
977	GKR 196N	Ford DA2114 tractor	4.12.74.	£4261.09	21340	W
976	GKR 197N	Ford DA2114 tractor	4.12.74.	£4261.09	21340	W
112	HKE 26N	Ford DA2114 tractor	1.1.75.	£4273.59	21340	N
17	HKE 27N	Ford DA2418 tractor	1.1.75.	£5876.14	24390	A
162	HKE 28N	Ford DA2418 tractor	1.1.75.	£5876.14	24390	G
733	HKE 29N	Ford DA2114 tractor	1.1.75.	£4273.59	21340	T
113	HKK 499N	Ford DA2114 tractor	10.1.75.	£4166.49	21340	N
114	HKL 856N	Ford DA2114 tractor	1.2.75.	£4261.09	21340	N
19	HKL 858N	Ford DA2418 tractor	1.2.75.	£5876.14	24390	A
20	HKM 314N	Ford DA2418 tractor	1.2.75.	£5876.14	24390	A
151	HKM 315N	Ford DA2418 tractor	1.2.75.	£6603.07	24390	L
735	HKP 181N	Ford DA2114 tractor	1.3.75.	£4699.52	21340	T
152	HKP 183N	Ford DA2418 tractor	1.3.75.	£6626.87	24390	L
23	HKP 184N	Ford DA2418 tractor	1.3.75.	£5876.14	24390	A
25	HKP 185N	Ford DA2418 tractor	1.3.75.	£6626.87	24390	A
116	HKP 186N	Ford DA2114 tractor	1.3.75.	£4473.66	21340	N
24	HKP 187N	Ford DA2418 tractor	1.3.75.	£6626.87	24390	A
979	HKP 874N	Ford DA2114 tractor	3.3.75.	£4691.10	21340	W
164	HKP 875N	Ford DA2418 tractor	3.3.75.	£6626.87	24390	G
978	HKP 876N	Ford DA2114 tractor	3.3.75.	£4261.09	21340	W
981	HKR 959N	Ford DA2114 tractor	12.3.75.	£4703.02	21340	W
980	HKR 960N	Ford DA2114 tractor	12.3.75.	£4261.09	21340	W
119	JKJ 115N	Ford DA2114 tractor	1.4.75.	£4703.02	21340	N
118	JKJ 116N	Ford DA2114 tractor	1.4.75.	£4699.53	21340	N
982	JKJ 117N	Ford DA2114 tractor	1.4.75.	£4703.02	21340	W
983	JKJ 118N	Ford DA2114 tractor	1.4.75.		21340	W

Appendix 19 continued:

Fleet No	Reg'n No	Make, Model and Type	Date Reg'd	Orig Cost	GVW/GTW	D
121	JKJ 936N	Ford DA2114 tractor	4.4.75.	£4699.52	21340	N
120	JKJ 937N	Ford DA2114 tractor	4.4.75.	£4699.52	21340	N
738	JKJ 938N	Ford DA2114 tractor	4.4.75.	£4689.00	21340	T
736	JKJ 939N	Ford DA2114 tractor	4.4.75.	£4703.02	21340	T
737	JKJ 940N	Ford DA2114 tractor	4.4.75.	£4689.00	21340	T
950	JKK 310N	Ford DA2114 tractor	8.4.75.	£4703.02	21340	W
951	JKK 311N	Ford DA2114 tractor	8.4.75.	£4703.02	21340	W
125	JKK 312N	Ford DA2114 tractor	8.4.75.		21340	N
122	JKK 313N	Ford DA2114 tractor	8.4.75.	£4699.52	21340	N
953	JKL 327N	Ford DA2114 tractor	1.5.75.	£4699.52	21340	W
952	JKL 328N	Ford DA2114 tractor	1.5.75.	£4699.53	21340	W
739	JKL 329N	Ford DA2114 tractor	1.5.75.	£4703.02	21340	T
742	JKL 756N	Ford DA2114 tractor	1.5.75.	£491x.xx	21340	T
740	JKL 757N	Ford DA2114 tractor	1.5.75.	£4699.52	21340	T
741	JKL 758N	Ford DA2114 tractor	1.5.75.	£4699.52	21340	T
743	JKN 229N	Ford DA2114 tractor	6.5.75.	£491x.xx	21340	T
126	JKN 231N	Ford DA2114 tractor	6.5.75.	£4934.30	21340	N
707	KKE 122N	Ford Escort van	15.5.75.	£1260.96	Insp.	T
2	KKL 168P	Leyland Sherpa 240 van	1.8.75.		Garage	A
744	MKR 992P	Ford DA1911 tractor	10.6.76.	£5243.31	19610	T
745	MKR 993P	Ford DA1911 tractor	10.6.76.	£5243.31	19610	T
153	MKR 994P	Scania LB81 tractor	23.3.76.	£10595.00	32520	L
928	MKR 995P	MAN 16.232 tractor	19.3.76.	£11528.20	32520	D
929	MKR 996P	MAN 16.232 tractor	19.3.76.	£11528.20	32520	D
930	MKR 997P	MAN 16.232 tractor	19.3.76.	£11528.20	32520	D
931	MKR 998P	MAN 16.232 tractor	17.3.76.	£11528.20	32520	D
932	MKR 999P	MAN 16.232 tractor	17.3.76.	£11528.20	32520	D
74	NKE 1P	Volvo F88 tractor	19.3.76.	£12925.40	32520	A
75	NKE 2P	Volvo F88 tractor	1.4.76.	£12925.40	32520	A
76	NKE 3P	Scania LB81 tractor	22.3.76.	£10595.00	32520	A
987	NKE 4P	Volvo F88 tractor	1.4.76.	£12595.00	32520	W
988	NKE 5P	Volvo F88 tractor	1.4.76.	£12595.00	32520	W
958	NKE 6P	Ford DA1911 tractor	5.5.76.	£5282.82	19610	W
959	NKE 7P	Ford DA1911 tractor	1.5.76.	£5282.82	19610	W
960	NKE 8P	Ford DA1911 tractor	10.5.76.	£5282.82	19610	W
961	NKE 9P	Ford DA1911 tractor	8.6.76.	£5397.07	19610	W
210	NKN 918P	Scania LB81 tractor	1.5.76.	£10415.04	32520	G
204	NKN 919P	Scania LB81 tractor	1.5.76.	£10415.04	32520	G
211	NKN 920P	Scania LB81 tractor	1.5.76.	£10415.04	32520	G
77	PKE 772R	Scania LB81 tractor	1.8.76.	£11011.00	32520	A
78	PKE 773R	Scania LB81 tractor	1.8.76.	£11011.00	32520	A
963	PKE 774R	Ford DA1911 tractor	1.9.76.	£5533.73	19610	W
964	PKE 775R	Ford DA1911 tractor	1.9.76.	£5533.73	19610	W
965	PKE 776R	Ford DA1911 tractor	8.9.76.	£5533.73	19610	W
1	PKK 889R	Ford Escort 45 van	1.8.76.	£1489.65	Garage	A
746	RKE 216R	Ford DA1911 tractor	1.10.76.	£5571.29	19610	T
151	RKE 217R	Scania LB81 tractor	7.10.76.	£11011.00	32520	L
152	RKE 218R	Scania LB81 tractor	7.10.76.	£11011.00	32520	L
129	RKE 219R	Leyland Clydesdale 4 whl rigid	1.11.76.	£7656.29	16260	A
966	RKK 844R	Ford Transit 90 van	1.11.76.	£2284.65	Samples	W
131	OVS 669R	Bedford TM 2300 tractor	3.12.76.		23000	N
K12	RKP 728R	Leyland Clydesdale 4 whl rigid	1.1.77.	£8922.30	16260	N
K14	RKP 729R	Leyland Clydesdale 4 whl rigid	1.1.77.	£8922.30	16260	N
130	SKL 498R	Ford DA2114 tractor	10.2.77.	£6220.01	21340	N
79	SKN 882R	Seddon Atk T36C250 tractor	1.3.77.	£13536.50	32520	A
80	SKN 883R	Seddon Atk T36C250 tractor	3.3.77.	£13536.50	32520	A

Appendix 19 continued:

Fleet No	Reg'n No	Make, Model and Type	Date Reg'd	Orig Cost	GVW/GTW	D
K15	TKL 156R	Leyland Clydesdale 4 whl rigid	3.5.77.	£9027.421	6260	N
K16	TKN 918R	Leyland Clydesdale 4 whl rigid	2.6.77.	£9027.42	16260	N
81	TKO 564R	Seddon Atk T38C290 tractor	13.6.77.	£14892.00	32520	A
-	TKP 160R	Ford Escort 45 van	1.7.77.	£1963.86	Insp.	T
3	TKP 161R	Leyland Marina 1300 van	1.7.77.	£1860.25	Depot	N
K17	TKP 649R	Leyland Clydesdale 4 whl rigid	1.7.77.	£9042.42	16260	N
-	UKL 473S	Leyland Sherpa van	1.8.77.		L D.Mill	
132	UKL 474S	Ford D1311 4 whl rigid c/side	1.8.77.	£7991.56	13470	N
133	UKL 475S	Ford D1311 4 whl rigid c/side	1.9.77.	£7991.56	13470	N
749	UKL 476S	Ford DA1911 tractor	1.8.77.	£6804.00	19610	T
K18	VKE 75S	Leyland Clydesdale 4 whl rigid	11.8.77.	£10061.62	16260	N
967	VKJ 241S	Ford D1311 4 whl rigid flat	1.9.77.	£6994.56	13470	W
K19	VKJ 242S	Ford D1311 4 whl rigid boxvan	6.9.77.	£7171.39	16260	N
K20	VKJ 243S	Ford D1311 4 whl rigid boxvan	1.9.77.	£7171.39	16260	N
82	VKJ 244S	ERF B Series 250 tractor	8.9.77.	£14835.00	32520	A
83	VKJ 245S	Seddon Atk T36C250 tractor	1.10.77.	£14612.00	32520	A
84	VKJ 246S	Seddon Atk T36C250 tractor	1.10.77.	£14612.00	32520	A
933	VKJ 247S	Seddon Atk T36C250 tractor	1.9.77.	£14612.00	32520	D
934	VKJ 248S	Seddon Atk T36C250 tractor	6.9.77.	£14612.00	32520	D
935	VKP 136S	Seddon Atk T36C250 tractor	1.11.77.	£14612.00	32520	D
936	VKP 137S	Seddon Atk T36C250 tractor	1.11.77.	£14612.00	32520	D
85	VKP 138S	Seddon Atk T36C250 tractor	1.12.77.	£14612.00	32520	A
86	VKP 139S	Seddon Atk T36C250 tractor	1.12.77.	£14612.00	32520	A
88	VKP 140S	ERF B Series 250 tractor	10.11.77.	£15439.00	32520	A
902	VKR 302S	Ford Transit 100 van	9.11.77.	£2835.47	Garage	D
90	WKJ 669S	ERF B Series 250 tractor	1.1.78.	£15839.00	32520	A
89	WKJ 670S	ERF B Series 250 tractor	1.1.78.	£15839.00	32520	A
91	WKN 272S	ERF B Series 250 tractor	1.2.78.	£15620.00	32520	A
92	WKN 273S	ERF B Series 250 tractor	1.2.78.	£15620.00	32520	A
93	XKL 532S	ERF B Series 250 tractor	1.4.78.	£15831.00	32520	A
154	XKL 533S	ERF B Series 250 tractor	1.5.78.	£15831.00	32520	L
156	XKL 534S	ERF B Series 250 tractor	1.5.78.	£15831.00	32520	L
763	XKL 535S	ERF B Series 250 tractor	1.5.78.	£15831.00	32520	T
764	XKL 536S	ERF B Series 250 tractor	1.5.78.	£15831.00	32520	T
989	XKL 537S	Volvo F10 tractor	5.5.78.	£18707.00	32520	W
990	XKL 538S	Volvo F10 tractor	5.5.78.	£18707.00	32520	W
94	XKL 539S	Volvo F10 tractor	1.6.78.	£18817.00	32520	A
95	XKL 540S	Volvo F10 tractor	1.6.78.	£18817.00	32520	A
96	XKL 541S	Volvo F10 tractor	1.6.78.	£18817.00	32520	A
97	XKL 542S	Volvo F10 tractor	1.7.78.	£18817.00	32520	A
750	YKK 64S	Ford DA2114 tractor	1.6.78.	£7881.86	21340	T
79	AKK 457T	Volvo F10 tractor	1.10.78.	£19090.00	32520	A
80	AKK 458T	Volvo F10 tractor	1.10.78.	£19090.00	32520	A
968	AKK 459T	Ford DA2114 tractor	1.9.78.	£8162.06	21340	W
710	AKK 460T	Ford DA2114 tractor	1.9.78.	£8162.86	21340	T
765	AKK 461T	MAN 280FTN tractor	4.9.78.	£18000.00	32520	T
766	AKK 462T	MAN 280FTN tractor	1.10.78.	£18000.00	32520	T
937	AKK 463T	MAN 280FTN tractor	1.11.78.	£18000.00	32520	D
938	AKK 464T	MAN 280FTN tractor	1.11.78.	£18000.00	32520	D
4	AKK 465T	Ford Escort 45 van	1.2.79.	£2261.27	Garage	A
957	AKK 466T	Ford Transit 100 van	1.3.79.	£3344.05	Samples	W
969	AKK 467T	Ford DA2114 tractor 2 spd axle	4.5.79.	£9266.74	21340	W
962	AKK 468T	Ford DA2114 tractor 2 spd axle	1.4.79.	£9266.75	21340	W
123	AKK 469T	Ford DA2114 tractor	1.4.79.	£8924.68	21340	N
124	AKK 470T	Ford DA2114 tractor	1.4.79.	£8924.68	21340	N
134	AKK 472T	Ford DA2114 tractor 2 spd axle	1.4.79.	£9266.75	21340	N

Appendice 19 continued:

Fleet No	Reg'n No	Make, Model and Type	Date Reg'd	Orig Cost	GVW/GTW	D
991	DKK 36T	Volvo F10-32 tractor	4.5.79.	£20406.00	32520	W
992	DKK 37T	Volvo F10-32 tractor	4.5.79.	£20406.00	32520	W
939	DKK 38T	MAN 16.280FTN tractor	4.5.79.	£19723.64	32520	D
994	DKK 39T	Ford DA2114 tractor 2 spd axle	4.5.79.	£9266.75	21340	W
709	DKK 40T	Ford DA2114 tractor 2 spd axle	4.5.79.	£9266.75	21340	T
-	DKK 41T	Ford Escort 45 van	1.6.79.	£2271.42	Insp.	T
K21	DKK 42T	Leyland Boxer BX20YF 4wl rigid	21.5.79.	£8500.00	20000	N
711	EKP 44T	Ford DA2418 tractor	6.7.79.	£11654.27	24390	T
995	EKP 45T	Ford DA2418 tractor	6.7.79.	£11654.27	24390	W
217	FKP 332V	Scania LB81 tractor	8.11.79.	£16165.00	32520	G
218	FKP 333V	Scania LB81 tractor	1.12.79.	£16165.00	32520	G
219	FKP 334V	Scania LB81 tractor	1.12.79.	£16165.00	32520	G
705	FKP 335V	Ford Escort 45 van	1.12.79.	£2587.09	Depot	T
K22	FKP 336V	Leyland Clydesdale 4 whl rigid	1.2.80.	£13366.75	16260	N
51	FKP 337V	Scania LB81 tractor	1.12.79.	£16200.00	32520	A
52	FKP 338V	Scania LB81 tractor	1.12.79.	£16200.00	32520	A
53	FKP 339V	Scania LB81 tractor	1.1.80.	£16165.00	32520	A
54	FKP 340V	Scania LB81 tractor	1.2.80.	£16165.00	32520	A
993	FKP 341V	Ford Escort 45 van	5.9.79.	£2467.15	Garage	W
996	GKP 582V	Volvo F10-32 tractor	1.1.80.	£22017.00	32520	W
997	GKP 583V	Volvo F10-32 tractor	1.1.80.	£22017.00	32520	W
55	GKP 584V	Volvo F10-32 tractor	1.1.80.	£22017.00	32520	A
56	GKP 585V	Volvo F10-32 tractor	1.1.80.	£22017.00	32520	A
780	GKP 586V	Ford D2418TR tractor	1.5.80.	£13570.32	24390	T
781	GKP 587V	Ford D2418TR tractor	1.4.80.	£13570.32	24390	T
782	GKP 588V	Ford D2418TR tractor	1.5.80.	£13570.32	24390	T
783	GKP 589V	Ford D2418TR tractor	7.5.80.	£13570.32	24390	T
784	GKP 590V	Ford D2418TR tractor	20.3.80.	£13570.32	24390	T
941	GKP 591V	Ford D2418TR tractor	1.4.80.	£13533.35	24390	W
942	GKP 592V	Ford D2418TR tractor	7.3.80.	£13533.35	24390	W
943	GKP 593V	Ford D2418TR tractor	1.2.80.	£13105.12	24390	W
944	GKP 594V	Ford D2418TR tractor	8.4.80.	£13533.35	24390	W
945	GKP 595V	Ford D2418TR tractor	1.2.80.	£13105.12	24390	W
140	GKP 596V	Ford D2418TR tractor	14.4.80.	£13291.72	24390	N
141	GKP 597V	Ford D2418TR tractor	14.4.80.	£13291.72	24390	N
142	GKP 598V	Ford D2418TR tractor	1.5.80.	£13291.72	24390	N
143	GKP 599V	Ford D2418TR tractor	14.4.80.	£13291.72	24390	N
144	GKP 600V	Ford D2418TR tractor	1.4.80.	£13291.72	24390	N
145	GKP 601V	Ford D2418TR tractor	14.4.80.	£13291.72	24390	N
146	GKP 602V	Ford D2418TR tractor	1.5.80.	£13291.72	24390	N
785	GKP 603V	Ford D2418TR tractor	1.4.80.	£13291.72	24390	T
946	GKP 604V	Ford D2418TR tractor	11.6.80.	£13715.02	24390	W
947	GKP 605V	Ford D2418TR tractor	11.6.80.	£13715.02	24390	W
948	GKP 606V	Ford D2418TR tractor	11.6.80.	£13715.02	24390	W
949	GKP 607V	Ford D2418TR tractor	6.5.80.	£13715.02	24390	W
708	HKO 359V	Leyland Marina pickup	1.2.80.	£2670.66	Garage	T
57	PGF 960V	Leyland Roadtrain 16-28 tractor	4.5.80.	£17250.00	32520	A
58	PGF 967V	Leyland Roadtrain 16-28 tractor	1.6.80.	£17250.00	32520	A
60	UGN 92W	Leyland Roadtrain 16-28 tractor	4.11.80.	£19500.00	32520	A
197	JKP 626V	Ford Transit 130 van	1.4.80.	£5258.92	Garage	G
62	JKP 670V	Foden Fleetmaster 255E tractor	1.6.80.	£17000.00	32520	A
-	NKP 833W	Ford Escort 45 van	28.11.80.	£2929.84	Insp.	T
147	OKJ 684W	Leyland Clydesdale tractor	20.1.81.	£12300.00	24390	N
148	OKJ 685W	Leyland Clydesdale tractor	13.1.81.	£12300.00	24390	N
149	OKJ 686W	Leyland Clydesdale tractor	13.1.81.	£12300.00	24390	N
139	SNM 768W	Dodge G26 Perkins V8-540 trac.	1.5.81.	£11000.00	26420	N

Appendix 19 continued:

Fleet No	Reg'n No	Make, Model and Type	Date Reg'd	Orig Cost	GVW/GTW	D
120	SKN 721X	Leyland Clydesdale tractor	1.8.81.	£12550.00	24390	N
121	SKN 722X	Leyland Clydesdale tractor	1.8.81.	£12550.00	24390	N
786	SKN 723X	Leyland Clydesdale tractor	6.8.81.	£12550.00	24390	T
787	SKN 724X	Leyland Clydesdale tractor	6.8.81.	£12550.00	24390	T
63	SKN 725X	Leyland Roadtrain 16-28 tractor	6.8.81.	£20250.00	32520	A
64	SKN 726X	Leyland Roadtrain 16-28 tractor	6.8.81.	£20250.00	32520	A
788	SKN 727X	Leyland Clydesdale tractor	1.9.81.	£12550.00	24390	T
769	SKN 728X	MAN 16.280FTN tractor	6.8.81.	£20500.00	32520	T
770	SKN 729X	MAN 16.280FTN tractor	6.8.81.	£20500.00	32520	T
771	SKN 730X	MAN 16.280FTN tractor	6.8.81.	£20500.00	32520	T
789	TKP 78X	Leyland Clydesdale tractor	1.9.81.	£12550.00	24390	T
125	TKP 79X	Leyland Clydesdale tractor	1.9.81.	£12550.00	24390	N
790	TKP 80X	Leyland Clydesdale tractor	1.1.82.	£12550.00	24390	T
956	TKP 81X	Ford Transit 100 van	12.10.81.	£5010.63	Samples	W
772	HEU 860X	Leyland Roadtrain T45 tractor	5.10.81.	£21206.00	32520	T
773	VKK 278X	Leyland Roadtrain 16-28 tractor	5.7.82.	£20625.00	32520	T
774	VKK 279X	Leyland Roadtrain 16-28 tractor	5.7.82.	£20625.00	32520	T
775	VKK 280X	Leyland Roadtrain 16-28 tractor	5.7.82.	£20625.00	32520	T
K1	VKK 281X	Leyland Clydesdale 4 whl rigid	1.12.81.	£14500.00	16260	N
K2	VKK 282X	Leyland Clydesdale 4 whl rigid	1.12.81.	£14500.00	16260	N
K3	VKK 283X	Leyland Clydesdale 4 whl rigid	1.1.82.	£14500.00	16260	N
K4	VKK 284X	Leyland Clydesdale 4 whl rigid	5.1.82.	£14500.00	16260	N
K5	VKK 285X	Leyland Clydesdale 4 whl rigid	1.1.82.	£14500,00	16260	N
K6	VKK 286X	Leyland Clydesdale 4 whl rigid	5.1.82.	£14500.00	16260	N
K7	VKK 287X	Leyland Clydesdale 4 whl rigid	1.1.82.	£14500.00	16260	N
K8	VKK 288X	Leyland Clydesdale 4 whl rigid	1.1.82.	£14500.00	16260	N
776	VKK 291X	Leyland Roadtrain 16-28 tractor	5.7.82.	£20625.00	32520	T
923	YKN 441X	Leyland Roadtrain 16-28 tractor	5.7.82.	£20625.00	32520	D
922	YKN 442X	Leyland Roadtrain 16-28 tractor	5.7.82.	£20625.00	32520	D
126	DVW 448X	Ford Cargo 2517C V8-504 trac.	7.7.82.	£15404.63	25000	N
127	DVW 451X	Ford Cargo 2517P tractor	14.7.82.	£14035.88	25000	N
4	BKR 399Y	Ford Transit 130 van	1.8.82.		Garage	A
5	DKM 995Y	Ford Escort 35 van	1.11.82.	£3573.62	Stores	A
6	DKM 996Y	Ford P100 pickup	1.11.82.	£3838.24	Garage	A
777	DKM 997Y	Leyland Roadtrain 16-28 tractor	5.11.82.	£20625.00	32520	T
924	DKM 998Y	Leyland Roadtrain 16-28 tractor	1.11.82.	£20625.00	32520	D
925	DKM 999Y	Leyland Roadtrain 16-28 tractor	1.11.82.	£20625.00	32520	D
950	DKN 411Y	Leyland Cruiser 16-15 tractor	3.11.82.	£15450.00	24390	W
791	EKR 973Y	Leyland Cruiser 16-15 tractor	25.1.83.	£15818.00	24390	T
952	FKR 912Y	Leyland Cruiser 16-15 tractor	10.3.83.	£16248.50	24390	W
953	FKR 913Y	Leyland Cruiser 16-15 tractor	10.3.83.	£16248.50	24390	W
954	FKR 914Y	Leyland Cruiser 16-15 tractor	10.3.83.	£16248.50	24390	W
955	FKR 915Y	Leyland Cruiser 16-15 tractor	10.3.83.	£16248.50	24390	W
966	FKR 916Y	Leyland Cruiser 16-15 tractor	10.3.83.	£16248.50	24390	W
793	B163 VKN	Leyland Cruiser 16-15 tractor	1.1.85.	£16823.98	24390	T
792	B164 VKN	Leyland Cruiser 16-15 tractor	1.1.85.	£16823.98	24390	T
K12	B997 XKN	Leyland Freighter 4 whl rigid	1.4.85.	£19376.00	16260	N
K14	B998 XKN	Leyland Freighter 4 whl rigid	1.4.85.	£19376.00	16260	N
958	B232 WKO	Ford Transit 100 van	1.7.85.	£6381.95	Samples	W
701	C484 AFB	FreightRover Sherpa255 dropside	1.8.85.	£5741.00	Garage	T
794	C806 BKN	Leyland Cruiser 16-17 tractor	1.9.85.	£18390.30	24390	T
798	C807 BKN	Leyland F'ter 4whl rigid c/side	1.9.85.	£22405.38	16260	T
799	C808 BKN	Leyland F'ter 4whl rigid c/side	1.9.85.	£22405.38	16260	T
128	C809 BKN	Leyland Cruiser 16-17 tractor	1.10.85.	£18390.30	24390	N
66	C703 ULE	ERF CP38C290 6x2 tractor	21.11.85.	£25000.00	38000	A
65	C522 JOO	Leyland Roadtrain 17-28 tractor	3.12.85.	£25357.00	32520	A

Appendix 19 continued:

Fleet No	Reg'n No	Make, Model and Type	Date Reg'd	Orig Cost	GVW/GTW	D
130	C231 GKE	Leyland F'ter 4whl rigid c/side	1.4.86.	£22555.00	16260	N
131	C232 GKE	Leyland F'ter 4whl rigid c/side	1.4.86.	£23028.00	16260	N
970	C232 GKE	Leyland F'ter 4whl rigid c/side	1.4.86.	£23028.00	16260	W
971	C234 GKE	Leyland F'ter 4whl rigid c/side	1.4.86.	£23028.00	16260	W
967	C235 GKE	Leyland Cruiser 16-17 tractor	11.4.86.	£19958.38	24390	W
968	C997 GKP	Leyland Cruiser 16-17 tractor	1.5.86.	£19958.38	24390	W
132	C311 GKR	Leyland Cruiser 16-17 tractor	13.5.86.	£19958.38	24390	N
133	C312 GKR	Leyland Cruiser 16-17 tractor	1.6.86.	£19958.38	24390	N
134	C313 GKR	Leyland Cruiser 16-17 tractor	1.7.86.	£19958.38	24390	N
135	C314 GKR	Leyland Cruiser 16-17 tractor	1.7.86.	£19958.38	24390	N
972	C315 GKR	Leyland Cruiser 16-17 tractor	1.6.86.	£19958.38	24390	W
973	C316 GKR	Leyland Cruiser 16-17 tractor	10.6.86.	£19958.38	24390	W
795	C317 GKR	Leyland Cruiser 16-17 tractor	14.5.86.	£19958.38	24390	T
796	C318 GKR	Leyland Cruiser 16-17 tractor	13.6.86.	£19958.38	24390	T
797	C319 GKR	Leyland Cruiser 16-17 tractor	13.6.86.	£19958.38	24390	T
67	C705 MTW	Leyland Roadtrain 20-32 6x2 tr.	1.7.86.	£33159.50	38000	A
783	D847 KKN	Leyland Cruiser 16-17 tractor	10.11.86.	£19958.38	24390	T
136	D848 KKN	Leyland Cruiser 16-17 tractor	24.11.86.	£20038.38	24390	N
220	D849 KKN	Leyland Roadtrain 17-29 tractor	24.11.86.	£26209.50	32520	G
50	D850 KKN	Leyland F'ter 4whl rigid c/side	17.10.86.	£23997.25	16260	N
68	D851 KKN	Leyland Roadtrain 20-32 6x2 tr.	9.9.86.	£33159.50	38000	A
69	D852 KKN	Leyland Roadtrain 20-32 6x2 tr.	9.9.86.	£33159.50	38000	A
70	D853 KKN	Leyland Roadtrain 20-29 6x2 tr.	1.10.86.	£31827.00	38000	A
71	D854 KKN	Leyland Roadtrain 20-29 6x2 tr.	1.11.86.	£31827.00	38000	A
72	D855 KKN	Leyland Roadtrain 20-29 6x2 tr.	1.11.86.	£31827.00	38000	A
73	D188 TOO	Leyland Roadtrain 20-32 6x2 tr.	1.2.87.	£35837.38	38000	A
782	D145 OKP	Leyland Cruiser 16-17 tractor	3.4.87.	£21390.00	24390	T
974	D296 PKL	Leyland Cruiser 16-17 tractor	12.5.87.	£21475.00	24390	W
975	D297 PKL	Leyland Cruiser 16-17 tractor	13.5.87.	£21475.00	24390	W
750	D298 PKL	Leyland Cruiser 16-17 tractor	13.5.87.	£21475.00	24390	T
74	D299 PKL	ERF E14 32TT 6x2 tractor	1.6.87.	£35203.25	38000	A
75	D300 PKL	ERF E14 32TT 6x2 tractor	3.7.87.	£37468.50	38000	A
751	D659 RKE	Leyland Cruiser 16-17 tractor	10.7.87.	£21475.00	24390	T
977	D731 RKE	Leyland Cruiser 16-17 tractor	3.7.87.	£21475.00	24390	W
976	D732 RKE	Leyland Cruiser 16-17 tractor	3.7.87.	£21475.00	24390	W
221	E336 TKE	Leyland Roadtrain 20-32 6x2 tr.	1.8.87.	£37468.50	38000	G
222	E337 TKE	Leyland Roadtrain 20-32 6x2 tr.	17.8.87.	£37468.50	38000	G
978	E338 TKE	Mercedes 16-17S/32 tractor	1.8.87.	£21446.00	24390	W
979	E339 TKE	Mercedes 16-17S/32 tractor	1.8.87.	£21446.00	24390	W
752	E340 TKE	Leyland Cruiser 16-17 tractor	17.8.87.	£21475.00	24390	T
76	E341 TKE	ERF E14 32TT 6x2 tractor	1.11.87.	£36958.00	38000	A
77	E342 TKE	ERF E14 32TT 6x2 tractor	10.11.87.	£36958.00	38000	A
778	E343 TKE	ERF E14 32TT 6x2 tractor	10.11.87.	£36958.00	38000	T
926	E344 TKE	Leyland Roadtrain 20-32 6x2 tr.	17.10.87.	£37486.50	38000	D
927	E345 TKE	Leyland Roadtrain 20-32 6x2 tr.	17.10.87.	£37486.50	38000	D
706	E252 UKP	Leyland Cruiser 16-17 tractor	1.12.87.	£21210.00	24390	T
707	E253 UKP	Leyland Cruiser 16-17 tractor	1.12.87.	£21210.00	24390	T
111	E254 UKP	Leyland Cruiser 16-17 tractor	1.12.87.	£21210.00	24390	N
112	E255 UKP	Leyland Cruiser 16-17 tractor	1.12.87.	£21210.00	24390	N
K15	E256 UKP	Leyland F'ter 16-17 4 whl rigid	24.1.88.	£24640.00	16260	N
K16	E257 UKP	Leyland F'ter 16-17 4 whl rigid	17.2.88.	£24640.23	16260	N
3	E258 UKP	Bedford Astramax 560L van	3.12.87.	£5732.50	16260	A
754	E436 AKE	Leyland Cruiser 16-17 tractor	10.5.88.	£23129.38	24390	T
753	E437 AKE	Leyland Cruiser 16-17 tractor	10.5.88.	£23129.38	24390	T
779	E141 AKN	ERF E14 32TT 6x2 tractor	13.6.88.	£38460.00	38000	T
760	E142 AKN	ERF E14 32TT 6x2 tractor	17.7.88.	£38460.00	38000	T

Appendix 19 continued:

Fleet No	Reg'n No	Make, Model and Type	Date Reg'd	Orig Cost	GVW/GTW	D
761	E143 AKN	ERF E14 32TT 6x2 tractor	17.7.87.	£38460.00	38000	T
137	E144 AKN	Leyland Cruiser 16-17 tractor	1.7.88.	£23129.38	24390	N
138	E145 AKN	Leyland Cruiser 16-17 tractor	10.7.88.	£23129.38	24390	N
140	E146 AKN	Leyland Cruiser 16-17 tractor	10.7.88.	£23129.38	24390	N
141	E147 AKN	Leyland Cruiser 16-17 tractor	1.7.88.	£23129.38	24390	N
142	F551 CKR	Leyland Cruiser 16-17 tractor	1.8.88.	£23129.38	24390	N
143	F552 CKR	Leyland Cruiser 16-17 tractor	17.9.88.	£23129.38	24390	N
145	F553 CKR	Leyland Cruiser 16-17 tractor	17.9.88.	£23129.38	24390	N
223	F554 CKR	Leyland Roadtrain 20-32 6x2 tr.	10.9.88.	£38402.00	38000	G
224	F555 CKR	Leyland Roadtrain 20-32 6x2 tr.	10.9.88.	£38400.00	38000	G
901	F556 CKR	Bedford Astramax 560L van	1.9.88.	£5952.50	Depot	D
755	F557 CKR	Leyland Cruiser 16-17 tractor	17.11.88.	£23129.38	24390	T
756	F558 CKR	Leyland Cruiser 16-17 tractor	20.1.89.	£23129.38	24390	T
757	F559 CKR	Leyland Cruiser 16-17 tractor	20.1.89.	£23129.38	24390	T
79	F560 CKR	ERF E14 32TT 6x2 tractor	24.1.89.	£39519.00	38000	A
758	F351 GKN	Leyland Cruiser 16-17 tractor	1.2.89.	£23129.38	24000	T
959	F352 GKN	Ford Transit 160 van	1.5.89.	£10406.29	Samples	W
80	F353 GKN	ERF E10 32TT 6x2 tractor	17.5.89.	£37365.00	38000	A
81	F354 GKN	ERF E10 32TT 6x2 tractor	1.6.89.	£37365.00	38000	A
83	F355 GKN	ERF E14 32TT 6x2 tractor	17.5.89.	£39519.00	38000	A
780	F588 KKK	Leyland Cruiser 16-17 tractor	24.5.89.	£24091.63	24390	T
84	F589 KKK	ERF E14 32TT 6x2 tractor	1.6.89.	£39519.00	38000	A
85	F247 VVT	Foden S106TS L10 325 6x2 tr.	1.6.89.	£34250.00	38000	A
86	G865 SKE	ERF E14 32TT 6x2 tractor	5.1.90.	£41000.00	38000	A
759	G668 TKJ	ERF E8 - 265 tractor	10.2.90.	£30423.00	28000	T
981	H558 DKK	ERF E8 - 265 tractor	24.10.90.	£31708.00	28000	W
146	H559 DKK	ERF E8 - 265 tractor	22.10.90.	£31708.00	28000	N
960	H798 KVX	Bedford Astramax 560LD van	25.1.91.	£7354.40	Garage	W
225	H959 AKL	Foden S104 L10 325 4x2 tractor	15.4.91.	£37500.00	38000	G
982	J988 KKO	ERF E8 24ST tractor	9.7.91.	£31569.00	28000	W

The following ancillary vehicles were purchased secondhand during this period:

101	RKO 218R	International fork lift truck	1.12.76.		Garage	A
102	THV 611M	Blaw Knox R/master sweeper	19.12.73.		Site	A
103	YWV 954T	Bedford RL 4x4 gritter	1.11.78.		Site	A
9	D985 SHJ	Landrover 90 pickup	13.2.87.	£6750.00	Garage	A

NOTES :

1. 905 - TKL 869N was transferred in Dec 1979 to New Hythe renumbered 136.
2. 105 - TKN 591N and 112 - HKE 26N were later transferred to Wigan, renumbered 955 and 954.
3. 64 - TKN 592N was transferred to Wigan at an early date, renumbered 983.
4. 161 - GKP 647N was transferred to New Hythe and renumbered 137.
5. 151 - HKM 315N was transferred to Darwen, renumbered 907.
6. 152 - HKP 183N had a chequered career transferring to Darwen as 908, then to Wigan and finally to New Hythe, renumbered 135.
7. Wigan Volvos 987 - 992/996/997 - NKE 4/5P, XKL 537/538S, DKK 36/37T, GKP 582/583S were transferred to Aylesford in 1981, see chapter 15. Renumbered 40 to 47. 44 was then destroyed by fire at Histon, see photograph.
8. 129 - RKE 219R, replaced by 50 - D850 KKN were in Reed Medway Sacks livery.
9. Ford Transit vans at Wigan designated as Samples were on weekly hire to the Corrugated Cases factory and were regularly replaced due to high mileage.
10. Ford Escort van TKP 160R saw it's time out at Darwen as 909.
11. Leyland Sherpa van UKL 473S was hired to Lower Darwen Paper Mill and when the Mill closed, it was transferred to Thatcham as 704.

Appendix 19 continued:

NOTES continued:

12   The following were ex demonstrators or manufacturer's 'seed' vehicles:
     131 - OVS 669R, 57 - PGF 960V, 58 - PGF 967V, 60 - UGN 92W, 62 - JKP 670V, 139 - SNM768W,
     772 - HEU 860X, 126 - DVW 448X, 127 - DVW 451X, 65 - C522 JOO, 66 - C703 ULE, 67 - C705 MTW,
     73 - D188 TOO, 85 - F247 VVT.

13   K1 - K8/K12/K14 were fitted with Ray Smith demount systems. About the same time K22 - FKP 336V and
     K18 - VKE 75S were converted by Ray Smith for demount operations, renumbered K9 and K10. See Chapter 12.

14   65 - C522 JOO was transferred to Gravesend and later to Darwen but never renumbered.

15   67 - C705 MTW was the first 6x2 Roadtrain, built by Scammell Watford after collaboration with Reed Transport.

16   221 - E336 TKE was fitted with an experimental gearbox. It was stolen out of Greenhithe Depot. Subsequent
     identification using this gearbox eventually led to the successful prosecution of the thief.

17   222 - E337 TKE was later repainted in a Royal Blue livery for customer Empire Paper Mill. It carried 'EMPIRE'
     in the cabcap and the customer's logo on the cab doors, a peacock's fanned tail with EMPIRE and then PAPER
     MILL below.

18   80 - F353 GKN was transferred to Darwen but not renumbered.

19   759 - G668 TKJ ERF E8 originally had a short 3.2m wheelbase and was given Baico extension to 3.8m in
     December 1991, cost £2250, to allow for 13.6m trailers.

20   763 - XKL 535S was transferred to New Hythe for site shunting at Caradon Terrain, repainted in their livery and
     renumbered K11.

21   83/84 - VKJ 245/246S were transferred to Darwen and renumbered 920/921.

22   When London Depot closed on 3rd April 1981, it's vehicles were reallocated. 151 - RKE 217R and
     152 - RKE 218R were transferred to Aylesford keeping the same numbers. 154 - XKL 533S and 156 - XKL 534S
     transferred to Thatcham renumbered 767 and 768

Appendix 20 - Order of the Secretary of State for the Environment under Section 42 (see Chapter 14)

Order No VS 46/76

ROAD TRAFFIC ACT 1972

ORDER OF THE SECRETARY OF STATE FOR THE ENVIRONMENT UNER SECTION 42

The Secretary of State for the Environment, in exercise of his powers under section 42 of the Road Traffic Act 1972, hereby authorises for the period 9th to 13th August 1976(dates inclusive) the use on roads of the vehicle combination described in the Schedule hereto, notwithstanding that the combination does not comply with the requirements of Regulation 136 of the Motor Vehicles(Construction and Use)Regulations, 1973, as amended, subject to the following conditions:-

1. the combination shall be operated only by Reed Transport Ltd of Maidstone, Kent,

2. all axles of the combination, except the steering axle of the tractive unit, shall be fitted with anti-lock brakes,

3. the tractive unit shall be fitted with twin lens rear view mirrors,

4. the drawbar attaching the second trailer to the first semi trailer shall be either constructed or adapted so that the vertical oscillation of the coupling eye only occurs about one point,

5. the combination shall be fitted with additional lights to make it clearly conspicuous by night especially from the side,

6. the weight of the first trailer of the combination shall at all times be equal to, or greater than, that of the second trailer,

7. the combination shall only be used on the route described on Sheet 2 of this Order,

8. the combination shall not travel at a speed exceeding 30 mph on all purpose roads and not exceeding 40 mph on motorways.

Signed by the authority of the Secretary of State   29   July 1976

N.S.Despicht
N.S.Despicht
An Assistant Secretary in the Department of the Environment

SCHEDULE

One heavy motor car, being the tractive unit of an articulated vehicle, with the registration number MHS53P drawing the following trailers -
        semi trailer numbered OLN 9882/1
        dolly trailer   "   SGN 4188/01
        semi trailer   "   OLN 9882/2

Sheet 2

ROUTE REFERRED TO IN CONDITION 7 OF ORDER VS 46/76

On leaving the premises of Odhams (Watford) Ltd, St Albans Road, Watford Herts:-

Turn Right - A412 St Albans Road

Turn Right - A41 North Western Avenue

Join M1 - Junction 5 Northwards

Leave Motorway Junction 19

Join M6 - Northwards

Leave Motorway Junction 25

Turn Left - A49 Warrington Road to Goose Green

Turn Right - Into depot of Reed Transport Ltd, Goose Green, Wigan, Lancs.

Return by same route.

Appendix 21 - Perkins & Glover ledger pages 4 & 5 identifying the purchase price and acquisition dates of vehicles in the immediate years after World War Two as detailed in Appendix 3

Index